Cats and

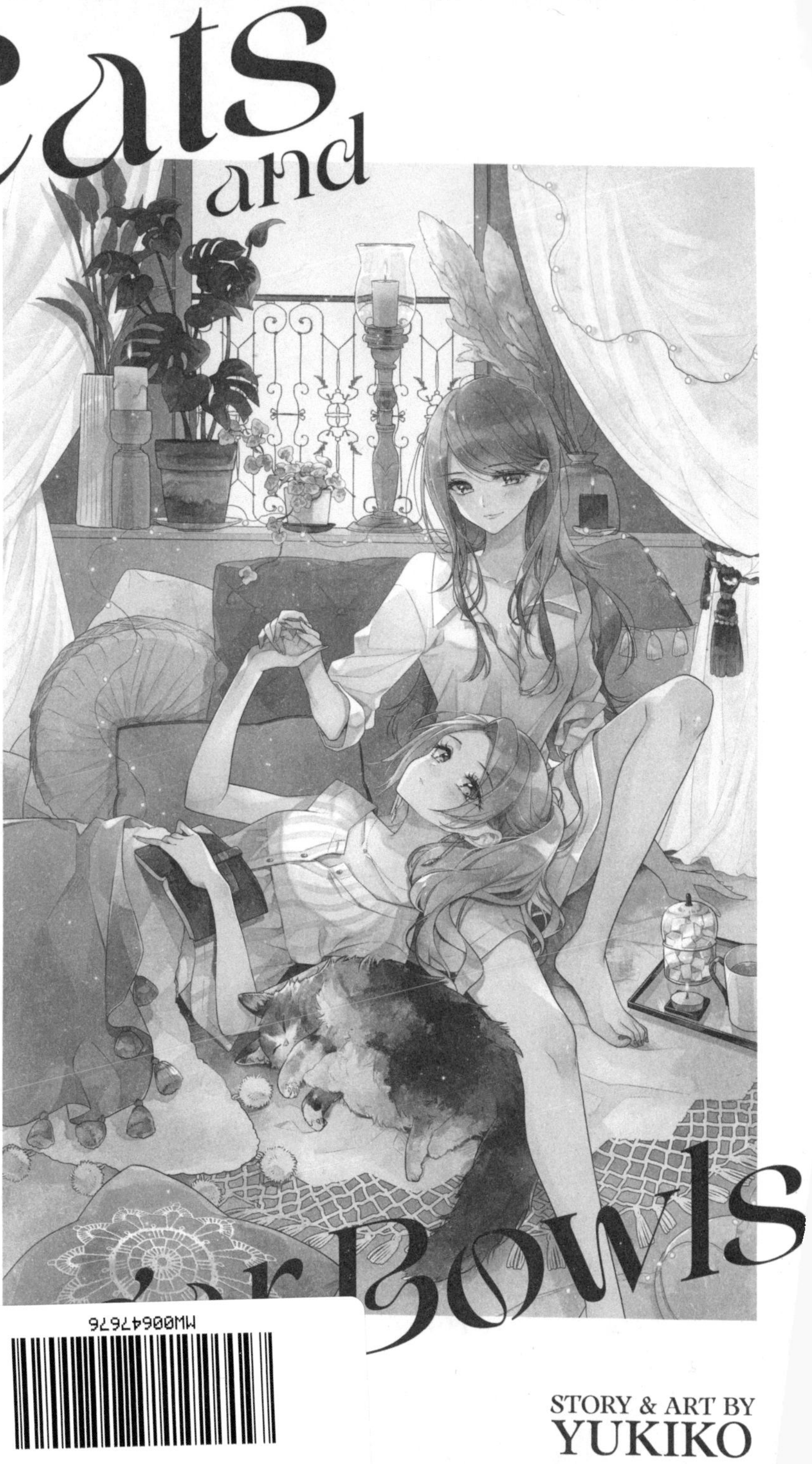

r Bowls

STORY & ART BY
YUKIKO

C O N T E N T S

003   [Watchful Cat]

019   [Crying of the Cat]

031   [The Phone and the Cat]

039   [Unbreakable Sugar Bowl]

075   [Silky]

083   [My Childhood Friend]

093   [One AM at the Laundromat]

103   [Killing Time of the Butterfly]

115   [The Ogre and the Mountain God]

122   [Afterword]

Watchful Cat

Cats and Sugar Bowls

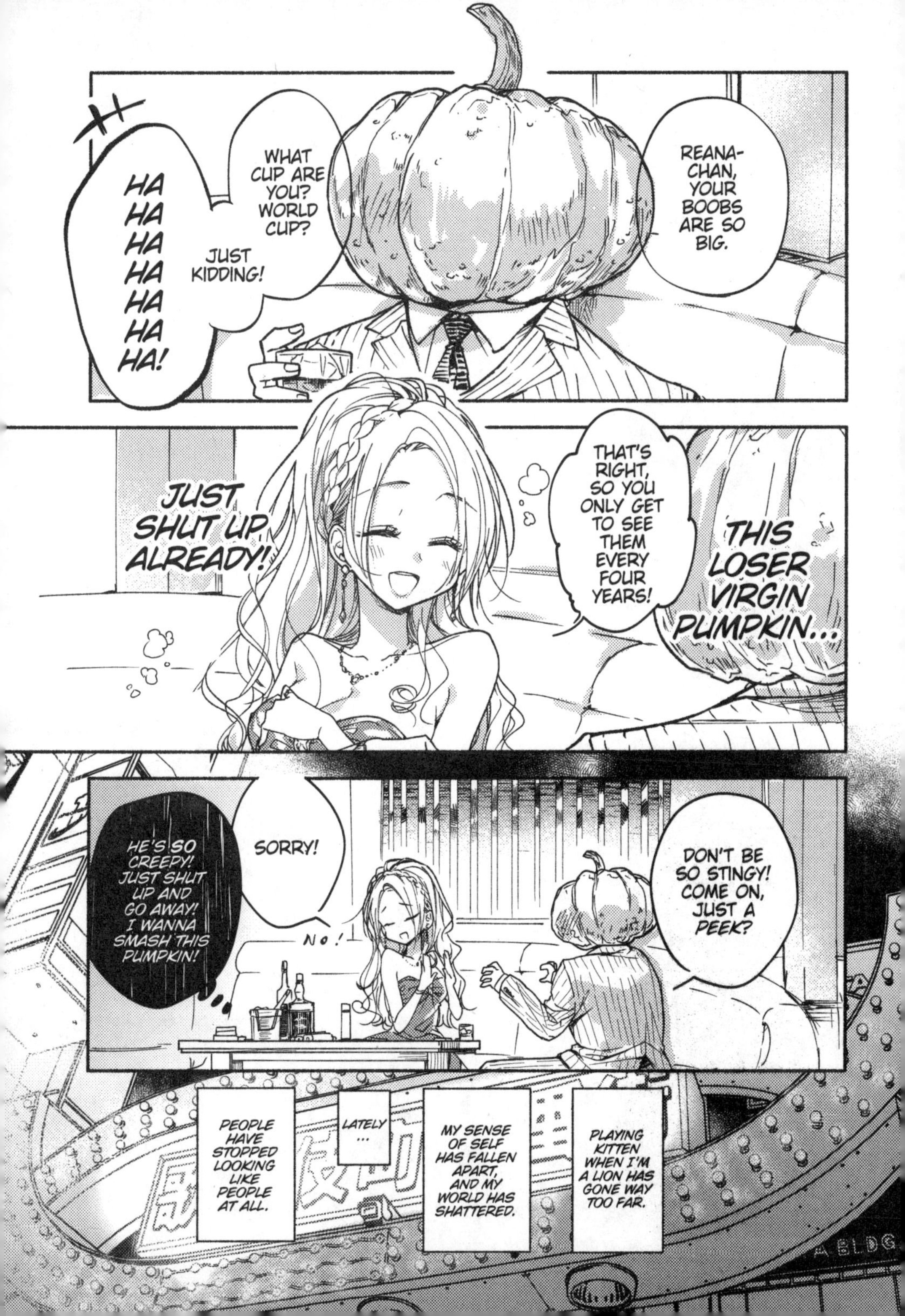

REANA-CHAN, YOUR BOOBS ARE SO BIG.
WHAT CUP ARE YOU? WORLD CUP?
JUST KIDDING!
HA HA HA HA HA HA HA HA!
THIS LOSER VIRGIN PUMPKIN...
THAT'S RIGHT, SO YOU ONLY GET TO SEE THEM EVERY FOUR YEARS!
JUST SHUT UP ALREADY!
DON'T BE SO STINGY! COME ON, JUST A PEEK?
NO!
SORRY!
HE'S SO CREEPY! JUST SHUT UP AND GO AWAY! I WANNA SMASH THIS PUMPKIN!
A BLDG
PLAYING KITTEN WHEN I'M A LION HAS GONE WAY TOO FAR.
MY SENSE OF SELF HAS FALLEN APART, AND MY WORLD HAS SHATTERED.
LATELY...
PEOPLE HAVE STOPPED LOOKING LIKE PEOPLE AT ALL.

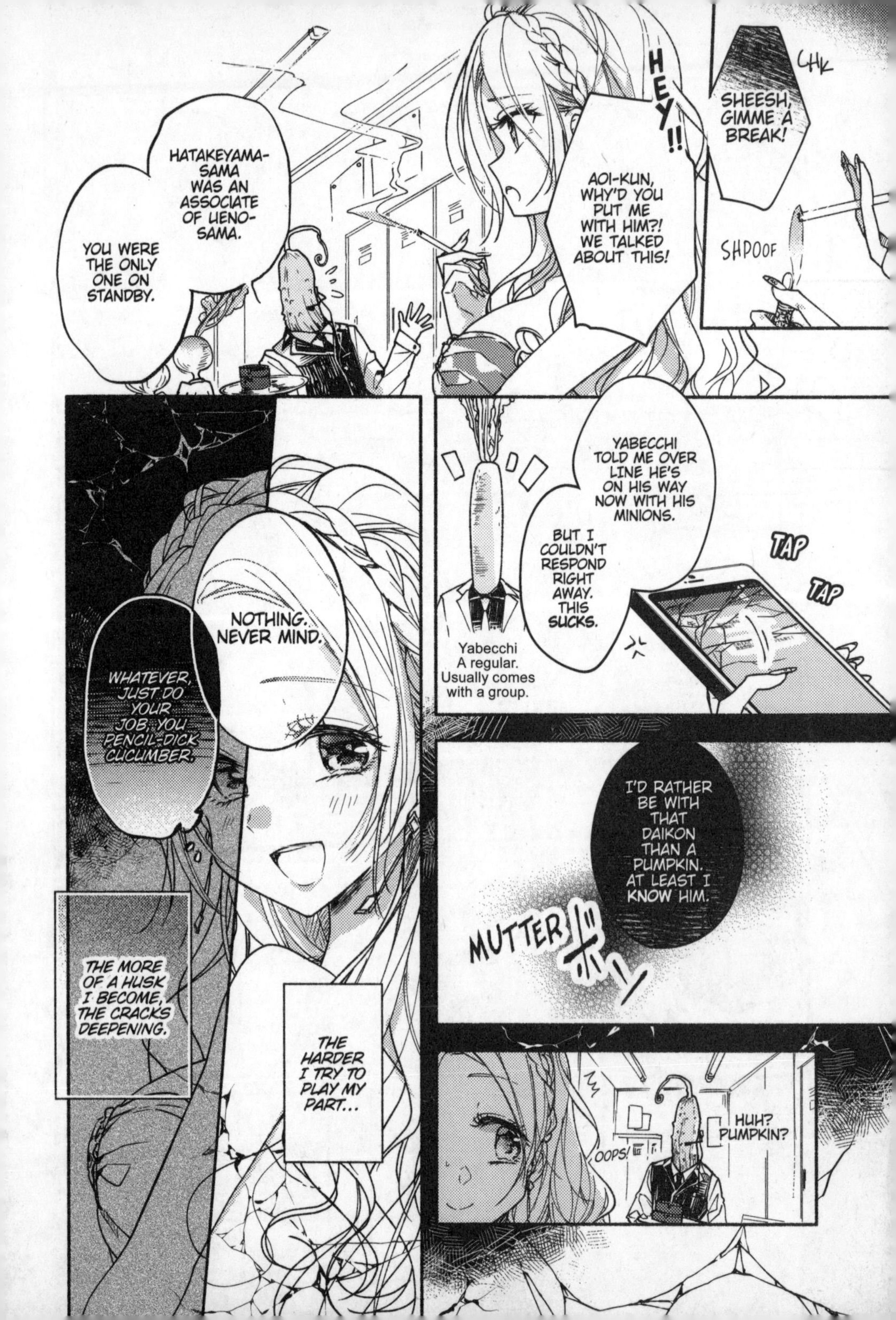
CHK
SHEESH, GIMME A BREAK!
SHPOOF
HEY!!
AOI-KUN, WHY'D YOU PUT ME WITH HIM?! WE TALKED ABOUT THIS!
HATAKEYAMA-SAMA WAS AN ASSOCIATE OF UENO-SAMA.
YOU WERE THE ONLY ONE ON STANDBY.
YABECCHI TOLD ME OVER LINE HE'S ON HIS WAY NOW WITH HIS MINIONS.
BUT I COULDN'T RESPOND RIGHT AWAY. THIS SUCKS.
TAP
TAP
Yabecchi A regular. Usually comes with a group.
I'D RATHER BE WITH THAT DAIKON THAN A PUMPKIN. AT LEAST I KNOW HIM.
MUTTER
HUH? PUMPKIN?
OOPS!
NOTHING. NEVER MIND.
WHATEVER, JUST DO YOUR JOB, YOU PENCIL-DICK CUCUMBER.
THE HARDER I TRY TO PLAY MY PART...
THE MORE OF A HUSK I BECOME, THE CRACKS DEEPENING.

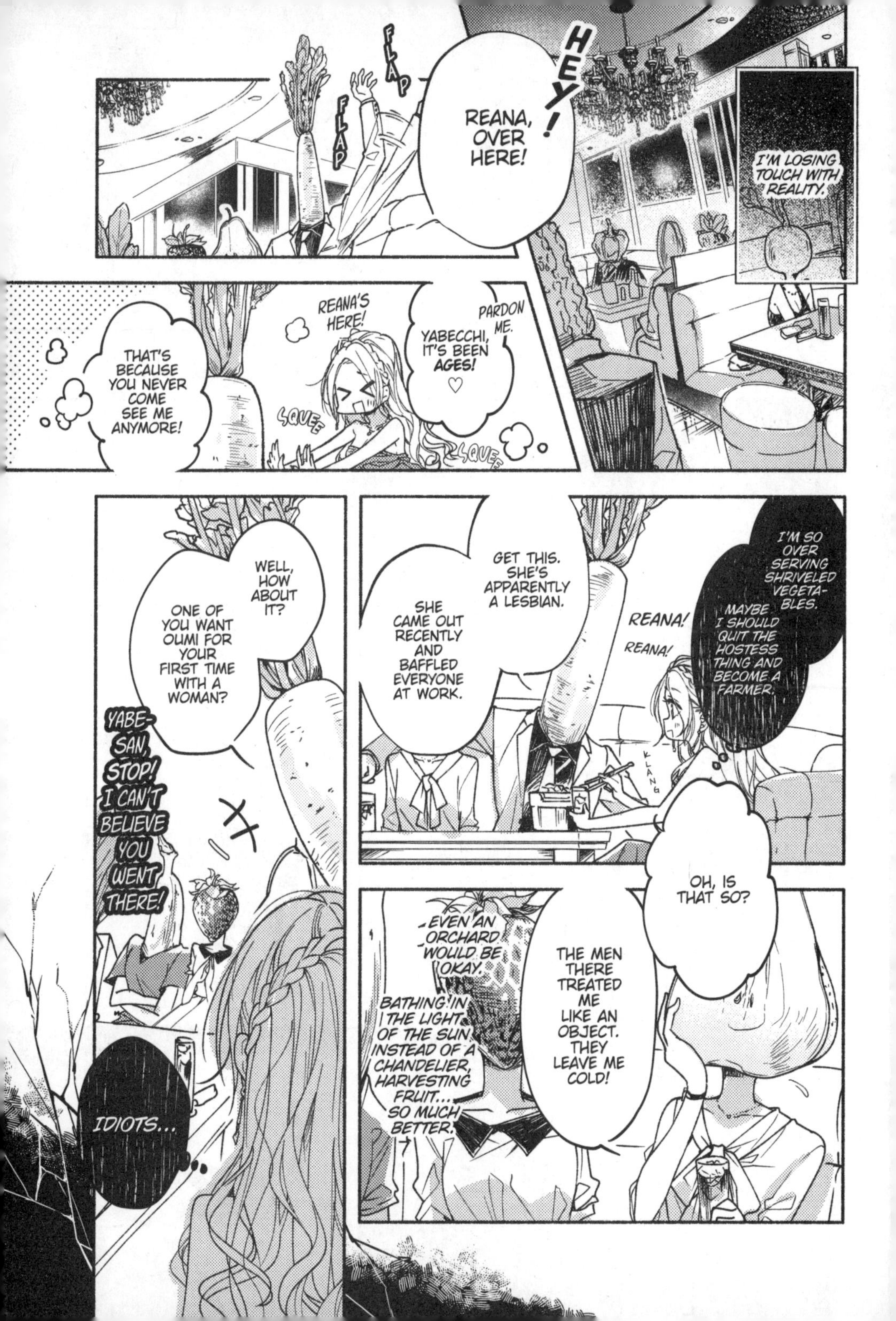
I'M LOSING TOUCH WITH REALITY.
HEY!
REANA, OVER HERE!
FLAP
FLAP
PARDON ME.
YABECCHI, IT'S BEEN AGES! ♡
REANA'S HERE!
SQUEE
SQUEE
THAT'S BECAUSE YOU NEVER COME SEE ME ANYMORE!
I'M SO OVER SERVING SHRIVELED VEGETABLES.
MAYBE I SHOULD QUIT THE HOSTESS THING AND BECOME A FARMER.
REANA!
REANA!
GET THIS. SHE'S APPARENTLY A LESBIAN.
SHE CAME OUT RECENTLY AND BAFFLED EVERYONE AT WORK.
KLANG
OH, IS THAT SO?
THE MEN THERE TREATED ME LIKE AN OBJECT. THEY LEAVE ME COLD!
EVEN AN ORCHARD WOULD BE OKAY.
BATHING IN THE LIGHT OF THE SUN INSTEAD OF A CHANDELIER, HARVESTING FRUIT... SO MUCH BETTER.
WELL, HOW ABOUT IT?
ONE OF YOU WANT OUMI FOR YOUR FIRST TIME WITH A WOMAN?
YABE-SAN, STOP! I CAN'T BELIEVE YOU WENT THERE!
IDIOTS...

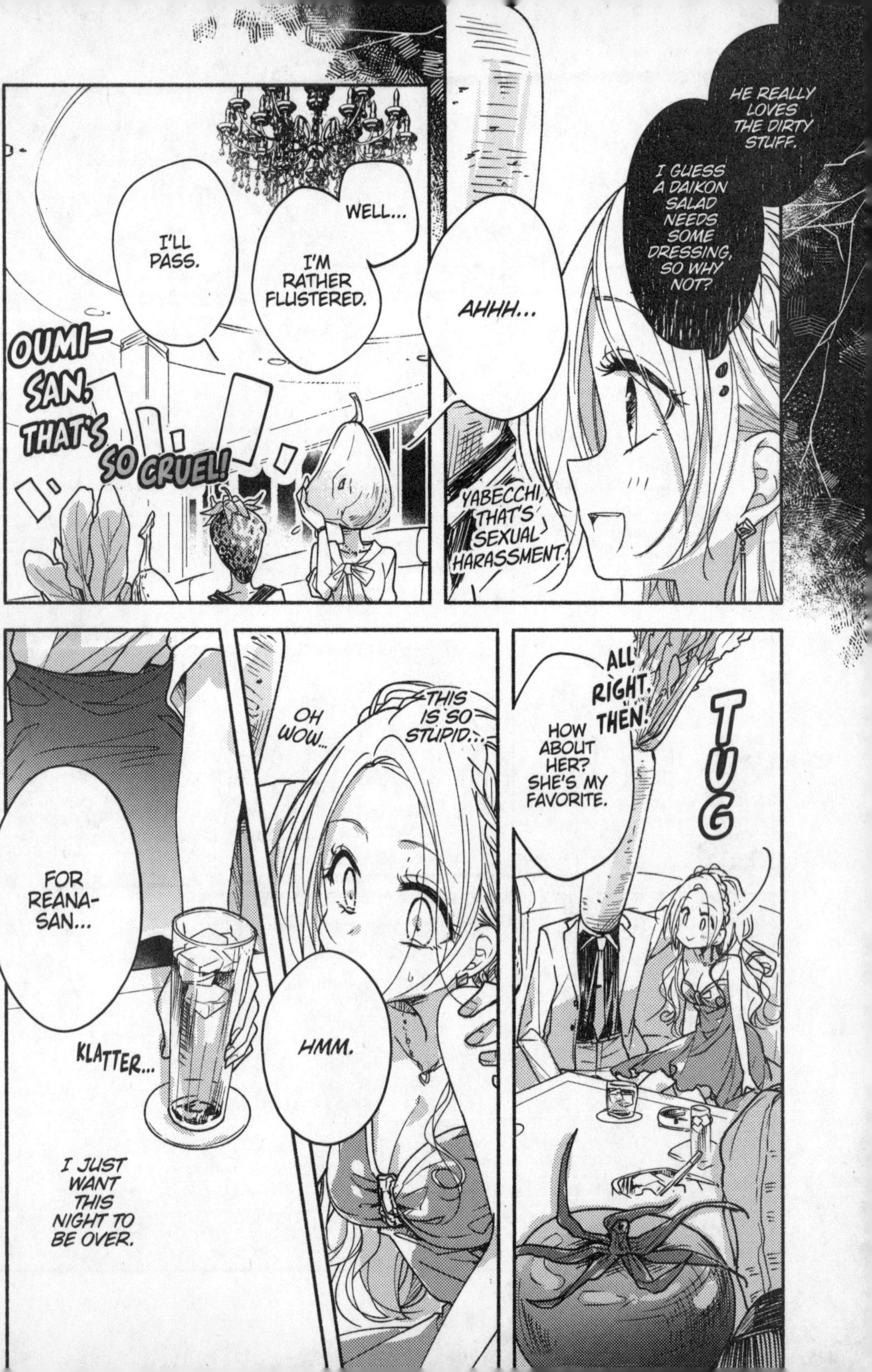
HE REALLY LOVES THE DIRTY STUFF.
I GUESS A DAIKON SALAD NEEDS SOME DRESSING, SO WHY NOT?
AHHH...
YABECCHI, THAT'S SEXUAL HARASSMENT.
WELL...
I'M RATHER FLUSTERED.
I'LL PASS.
OUMI-SAN, THAT'S SO CRUEL!
ALL RIGHT, THEN.
TUG
HOW ABOUT HER? SHE'S MY FAVORITE.
THIS IS SO STUPID...
OH WOW...
HMM.
FOR REANA-SAN...
KLATTER...
I JUST WANT THIS NIGHT TO BE OVER.

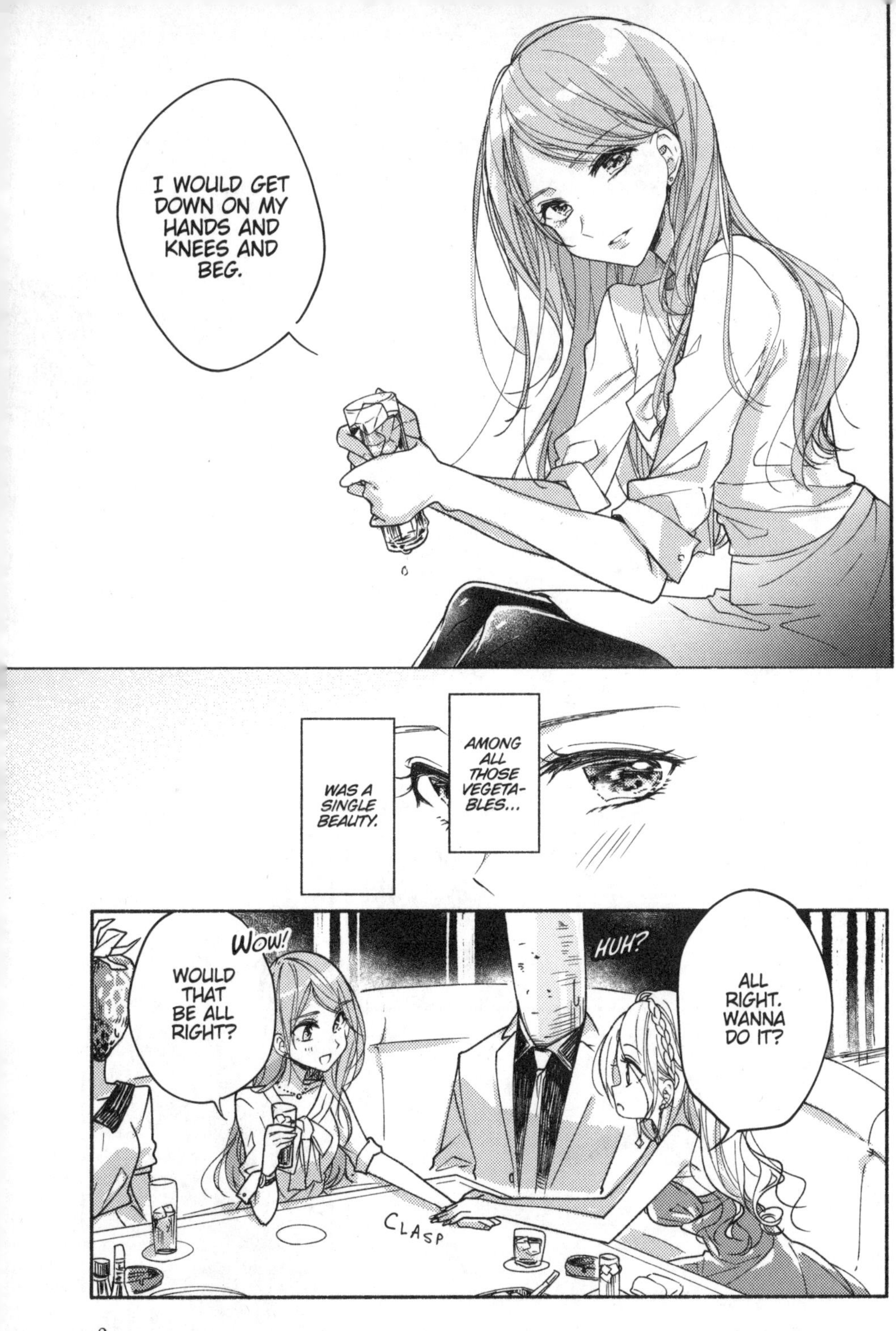
I WOULD GET DOWN ON MY HANDS AND KNEES AND BEG.
AMONG ALL THOSE VEGETA-BLES...
WAS A SINGLE BEAUTY.
ALL RIGHT. WANNA DO IT?
HUH?
WOW!
WOULD THAT BE ALL RIGHT?
CLASP

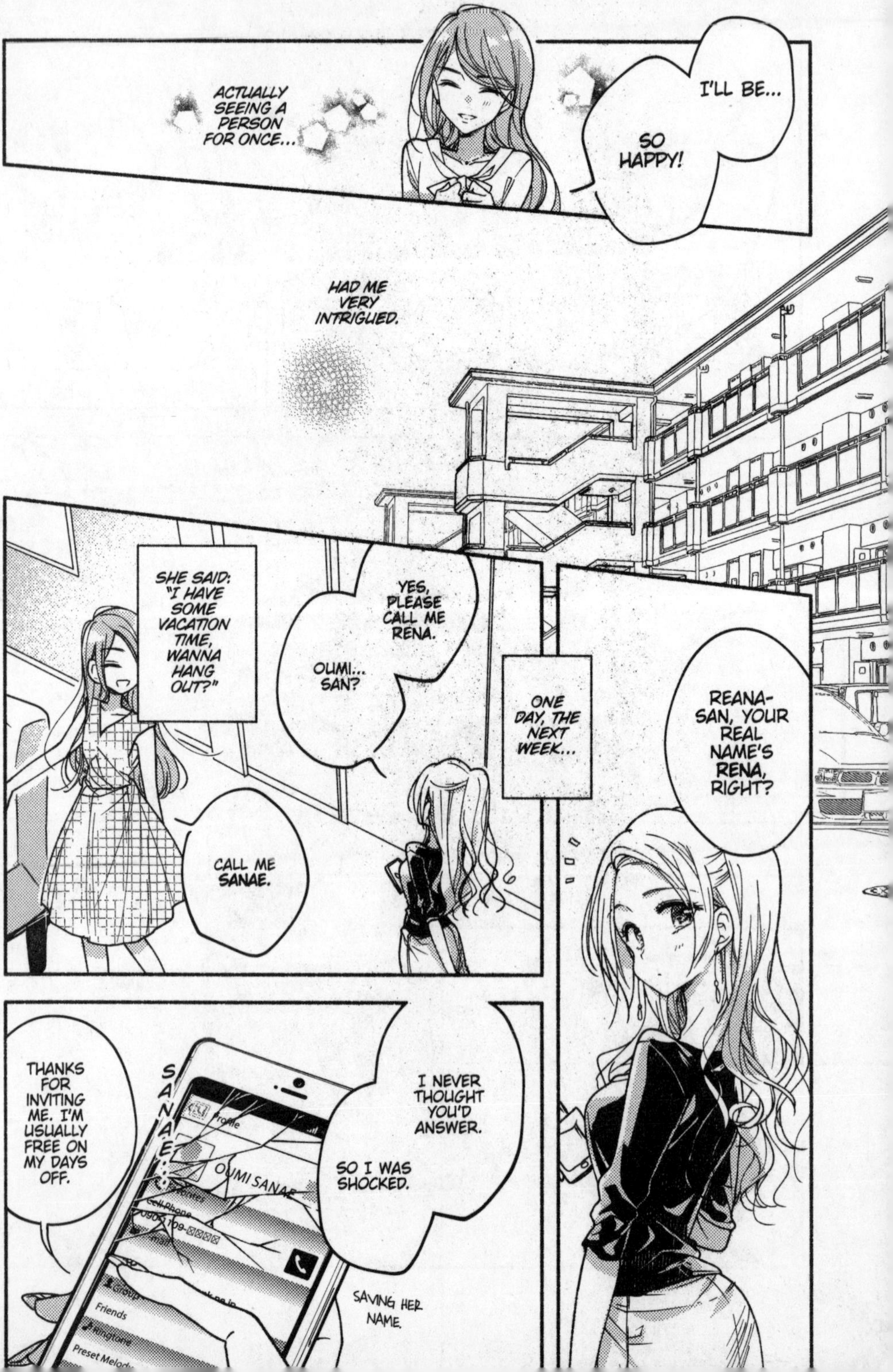
I'LL BE... SO HAPPY!
ACTUALLY SEEING A PERSON FOR ONCE...
HAD ME VERY INTRIGUED.
REANA-SAN, YOUR REAL NAME'S RENA, RIGHT?
ONE DAY, THE NEXT WEEK...
YES, PLEASE CALL ME RENA.
OUMI... SAN?
SHE SAID: "I HAVE SOME VACATION TIME, WANNA HANG OUT?"
CALL ME SANAE.
I NEVER THOUGHT YOU'D ANSWER.
SO I WAS SHOCKED.
THANKS FOR INVITING ME. I'M USUALLY FREE ON MY DAYS OFF.
SANAE...
Profile
OUMI SANAE
Cell Phone
Friends
Ringtone
Preset Melody
SAVING HER NAME.

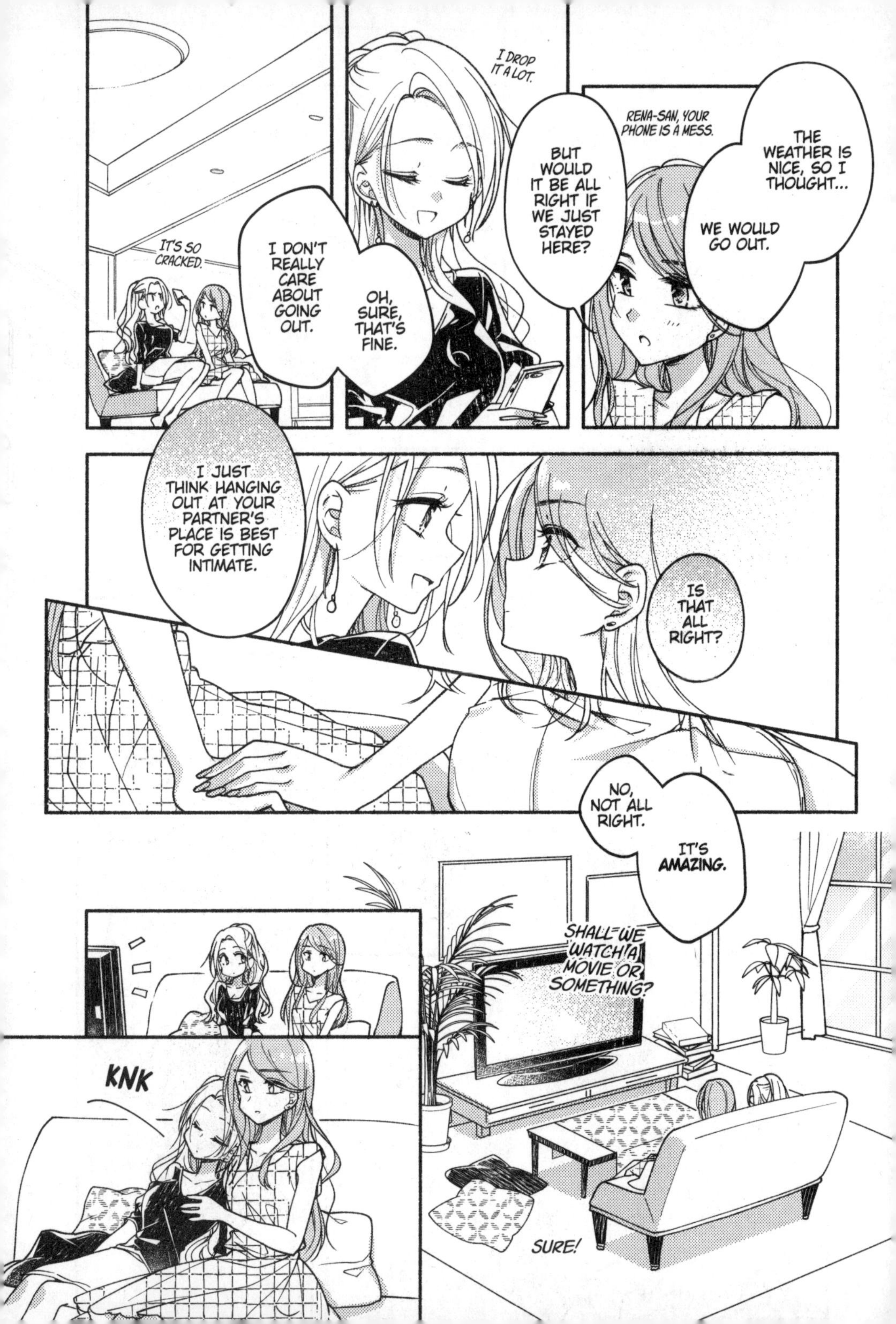
THE WEATHER IS NICE, SO I THOUGHT...
RENA-SAN, YOUR PHONE IS A MESS.
WE WOULD GO OUT.
BUT WOULD IT BE ALL RIGHT IF WE JUST STAYED HERE?
I DROP IT A LOT.
OH, SURE, THAT'S FINE.
I DON'T REALLY CARE ABOUT GOING OUT.
IT'S SO CRACKED.
I JUST THINK HANGING OUT AT YOUR PARTNER'S PLACE IS BEST FOR GETTING INTIMATE.
IS THAT ALL RIGHT?
NO, NOT ALL RIGHT.
IT'S AMAZING.
SHALL WE WATCH A MOVIE OR SOMETHING?
SURE!
KNK

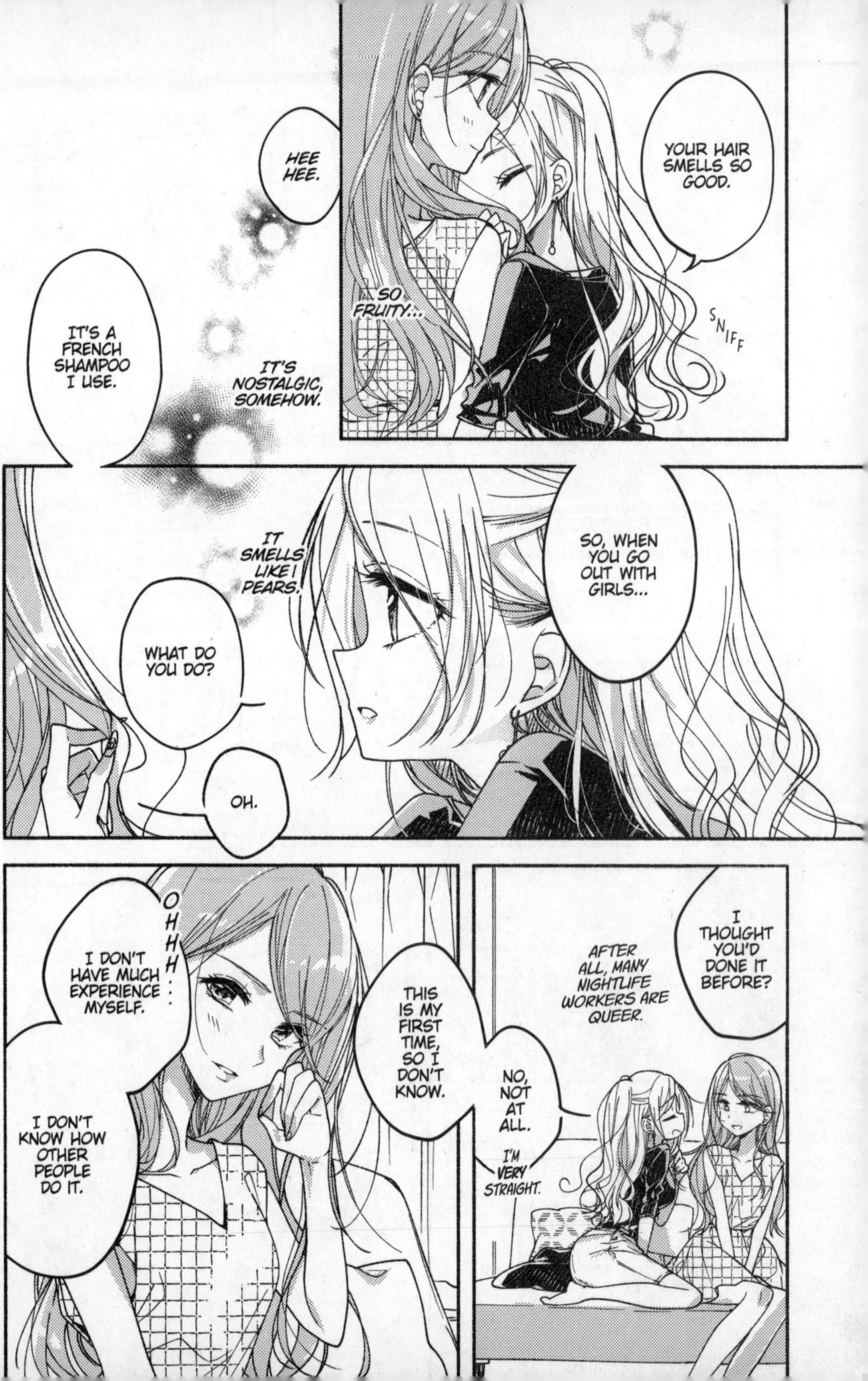
YOUR HAIR SMELLS SO GOOD.
HEE HEE.
SNIFF
SO FRUITY...
IT'S NOSTALGIC, SOMEHOW.
IT'S A FRENCH SHAMPOO I USE.
SO, WHEN YOU GO OUT WITH GIRLS...
IT SMELLS LIKE PEARS.
WHAT DO YOU DO?
OH.
I THOUGHT YOU'D DONE IT BEFORE?
AFTER ALL, MANY NIGHTLIFE WORKERS ARE QUEER.
NO, NOT AT ALL.
I'M VERY STRAIGHT.
THIS IS MY FIRST TIME, SO I DON'T KNOW.
OHHH...
I DON'T HAVE MUCH EXPERIENCE MYSELF.
I DON'T KNOW HOW OTHER PEOPLE DO IT.

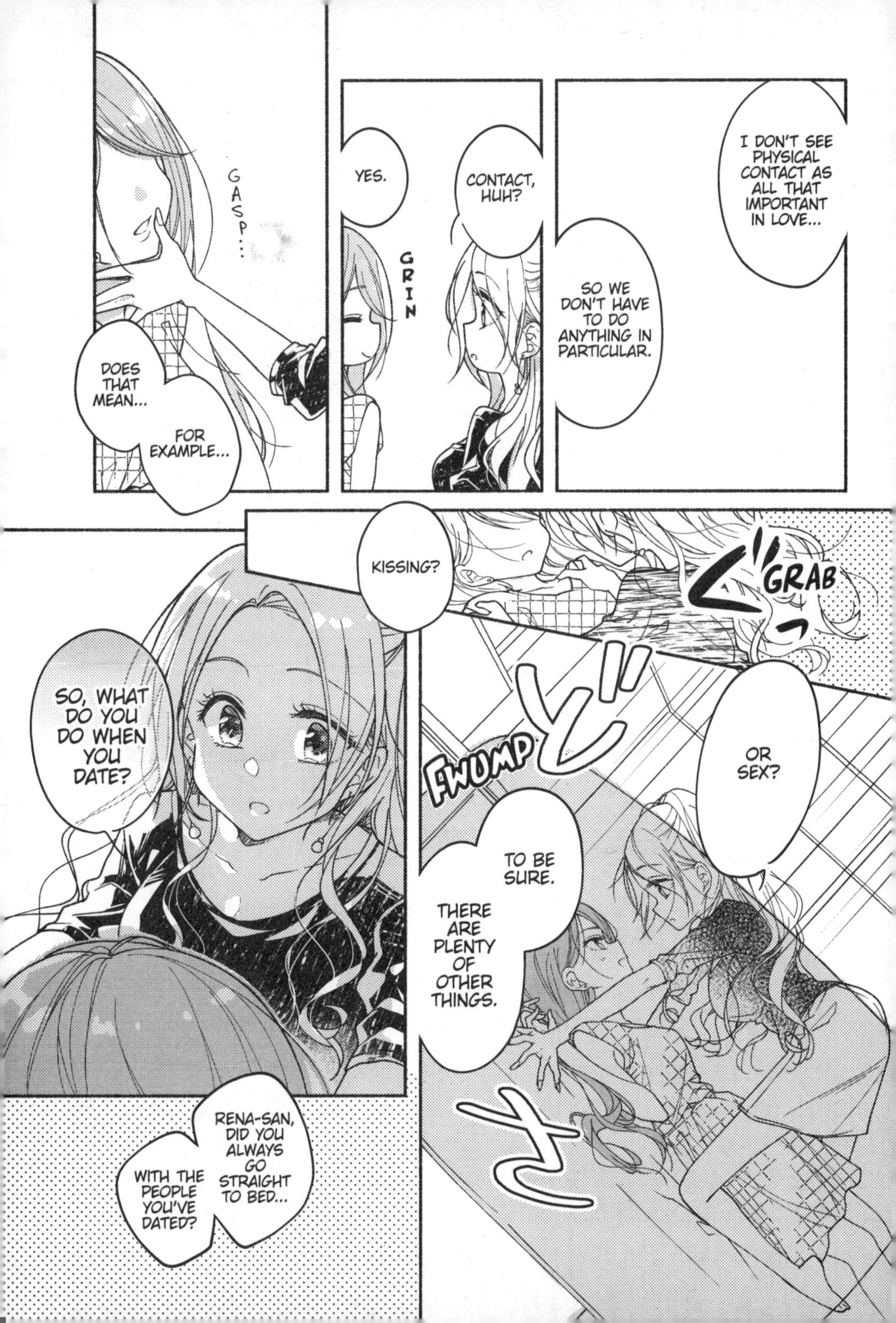
I DON'T SEE PHYSICAL CONTACT AS ALL THAT IMPORTANT IN LOVE...
SO WE DON'T HAVE TO DO ANYTHING IN PARTICULAR.
CONTACT, HUH?
YES.
GRIN
GASP...
DOES THAT MEAN...
FOR EXAMPLE...
KISSING?
GRAB
OR SEX?
FWUMP
TO BE SURE.
THERE ARE PLENTY OF OTHER THINGS.
SO, WHAT DO YOU DO WHEN YOU DATE?
RENA-SAN, DID YOU ALWAYS GO STRAIGHT TO BED...
WITH THE PEOPLE YOU'VE DATED?

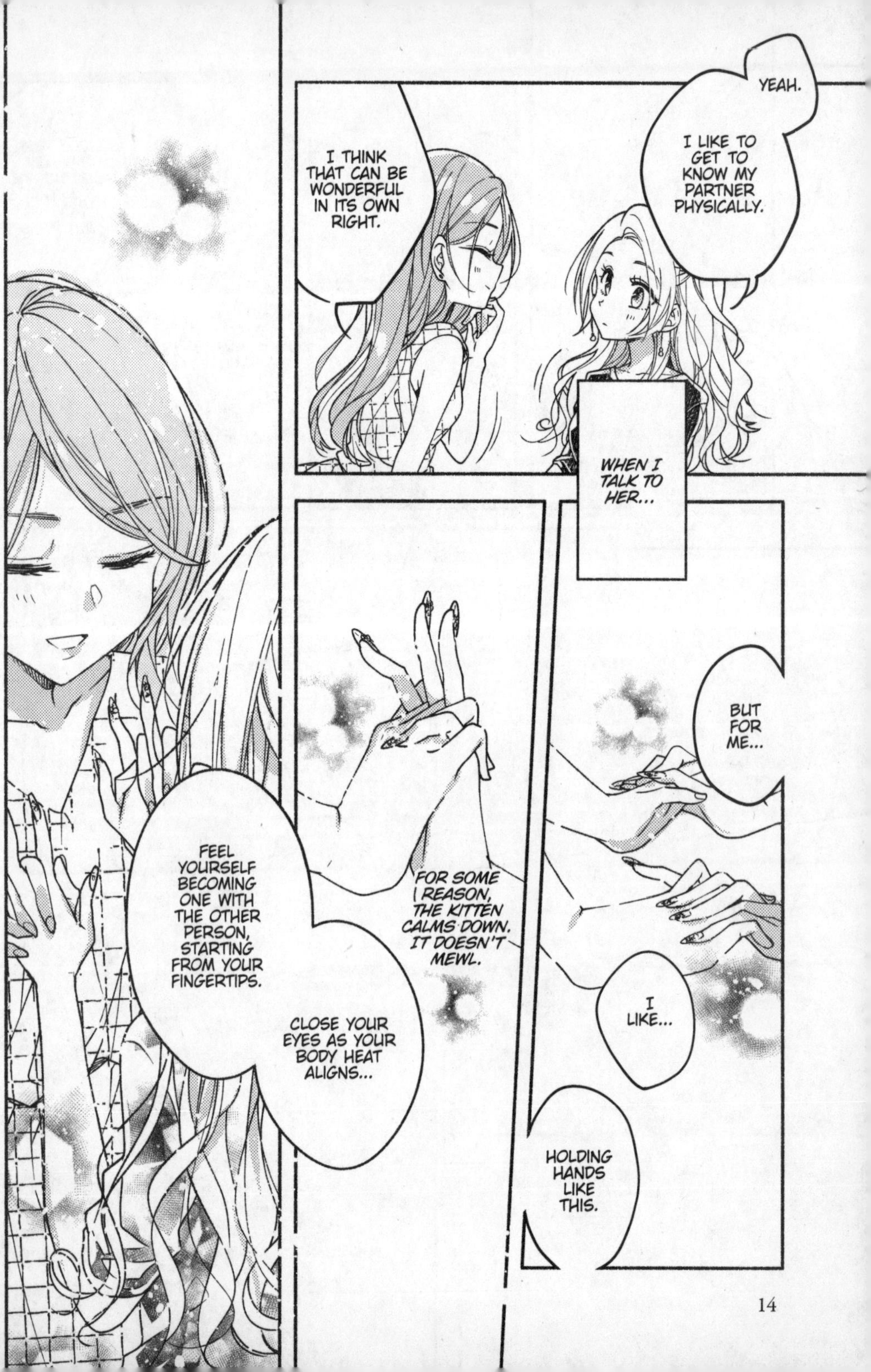
YEAH.
I LIKE TO GET TO KNOW MY PARTNER PHYSICALLY.
I THINK THAT CAN BE WONDERFUL IN ITS OWN RIGHT.
WHEN I TALK TO HER...
BUT FOR ME...
I LIKE...
HOLDING HANDS LIKE THIS.
FOR SOME REASON, THE KITTEN CALMS DOWN. IT DOESN'T MEWL.
FEEL YOURSELF BECOMING ONE WITH THE OTHER PERSON, STARTING FROM YOUR FINGERTIPS.
CLOSE YOUR EYES AS YOUR BODY HEAT ALIGNS...

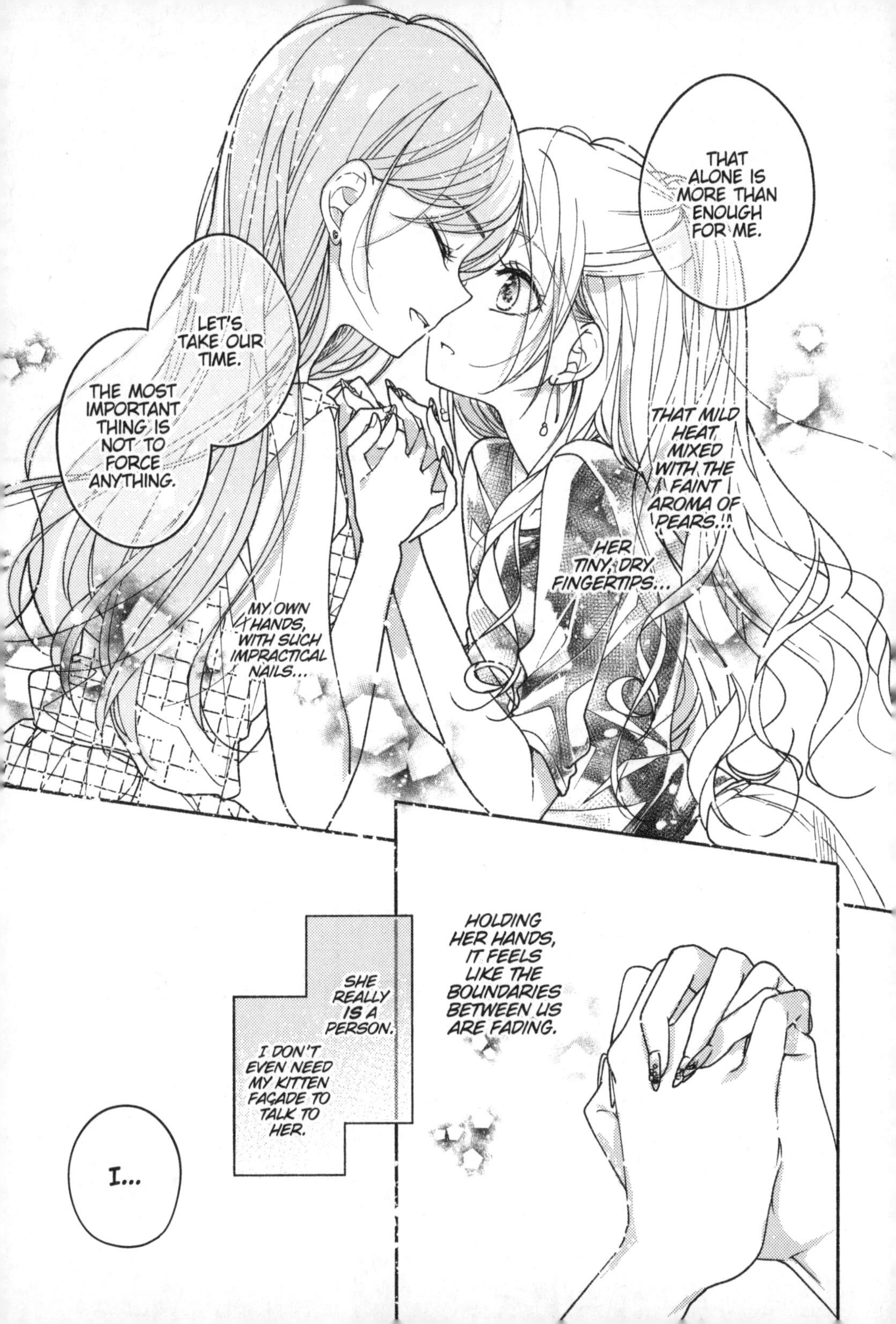
THAT ALONE IS MORE THAN ENOUGH FOR ME.
LET'S TAKE OUR TIME.
THE MOST IMPORTANT THING IS NOT TO FORCE ANYTHING.
THAT MILD HEAT MIXED WITH THE FAINT AROMA OF PEARS...
HER TINY, DRY FINGERTIPS...
MY OWN HANDS, WITH SUCH IMPRACTICAL NAILS...
HOLDING HER HANDS, IT FEELS LIKE THE BOUNDARIES BETWEEN US ARE FADING.
SHE REALLY IS A PERSON.
I DON'T EVEN NEED MY KITTEN FAÇADE TO TALK TO HER.
I...

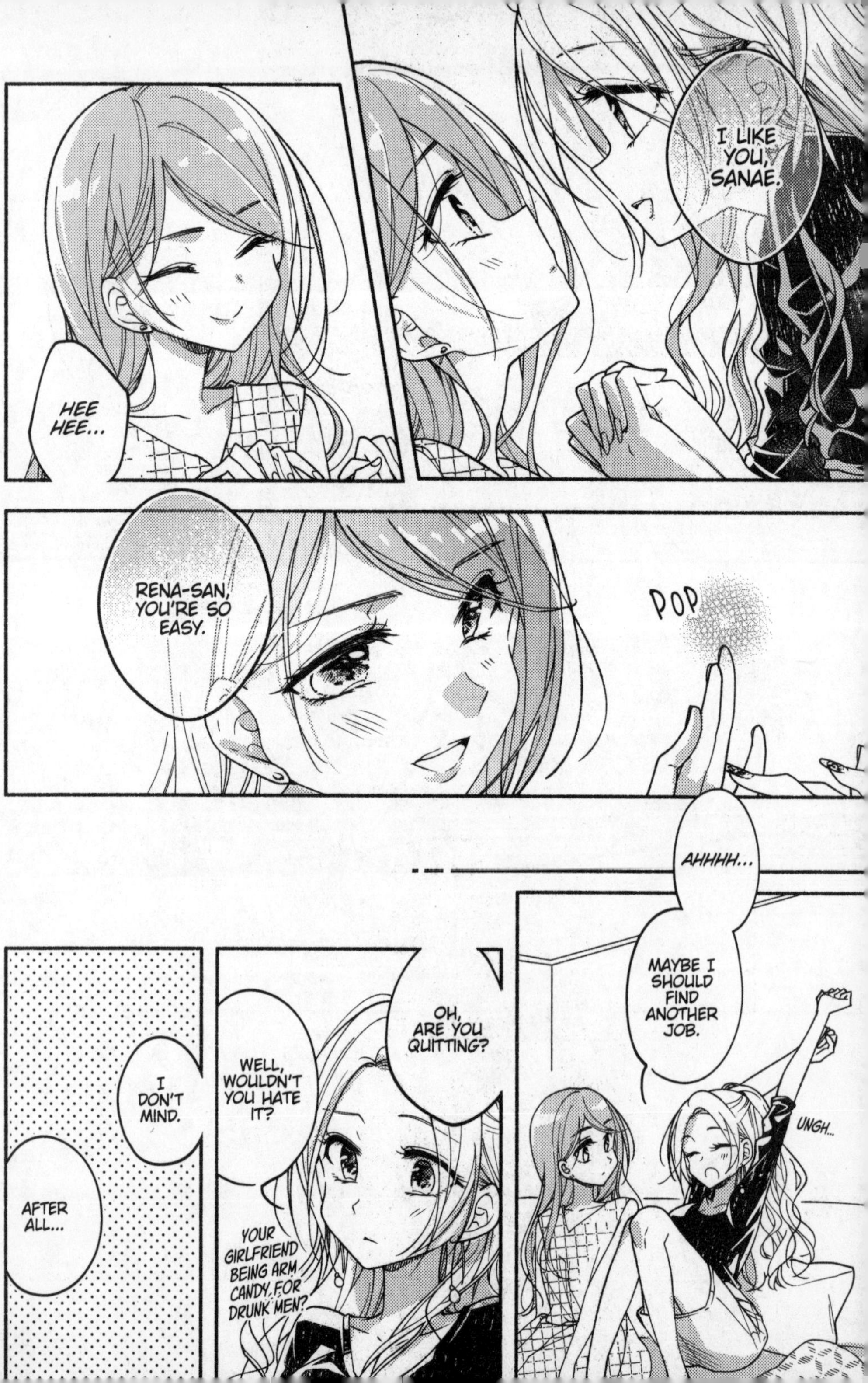
I LIKE YOU, SANAE.
HEE HEE...
RENA-SAN, YOU'RE SO EASY.
POP
AHHHH...
MAYBE I SHOULD FIND ANOTHER JOB.
UNGH...
OH, ARE YOU QUITTING?
WELL, WOULDN'T YOU HATE IT?
YOUR GIRLFRIEND BEING ARM CANDY FOR DRUNK MEN?
I DON'T MIND.
AFTER ALL...

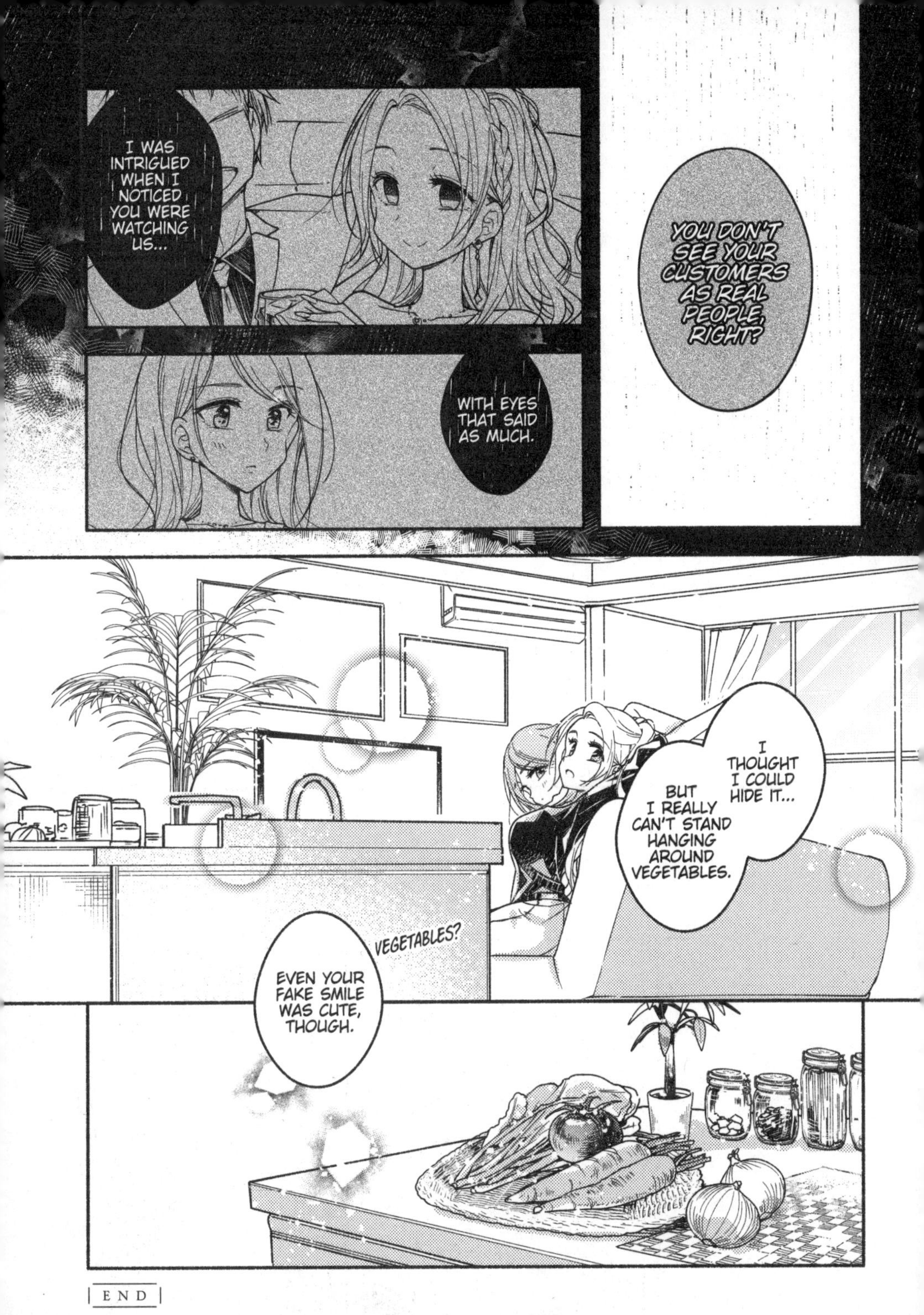
YOU DON'T SEE YOUR CUSTOMERS AS REAL PEOPLE, RIGHT?
I WAS INTRIGUED WHEN I NOTICED YOU WERE WATCHING US...
WITH EYES THAT SAID AS MUCH.
I THOUGHT I COULD HIDE IT...
BUT I REALLY CAN'T STAND HANGING AROUND VEGETABLES.
VEGETABLES?
EVEN YOUR FAKE SMILE WAS CUTE, THOUGH.

END

Cats *and* Sugar Bowls

Crying of the Cat

Cats and Sugar Bowls

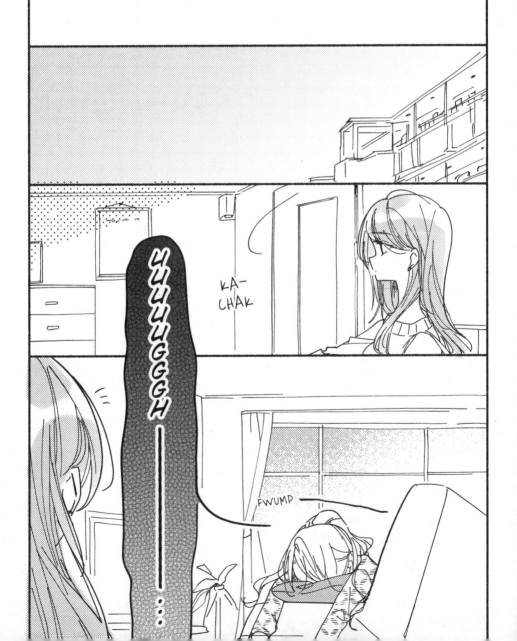

IT'S BEEN THREE MONTHS SINCE I WENT FROM BEING A HOSTESS TO WORKING AN OFFICE JOB.

I'VE BEEN SO GLOOMY, I'M AFRAID BLACK SMOKE WILL LEAK OUT OF MY EARS.

UUUUUGGGH......

KA-CHAK

FWUMP

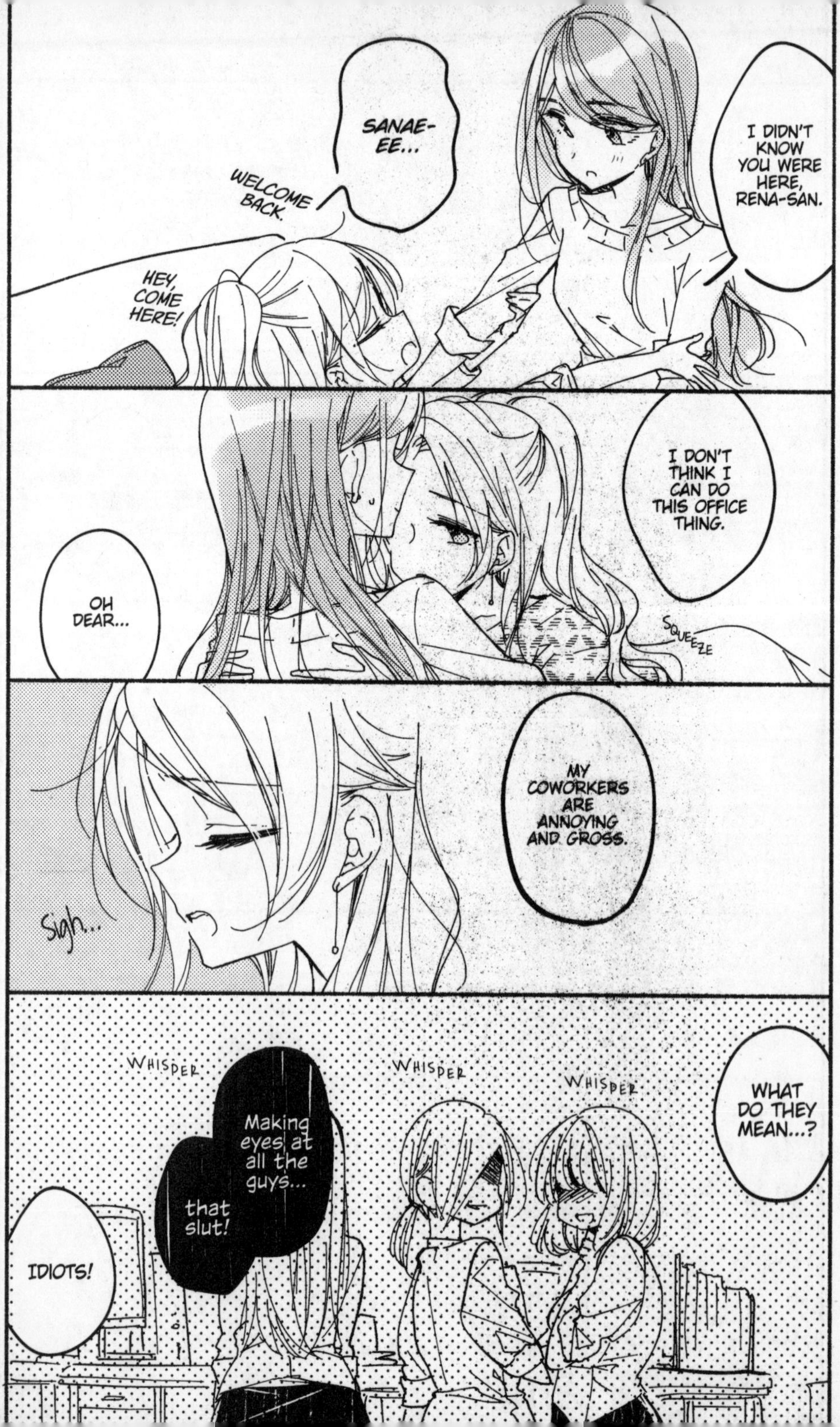
I DIDN'T KNOW YOU WERE HERE, RENA-SAN.
SANAE-EE...
WELCOME BACK.
HEY, COME HERE!
I DON'T THINK I CAN DO THIS OFFICE THING.
SQUEEZE
OH DEAR...
MY COWORKERS ARE ANNOYING AND GROSS.
Sigh...
WHAT DO THEY MEAN...?
WHISPER
WHISPER
WHISPER
Making eyes at all the guys...
that slut!
IDIOTS!

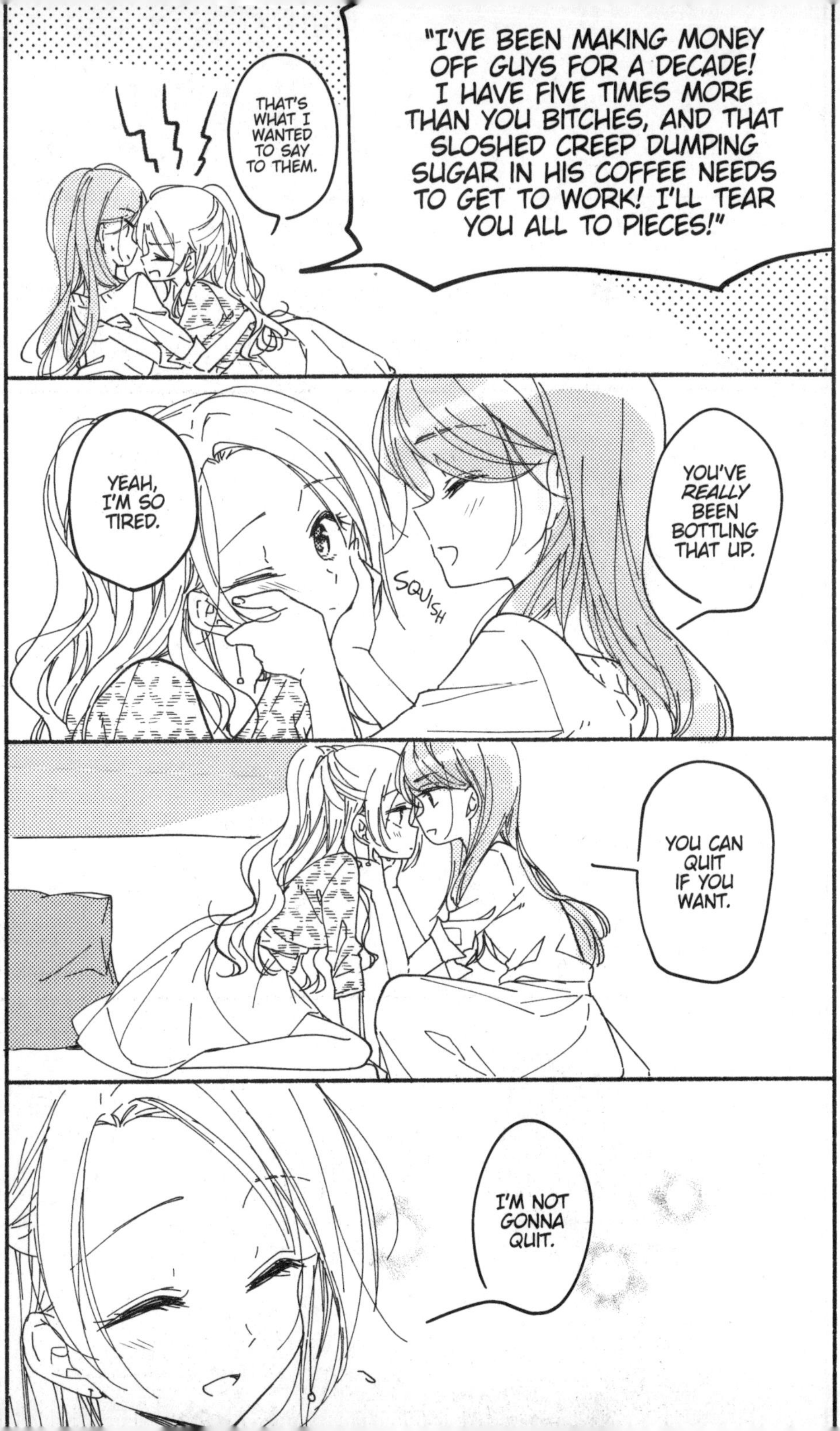
"I'VE BEEN MAKING MONEY OFF GUYS FOR A DECADE! I HAVE FIVE TIMES MORE THAN YOU BITCHES, AND THAT SLOSHED CREEP DUMPING SUGAR IN HIS COFFEE NEEDS TO GET TO WORK! I'LL TEAR YOU ALL TO PIECES!"
THAT'S WHAT I WANTED TO SAY TO THEM.
YOU'VE *REALLY* BEEN BOTTLING THAT UP.
SQUISH
YEAH, I'M SO TIRED.
YOU CAN QUIT IF YOU WANT.
I'M NOT GONNA QUIT.

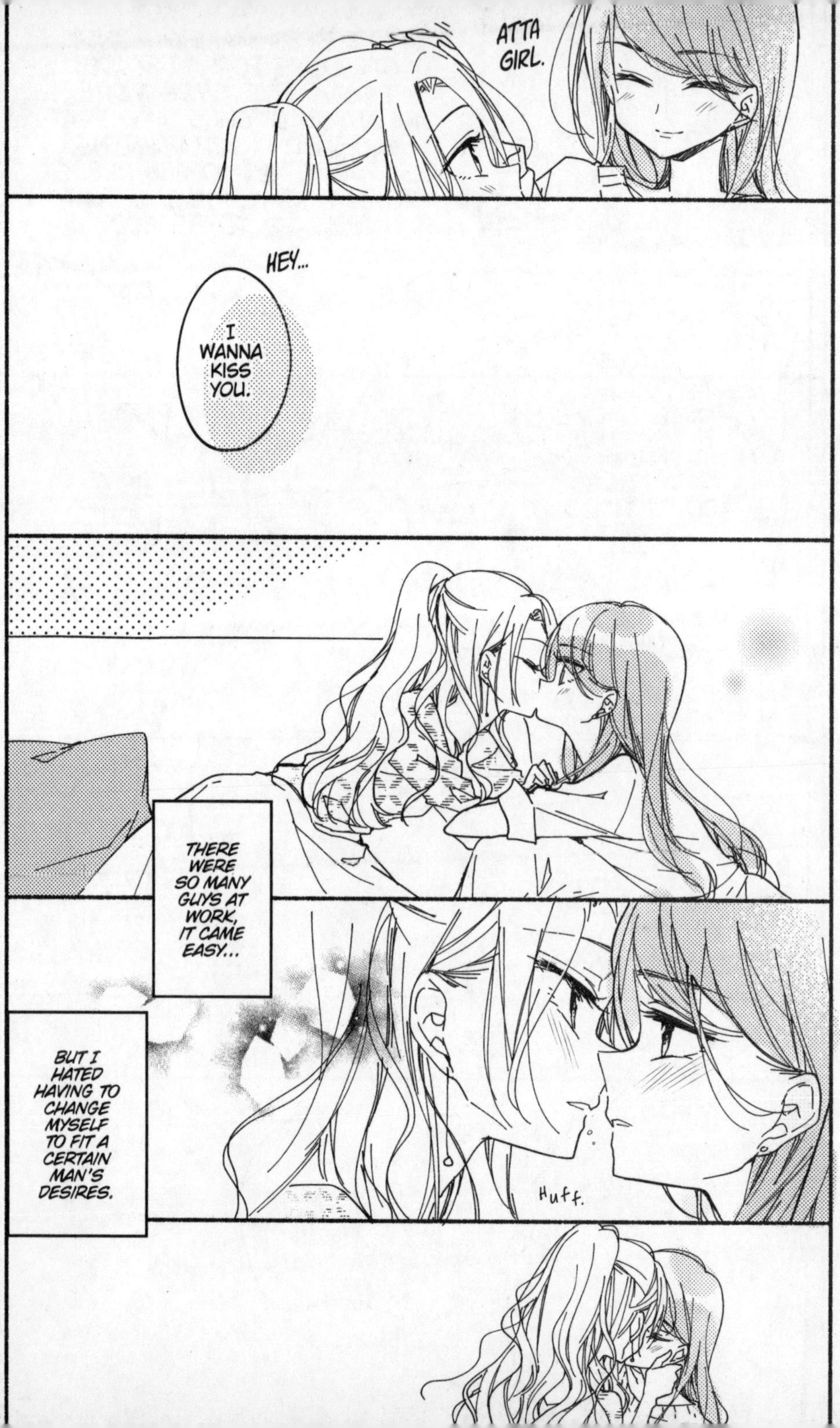
ATTA GIRL.
HEY...
I WANNA KISS YOU.
THERE WERE SO MANY GUYS AT WORK, IT CAME EASY...
BUT I HATED HAVING TO CHANGE MYSELF TO FIT A CERTAIN MAN'S DESIRES.
Huff.

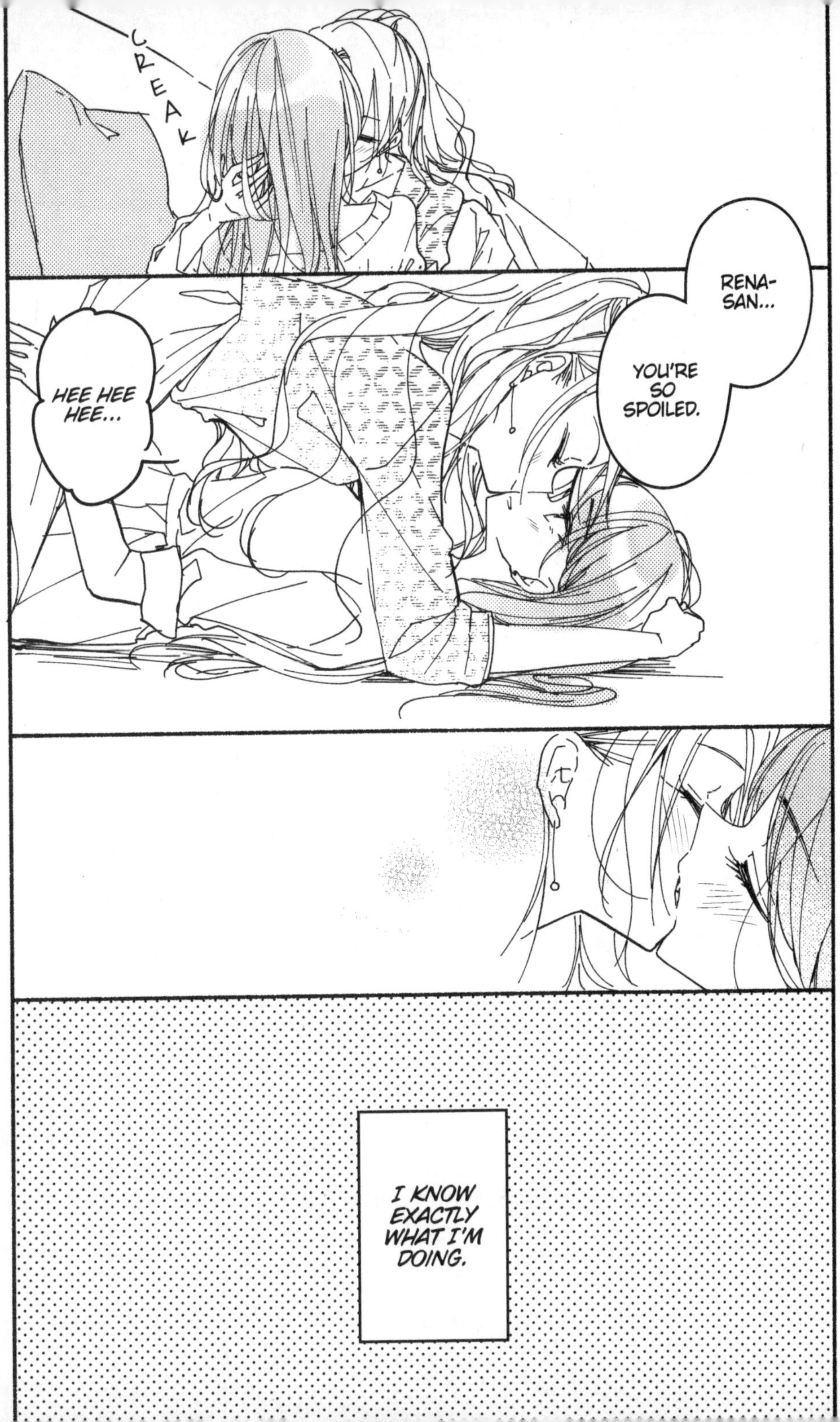
CREAK
RENA-SAN...
YOU'RE SO SPOILED.
HEE HEE HEE...
I KNOW EXACTLY WHAT I'M DOING.

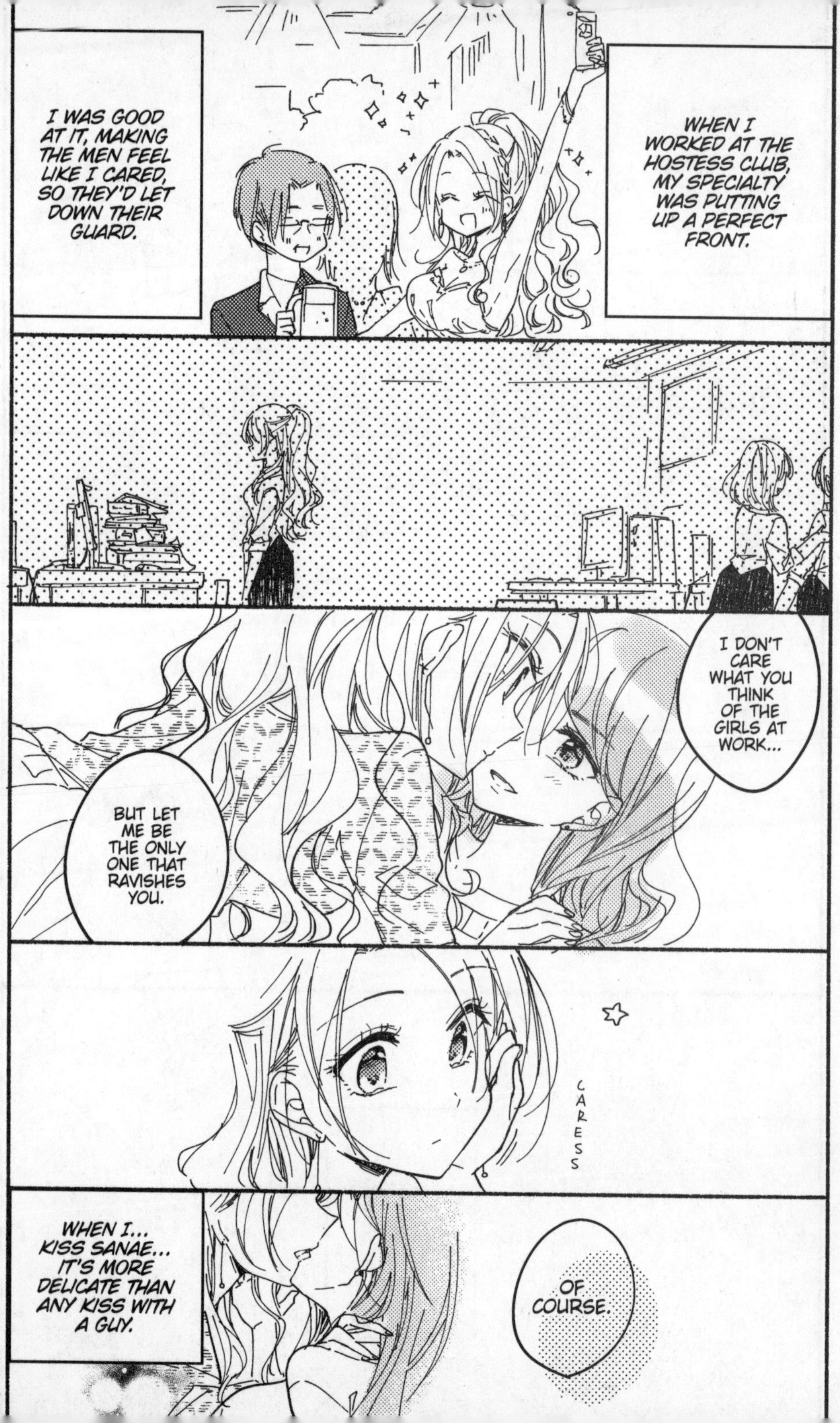

WHEN I WORKED AT THE HOSTESS CLUB, MY SPECIALTY WAS PUTTING UP A PERFECT FRONT.
I WAS GOOD AT IT, MAKING THE MEN FEEL LIKE I CARED, SO THEY'D LET DOWN THEIR GUARD.
I DON'T CARE WHAT YOU THINK OF THE GIRLS AT WORK...
BUT LET ME BE THE ONLY ONE THAT RAVISHES YOU.
CARESS
OF COURSE.
WHEN I... KISS SANAE... IT'S MORE DELICATE THAN ANY KISS WITH A GUY.

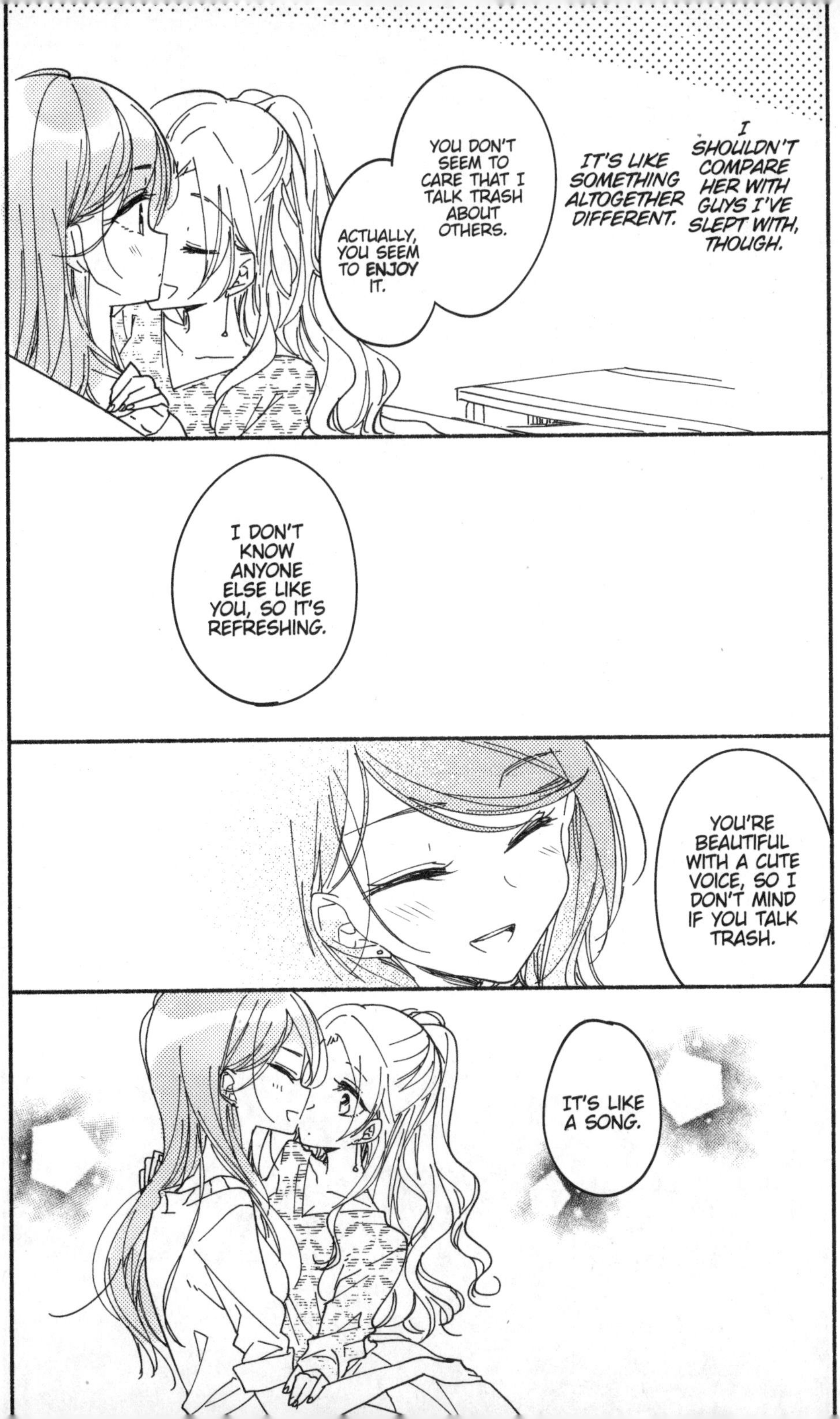
I SHOULDN'T COMPARE HER WITH GUYS I'VE SLEPT WITH, THOUGH.
IT'S LIKE SOMETHING ALTOGETHER DIFFERENT.
YOU DON'T SEEM TO CARE THAT I TALK TRASH ABOUT OTHERS.
ACTUALLY, YOU SEEM TO ENJOY IT.
I DON'T KNOW ANYONE ELSE LIKE YOU, SO IT'S REFRESHING.
YOU'RE BEAUTIFUL WITH A CUTE VOICE, SO I DON'T MIND IF YOU TALK TRASH.
IT'S LIKE A SONG.

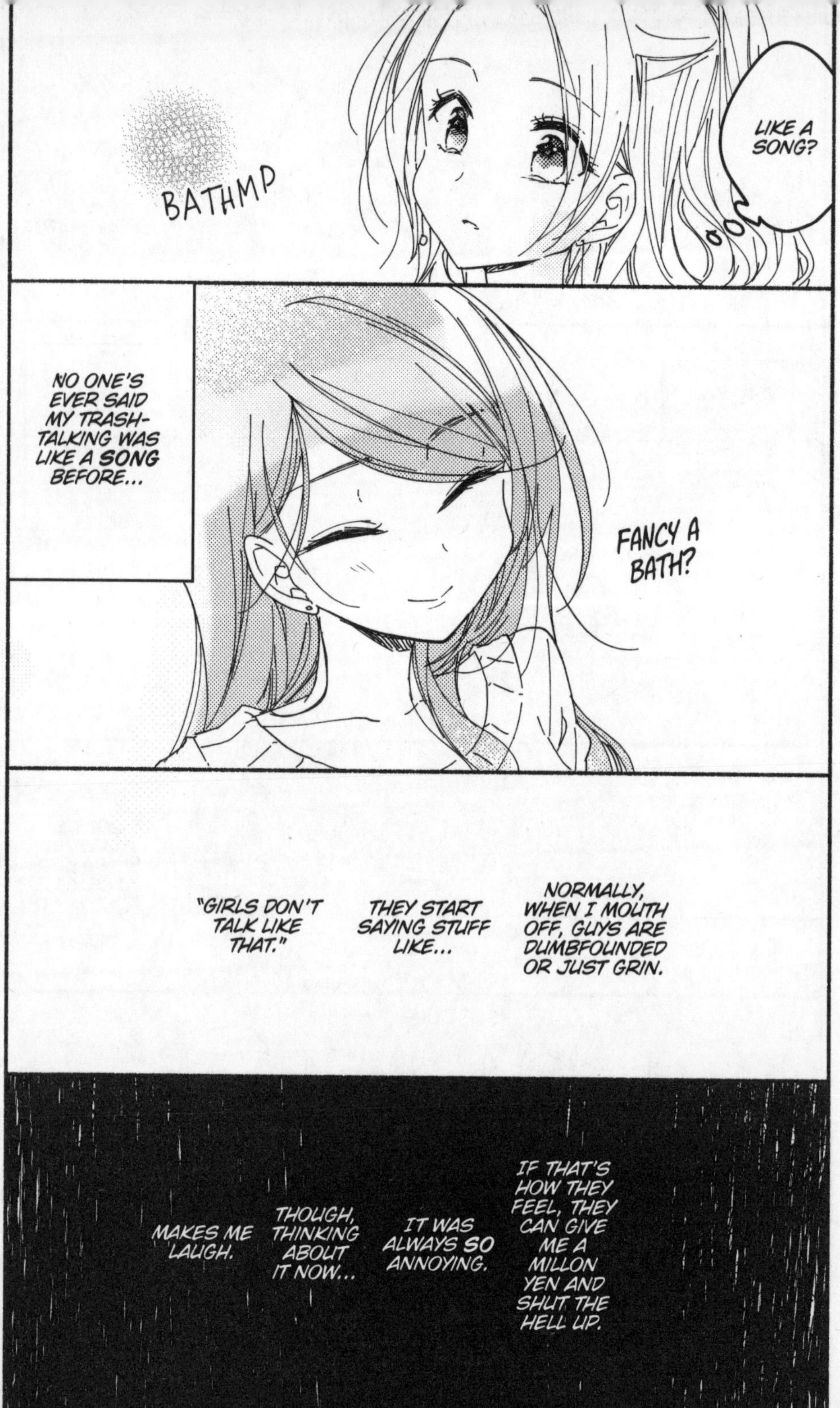
LIKE A SONG?
BATHMP
FANCY A BATH?
NO ONE'S EVER SAID MY TRASH-TALKING WAS LIKE A SONG BEFORE...
NORMALLY, WHEN I MOUTH OFF, GUYS ARE DUMBFOUNDED OR JUST GRIN.
THEY START SAYING STUFF LIKE...
"GIRLS DON'T TALK LIKE THAT."
IF THAT'S HOW THEY FEEL, THEY CAN GIVE ME A MILLON YEN AND SHUT THE HELL UP.
IT WAS ALWAYS SO ANNOYING.
THOUGH, THINKING ABOUT IT NOW...
MAKES ME LAUGH.

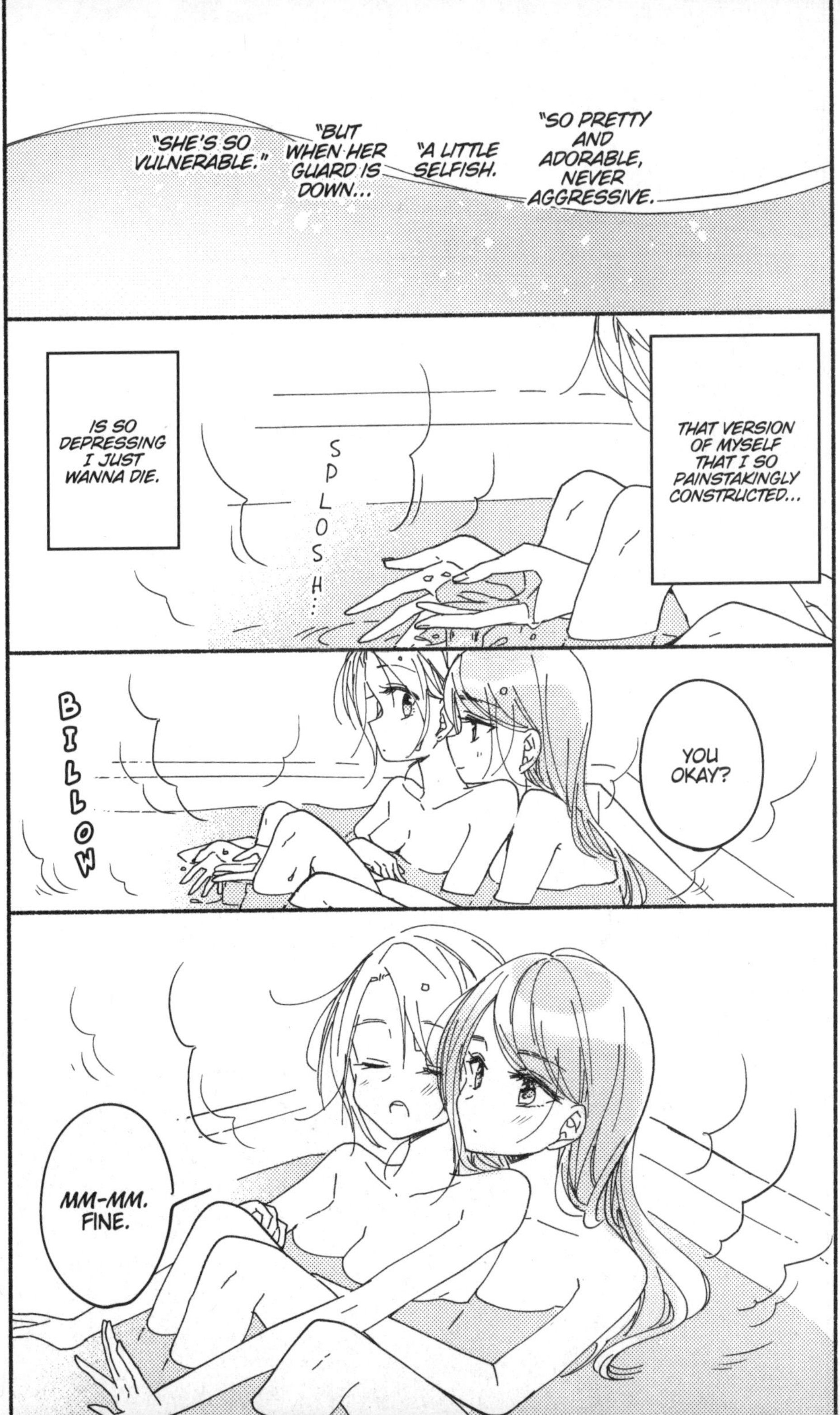
"SO PRETTY AND ADORABLE, NEVER AGGRESSIVE.
"A LITTLE SELFISH.
"BUT WHEN HER GUARD IS DOWN...
"SHE'S SO VULNERABLE."
THAT VERSION OF MYSELF THAT I SO PAINSTAKINGLY CONSTRUCTED...
SPLOSH...
IS SO DEPRESSING I JUST WANNA DIE.
YOU OKAY?
BILLOW
MM-MM. FINE.

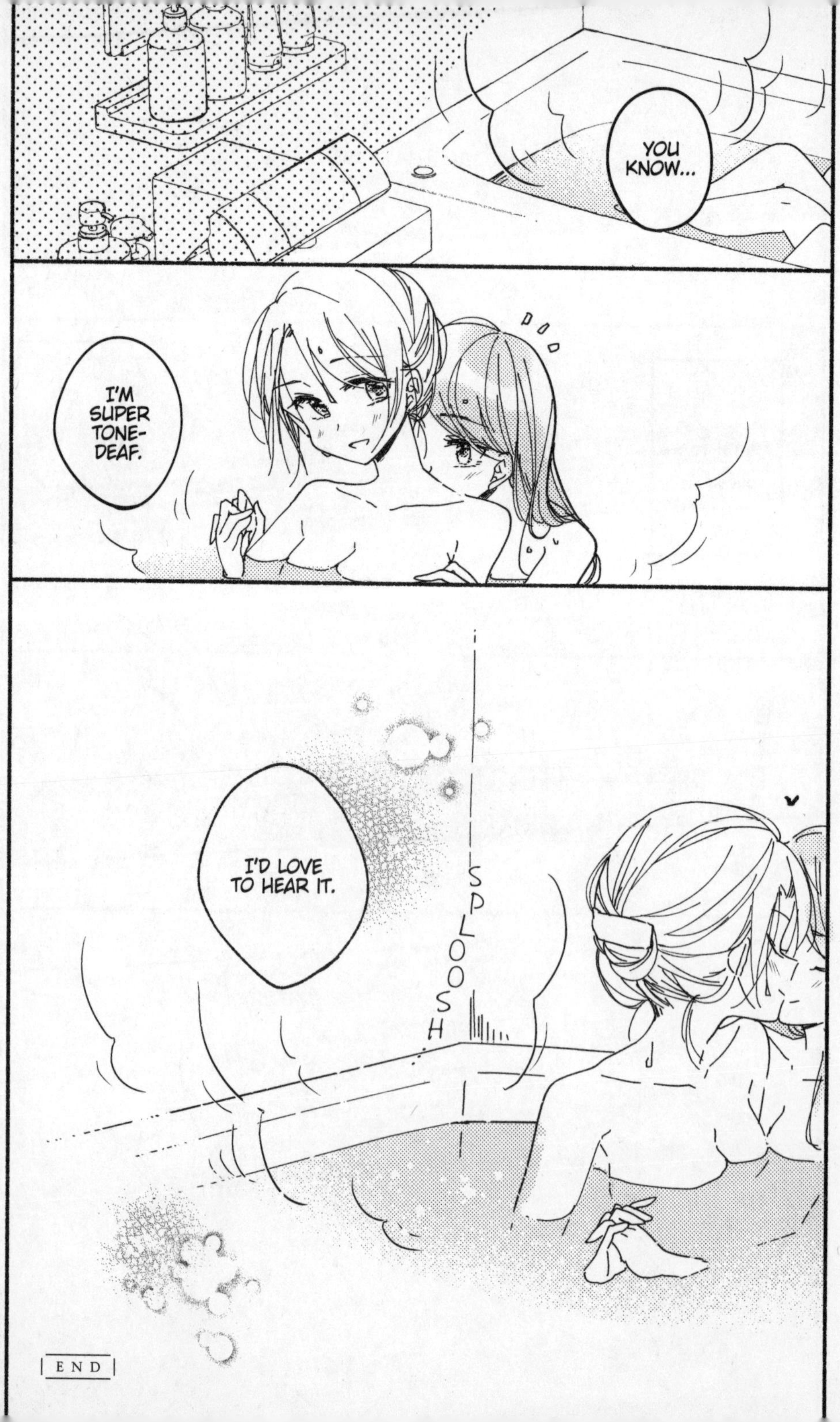
YOU KNOW...
I'M SUPER TONE-DEAF.
I'D LOVE TO HEAR IT.
SPLOOSH
END

The Phone and
the Cat

Cats and Sugar Bowls

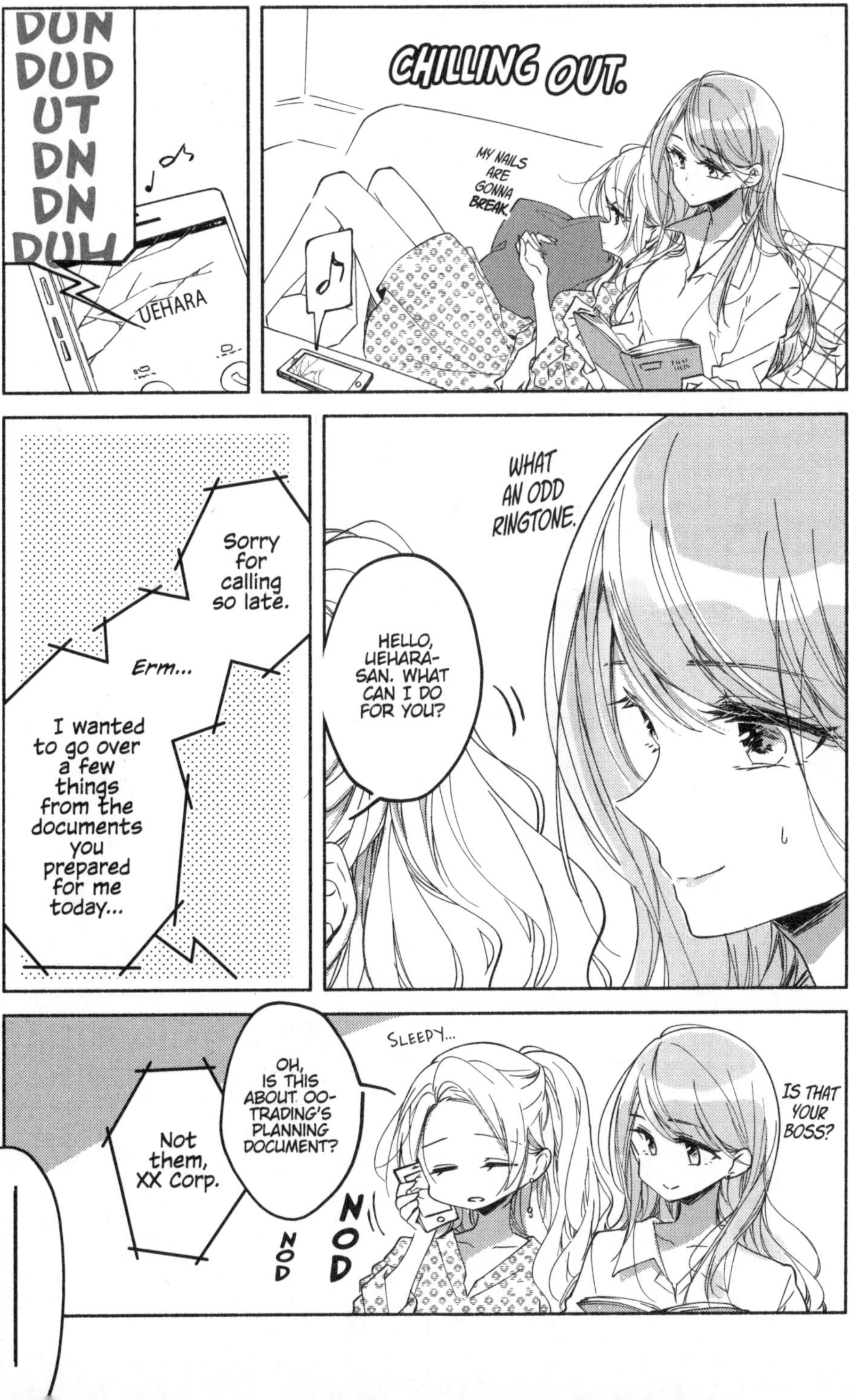
CHILLING OUT.
MY NAILS ARE GONNA BREAK.
DUN DUD UT DN DN DUH
UEHARA
WHAT AN ODD RINGTONE.
HELLO, UEHARA-SAN. WHAT CAN I DO FOR YOU?
Sorry for calling so late.
Erm...
I wanted to go over a few things from the documents you prepared for me today...
IS THAT YOUR BOSS?
SLEEPY...
OH, IS THIS ABOUT OO-TRADING'S PLANNING DOCUMENT?
NOD NOD
Not them, XX Corp.

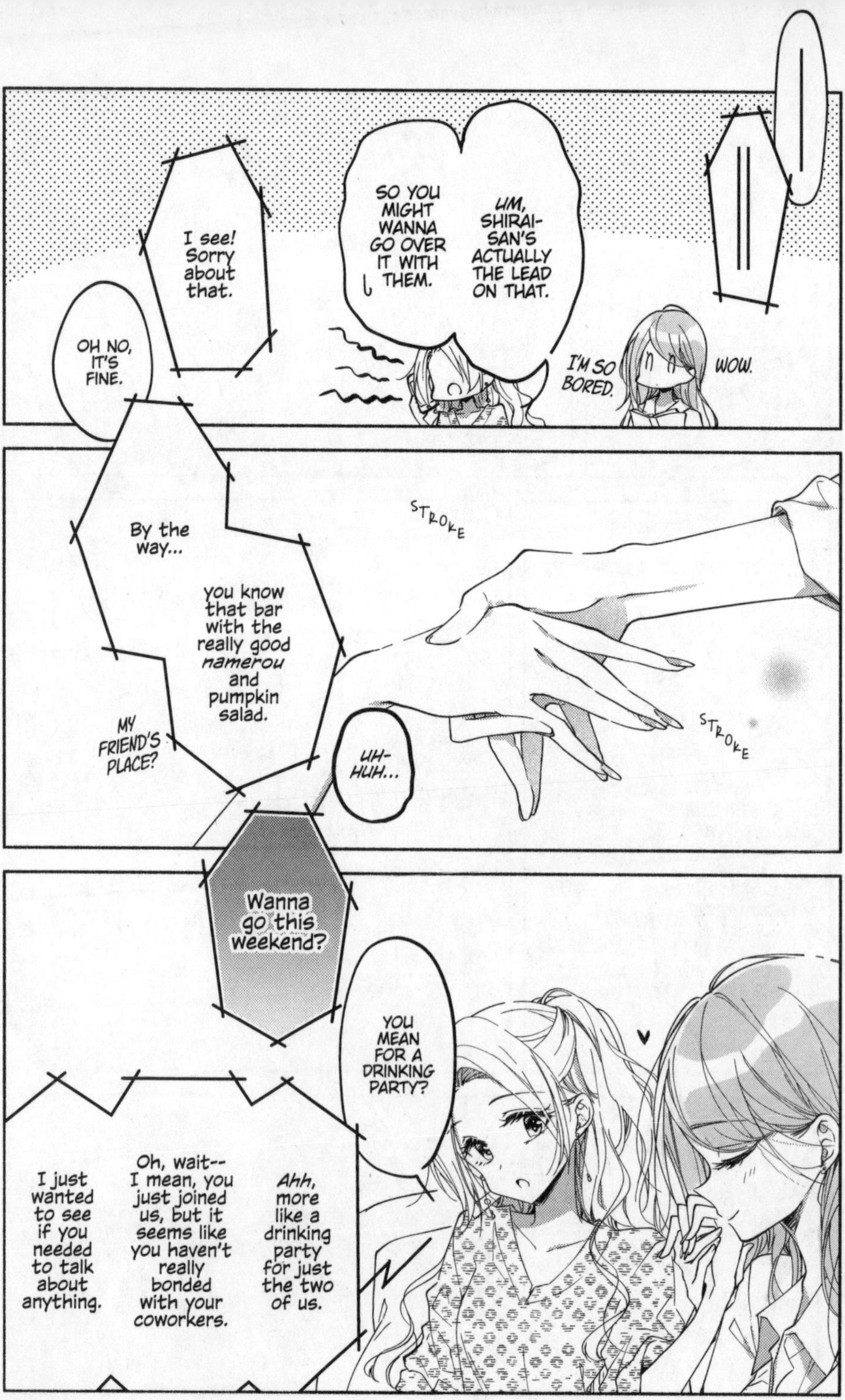
WOW.
I'M SO BORED.
UM, SHIRAI-SAN'S ACTUALLY THE LEAD ON THAT.
SO YOU MIGHT WANNA GO OVER IT WITH THEM.
I see! Sorry about that.
OH NO, IT'S FINE.
STROKE
STROKE
By the way...
you know that bar with the really good *namerou* and pumpkin salad.
UH-HUH...
MY FRIEND'S PLACE?
Wanna go this weekend?
YOU MEAN FOR A DRINKING PARTY?
Ahh, more like a drinking party for just the two of us.
Oh, wait-- I mean, you just joined us, but it seems like you haven't really bonded with your coworkers.
I just wanted to see if you needed to talk about anything.

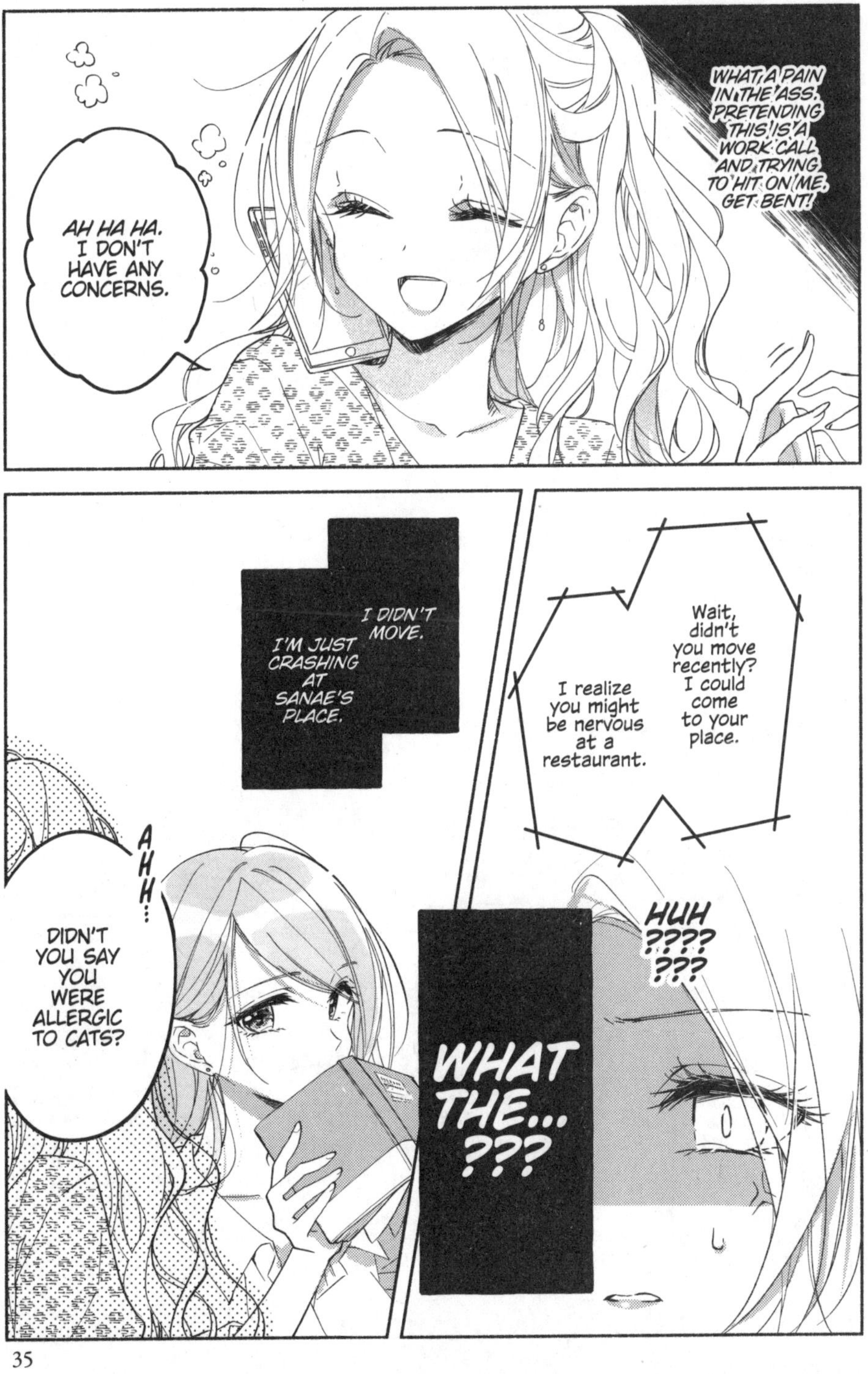
WHAT A PAIN IN THE ASS. PRETENDING THIS IS A WORK CALL AND TRYING TO HIT ON ME. GET BENT!
AH HA HA. I DON'T HAVE ANY CONCERNS.
Wait, didn't you move recently? I could come to your place.
I realize you might be nervous at a restaurant.
HUH ???? ???
WHAT THE... ???
I DIDN'T MOVE.
I'M JUST CRASHING AT SANAE'S PLACE.
AHH...
DIDN'T YOU SAY YOU WERE ALLERGIC TO CATS?

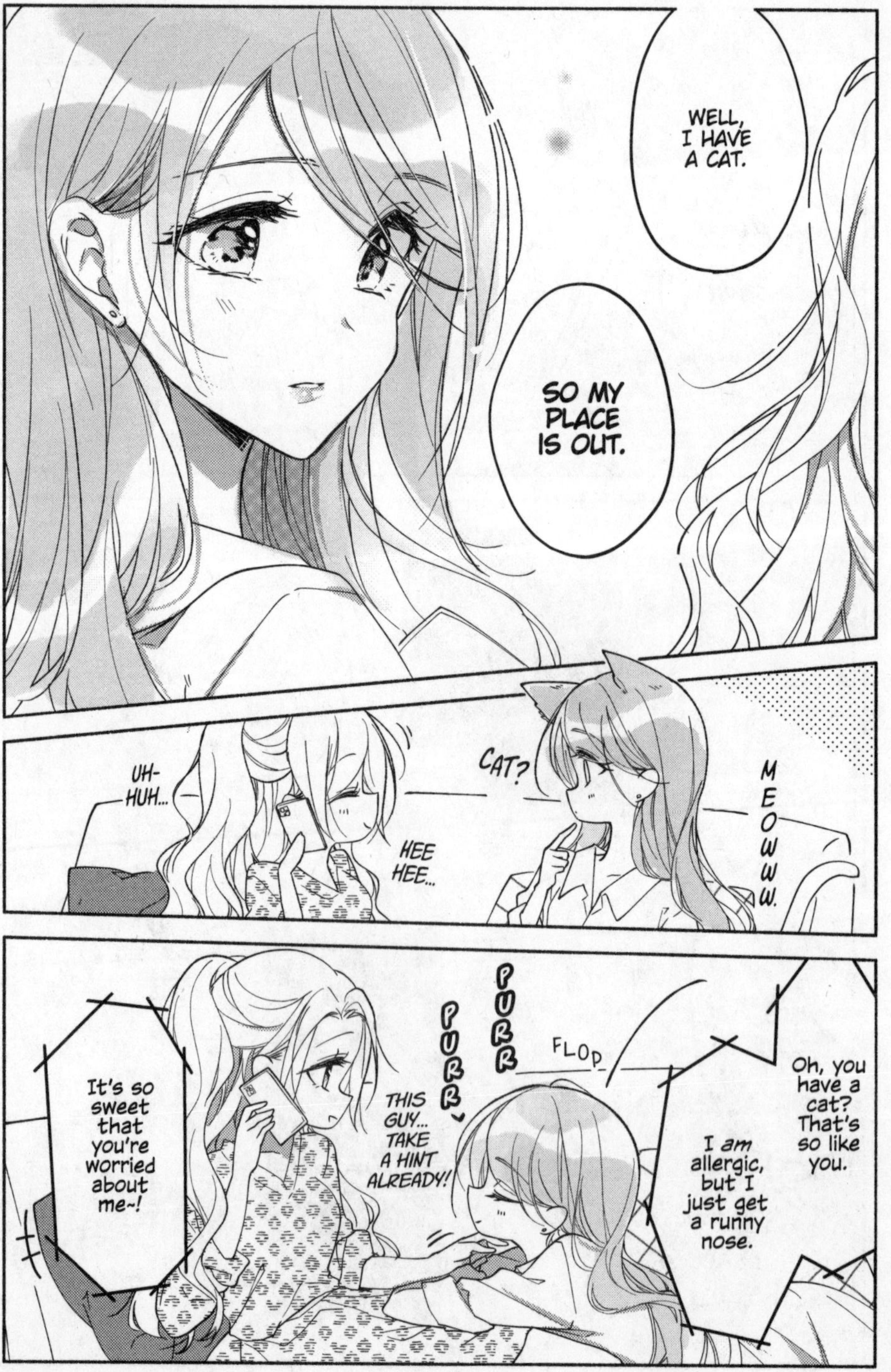
WELL, I HAVE A CAT.
SO MY PLACE IS OUT.
MEOWWW.
CAT?
UH-HUH...
HEE HEE...
Oh, you have a cat? That's so like you.
I *am* allergic, but I just get a runny nose.
FLOP
PURR
PURR
THIS GUY... TAKE A HINT ALREADY!
It's so sweet that you're worried about me~!

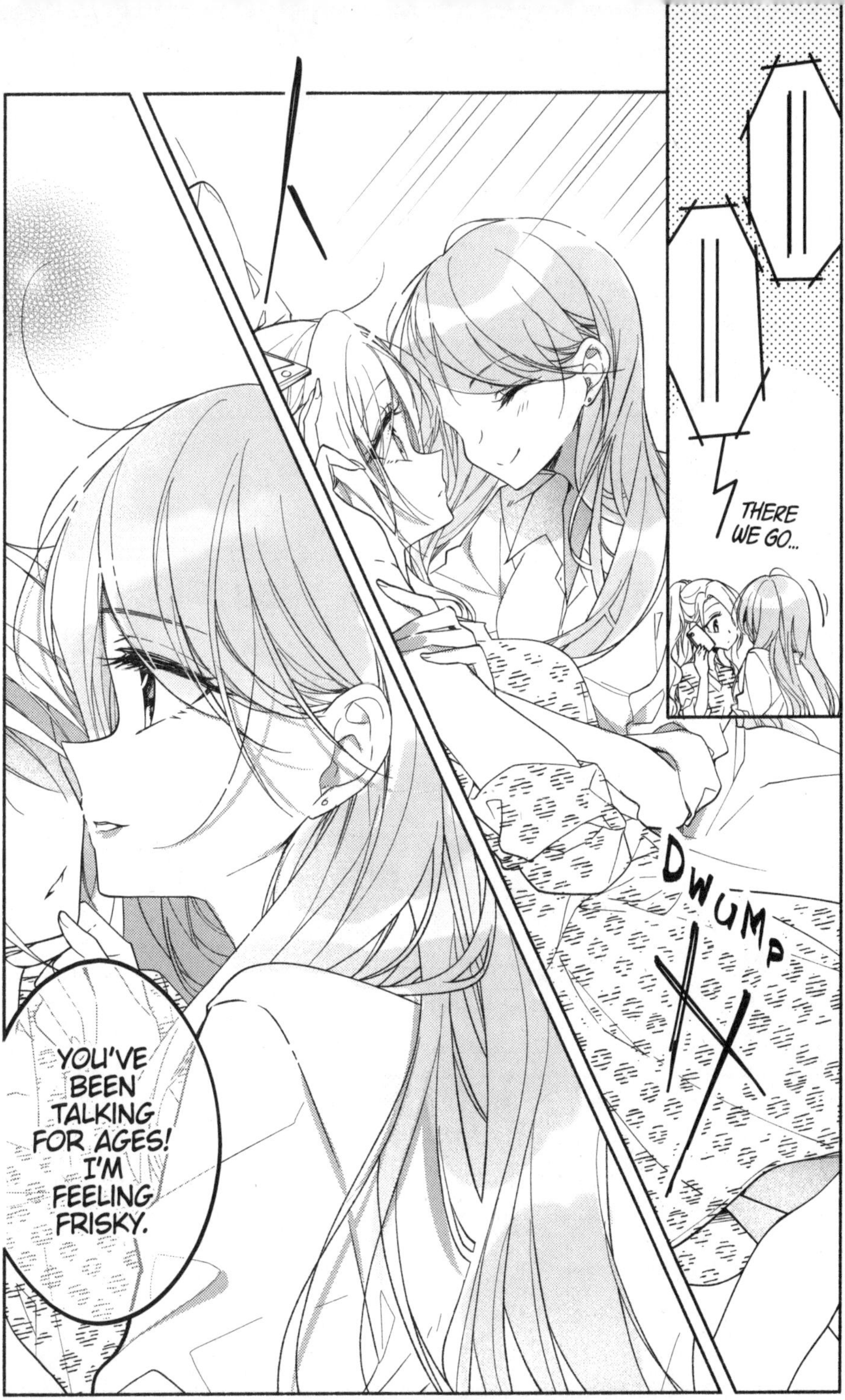
THERE WE GO...
DWUMP
YOU'VE BEEN TALKING FOR AGES! I'M FEELING FRISKY.

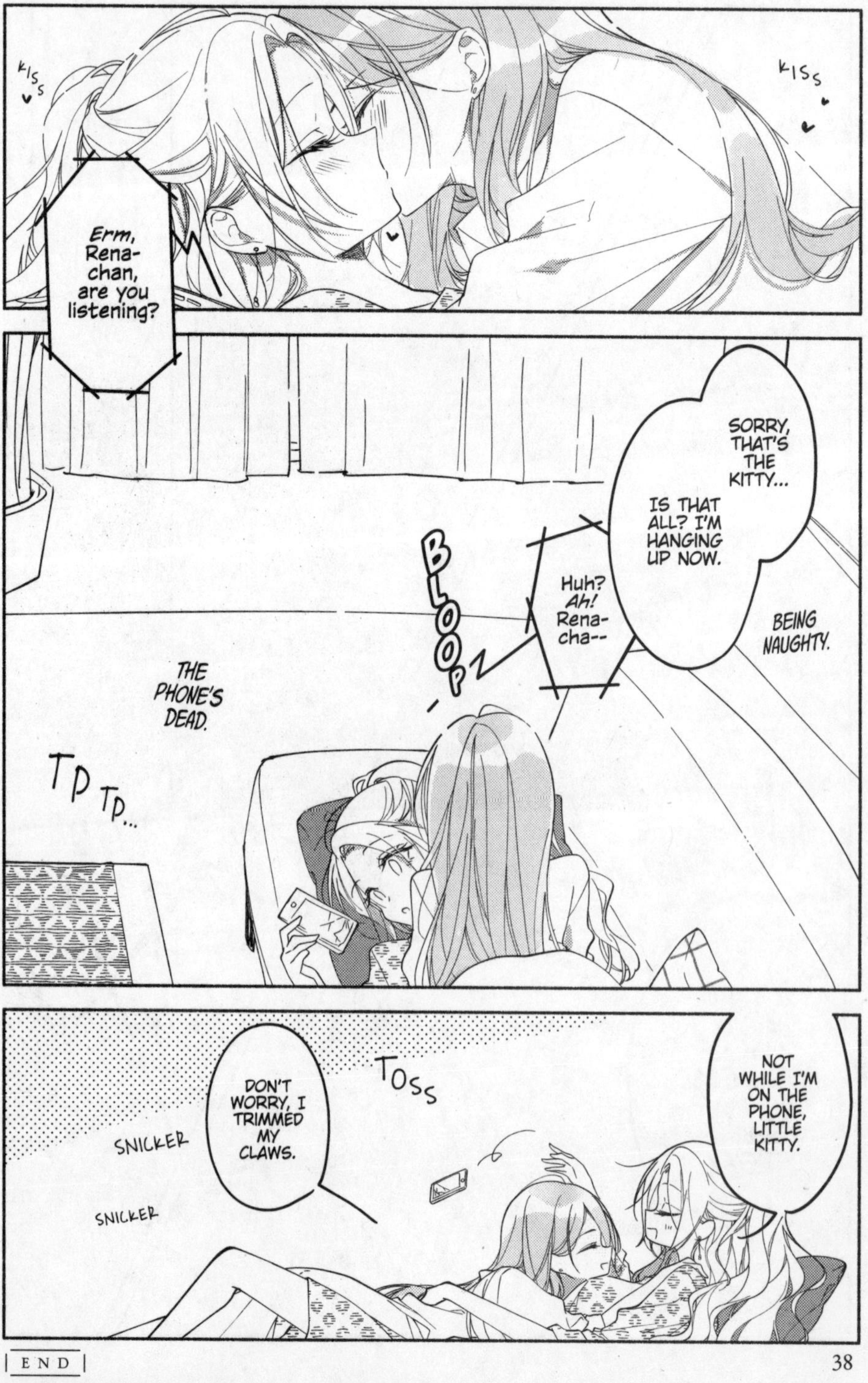

KISS
KISS
Erm, Rena-chan, are you listening?
SORRY, THAT'S THE KITTY...
BEING NAUGHTY.
IS THAT ALL? I'M HANGING UP NOW.
Huh? Ah! Rena-cha--
BLOOP
THE PHONE'S DEAD.
TP TP...
NOT WHILE I'M ON THE PHONE, LITTLE KITTY.
TOSS
DON'T WORRY, I TRIMMED MY CLAWS.
SNICKER
SNICKER

END

Unbreakable Sugar Bowl

Cats and Sugar Bowls

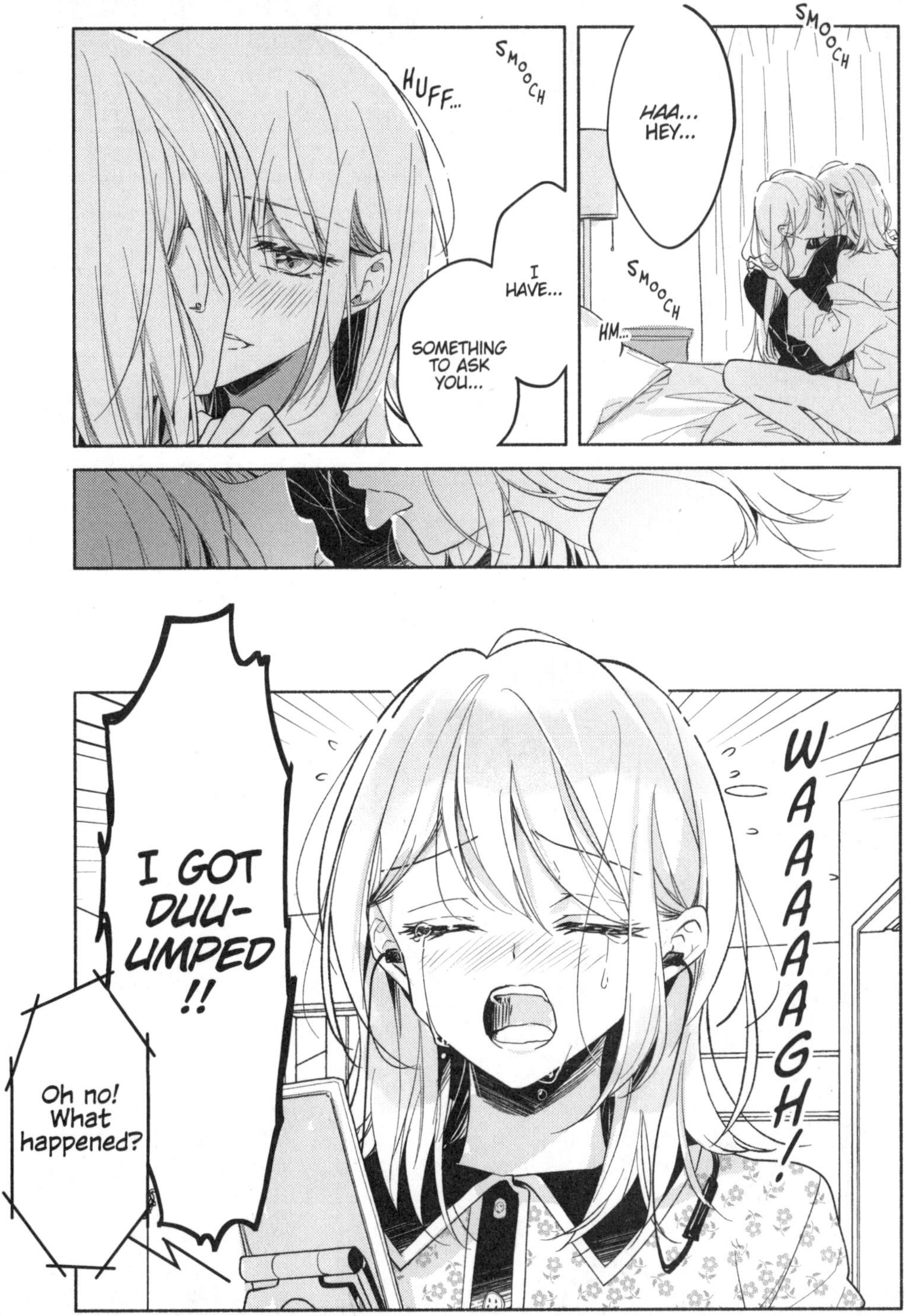
SMOOCH
HAA... HEY...
SMOOCH
HM...
HUFF...
SMOOCH
I HAVE...
SOMETHING TO ASK YOU...
WAAAAAAAGH!
I GOT DUU-UMPED!!
Oh no! What happened?

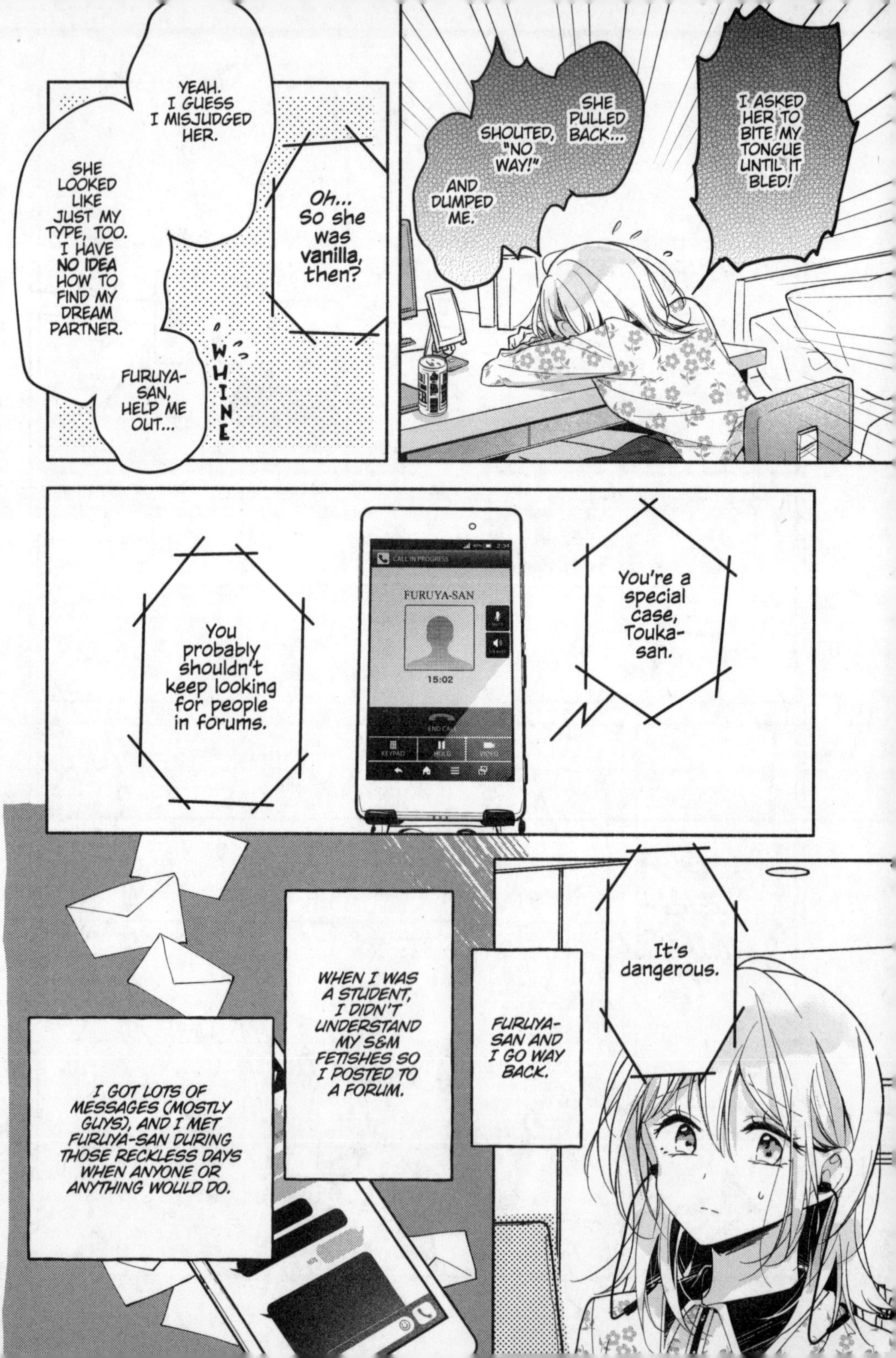
I ASKED HER TO BITE MY TONGUE UNTIL IT BLED!
SHE PULLED BACK...
SHOUTED, "NO WAY!"
AND DUMPED ME.
Oh... So she was vanilla, then?
YEAH. I GUESS I MISJUDGED HER.
SHE LOOKED LIKE JUST MY TYPE, TOO. I HAVE NO IDEA HOW TO FIND MY DREAM PARTNER.
WHINE
FURUYA-SAN, HELP ME OUT...
You're a special case, Touka-san.
CALL IN PROGRESS
FURUYA-SAN
15:02
END CALL
KEYPAD
HOLD
VIDEO
You probably shouldn't keep looking for people in forums.
It's dangerous.
FURUYA-SAN AND I GO WAY BACK.
WHEN I WAS A STUDENT, I DIDN'T UNDERSTAND MY S&M FETISHES SO I POSTED TO A FORUM.
I GOT LOTS OF MESSAGES (MOSTLY GUYS), AND I MET FURUYA-SAN DURING THOSE RECKLESS DAYS WHEN ANYONE OR ANYTHING WOULD DO.

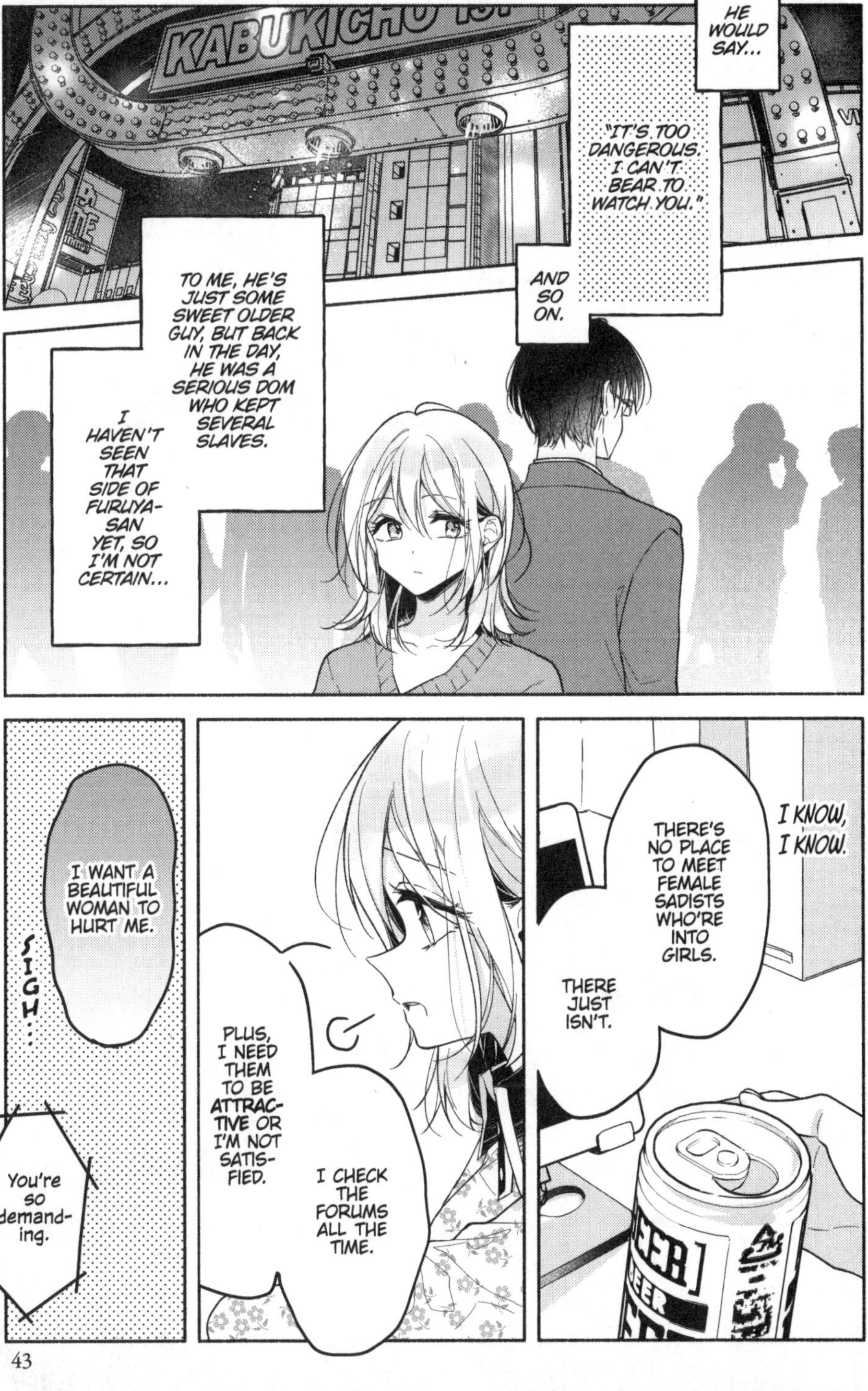
KABUKICHO
HE WOULD SAY...
"IT'S TOO DANGEROUS. I CAN'T BEAR TO WATCH YOU."
AND SO ON.
TO ME, HE'S JUST SOME SWEET OLDER GUY, BUT BACK IN THE DAY, HE WAS A SERIOUS DOM WHO KEPT SEVERAL SLAVES.
I HAVEN'T SEEN THAT SIDE OF FURUYA-SAN YET, SO I'M NOT CERTAIN...
I KNOW, I KNOW.
THERE'S NO PLACE TO MEET FEMALE SADISTS WHO'RE INTO GIRLS.
THERE JUST ISN'T.
PLUS, I NEED THEM TO BE **ATTRACTIVE** OR I'M NOT SATISFIED.
I CHECK THE FORUMS ALL THE TIME.
I WANT A BEAUTIFUL WOMAN TO HURT ME.
SIGH...
You're so demanding.

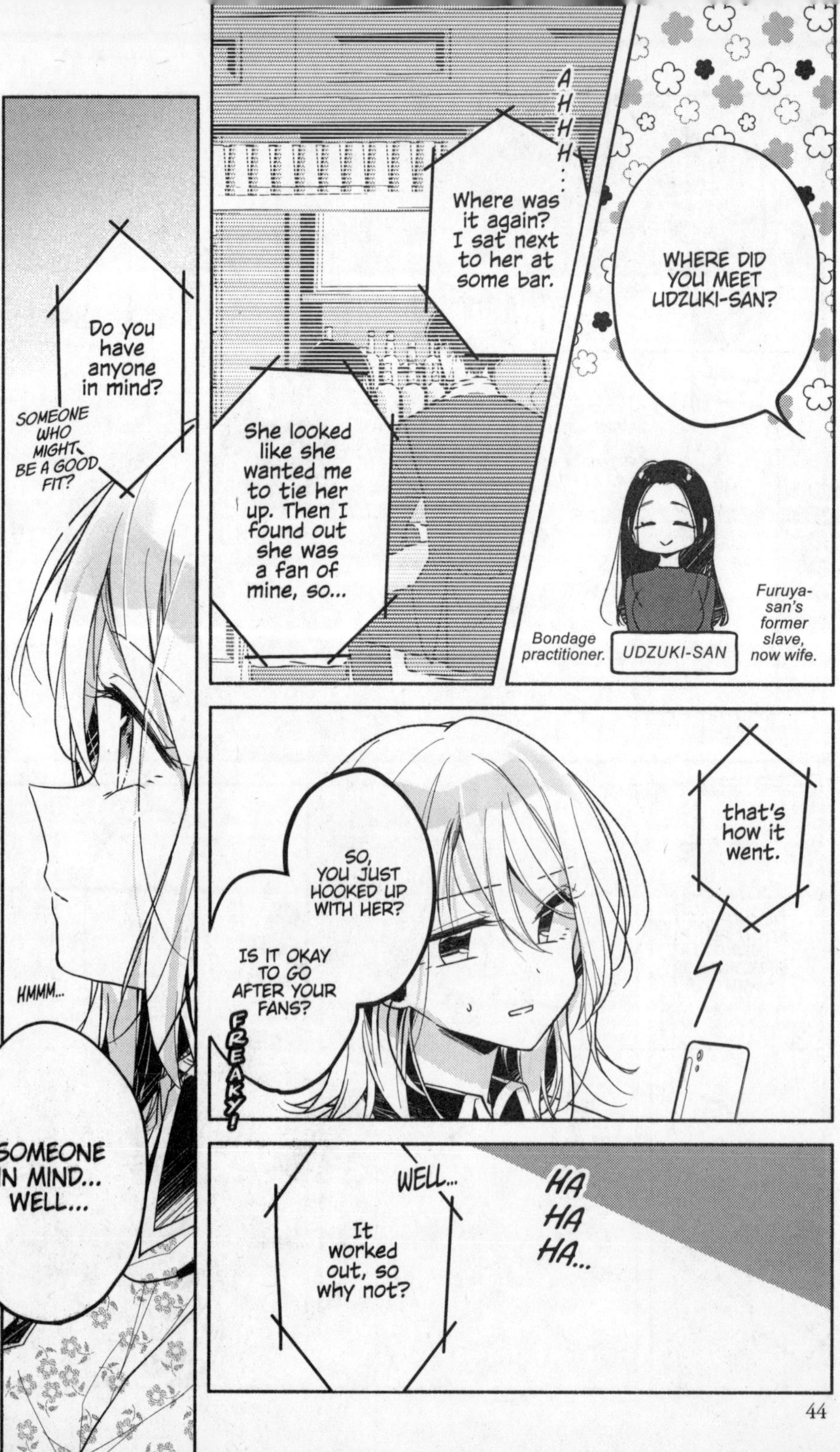
WHERE DID YOU MEET UDZUKI-SAN?
Bondage practitioner.
UDZUKI-SAN
Furuya-san's former slave, now wife.
AHHH...
Where was it again? I sat next to her at some bar.
She looked like she wanted me to tie her up. Then I found out she was a fan of mine, so...
that's how it went.
SO, YOU JUST HOOKED UP WITH HER?
IS IT OKAY TO GO AFTER YOUR FANS?
FREAKY!
HA HA HA...
WELL...
It worked out, so why not?
Do you have anyone in mind?
SOMEONE WHO MIGHT BE A GOOD FIT?
HMMM...
SOMEONE IN MIND... WELL...

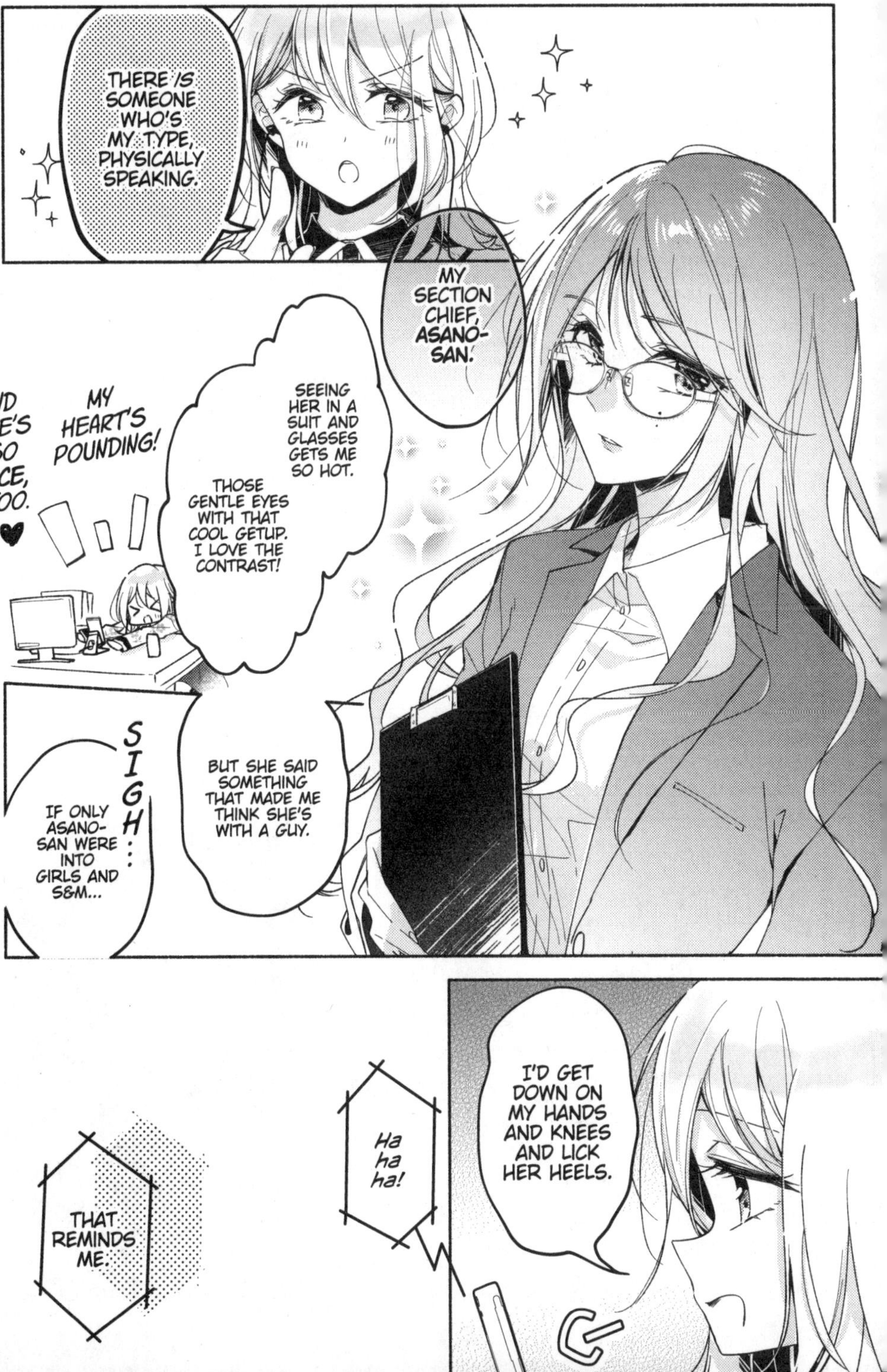
THERE IS SOMEONE WHO'S MY TYPE, PHYSICALLY SPEAKING.
MY SECTION CHIEF, ASANO-SAN.
SEEING HER IN A SUIT AND GLASSES GETS ME SO HOT.
THOSE GENTLE EYES WITH THAT COOL GETUP. I LOVE THE CONTRAST!
MY HEART'S POUNDING!
AND SHE'S SO NICE, TOO.
BUT SHE SAID SOMETHING THAT MADE ME THINK SHE'S WITH A GUY.
SIGH...
IF ONLY ASANO-SAN WERE INTO GIRLS AND S&M...
I'D GET DOWN ON MY HANDS AND KNEES AND LICK HER HEELS.
Ha ha ha!
THAT REMINDS ME.

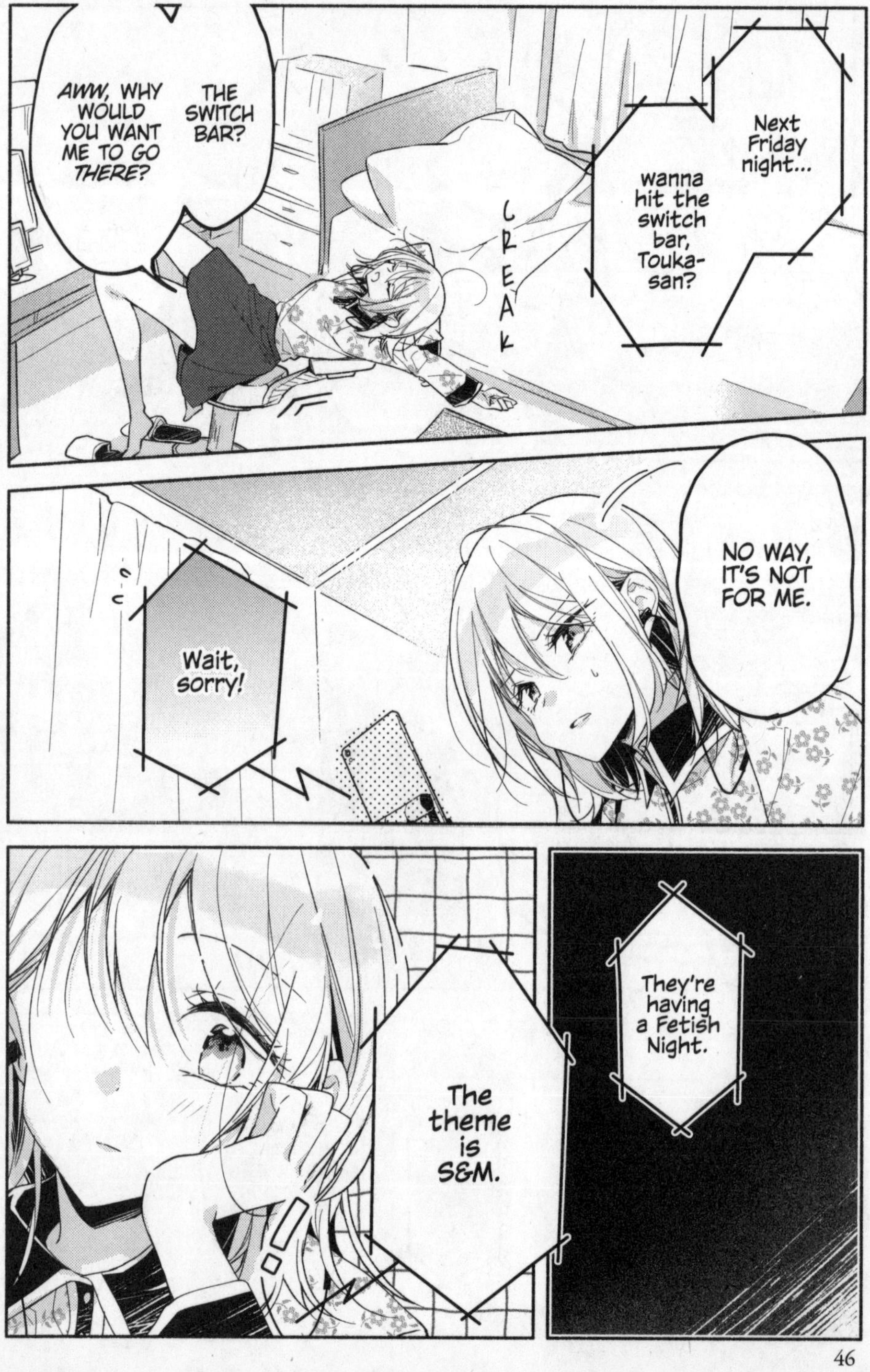
Next Friday night... wanna hit the switch bar, Touka-san?
THE SWITCH BAR?
AWW, WHY WOULD YOU WANT ME TO GO *THERE?*
CREAK
NO WAY, IT'S NOT FOR ME.
Wait, sorry!
They're having a Fetish Night.
The theme is S&M.

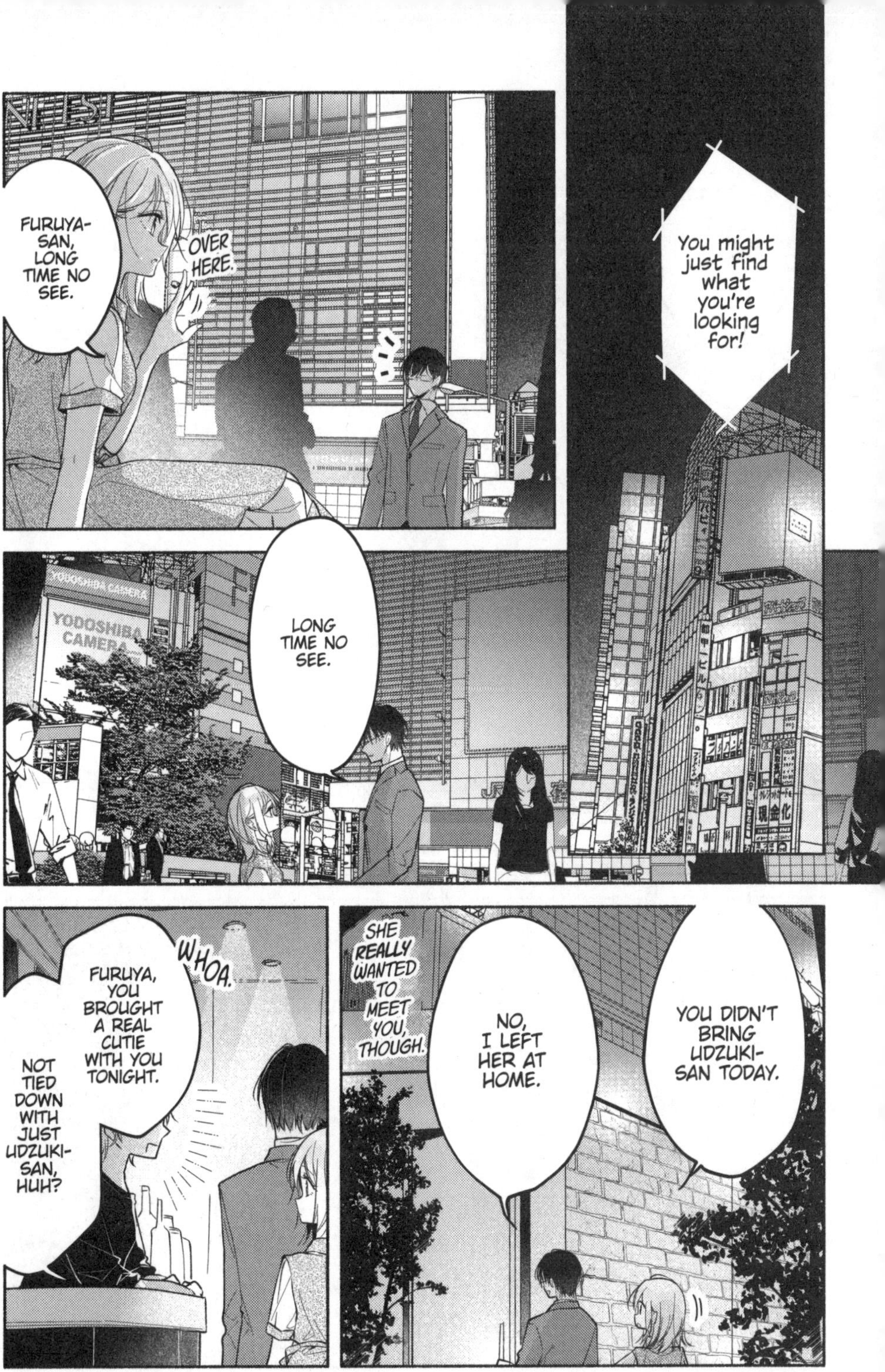
You might just find what you're looking for!
OVER HERE.
FURUYA-SAN, LONG TIME NO SEE.
LONG TIME NO SEE.
YOU DIDN'T BRING UDZUKI-SAN TODAY.
NO, I LEFT HER AT HOME.
SHE REALLY WANTED TO MEET YOU, THOUGH.
WHOA.
FURUYA, YOU BROUGHT A REAL CUTIE WITH YOU TONIGHT.
NOT TIED DOWN WITH JUST UDZUKI-SAN, HUH?

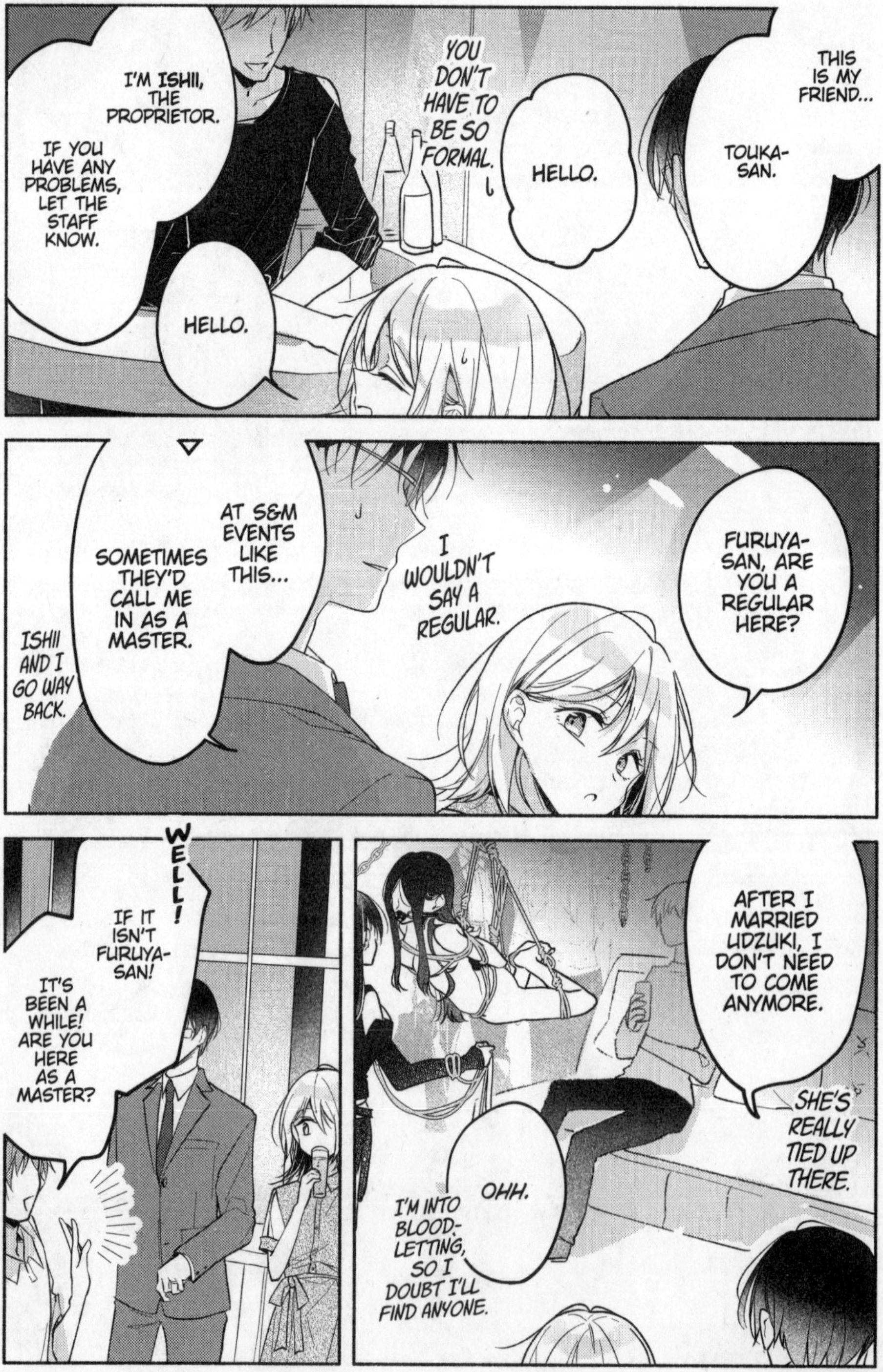
THIS IS MY FRIEND...
TOUKA-SAN.
HELLO.
YOU DON'T HAVE TO BE SO FORMAL.
I'M ISHII, THE PROPRIETOR.
IF YOU HAVE ANY PROBLEMS, LET THE STAFF KNOW.
HELLO.
FURUYA-SAN, ARE YOU A REGULAR HERE?
I WOULDN'T SAY A REGULAR.
AT S&M EVENTS LIKE THIS...
SOMETIMES THEY'D CALL ME IN AS A MASTER.
ISHII AND I GO WAY BACK.
AFTER I MARRIED UDZUKI, I DON'T NEED TO COME ANYMORE.
SHE'S REALLY TIED UP THERE.
OHH.
I'M INTO BLOOD-LETTING, SO I DOUBT I'LL FIND ANYONE.
WELL!
IF IT ISN'T FURUYA-SAN!
IT'S BEEN A WHILE! ARE YOU HERE AS A MASTER?

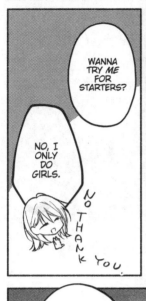

I DON'T DO THAT ANY-MORE.
I CAME TODAY TO HELP FIND HER SOMEONE.
OH, SHE'S A CUTIE.
YOU'LL HAVE YOUR PICK!
WANNA TRY *ME* FOR STARTERS?
NO, I ONLY DO GIRLS.
NO THANK YOU.
TODAY IS NOT MY DAY.
SO, WHICH WAY DO YOU GO?
I'M A MASOCHIST.
AHH...
I THINK THE NEW GIRL ITOU-SAN BROUGHT WITH HIM IS A SADIST.
WANT ME TO GET HER?
THIS GUY SURE TALKS A LOT...

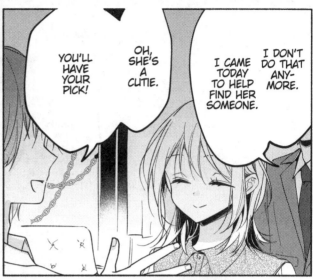

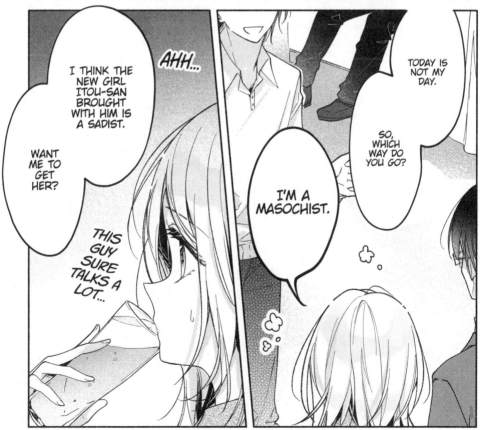

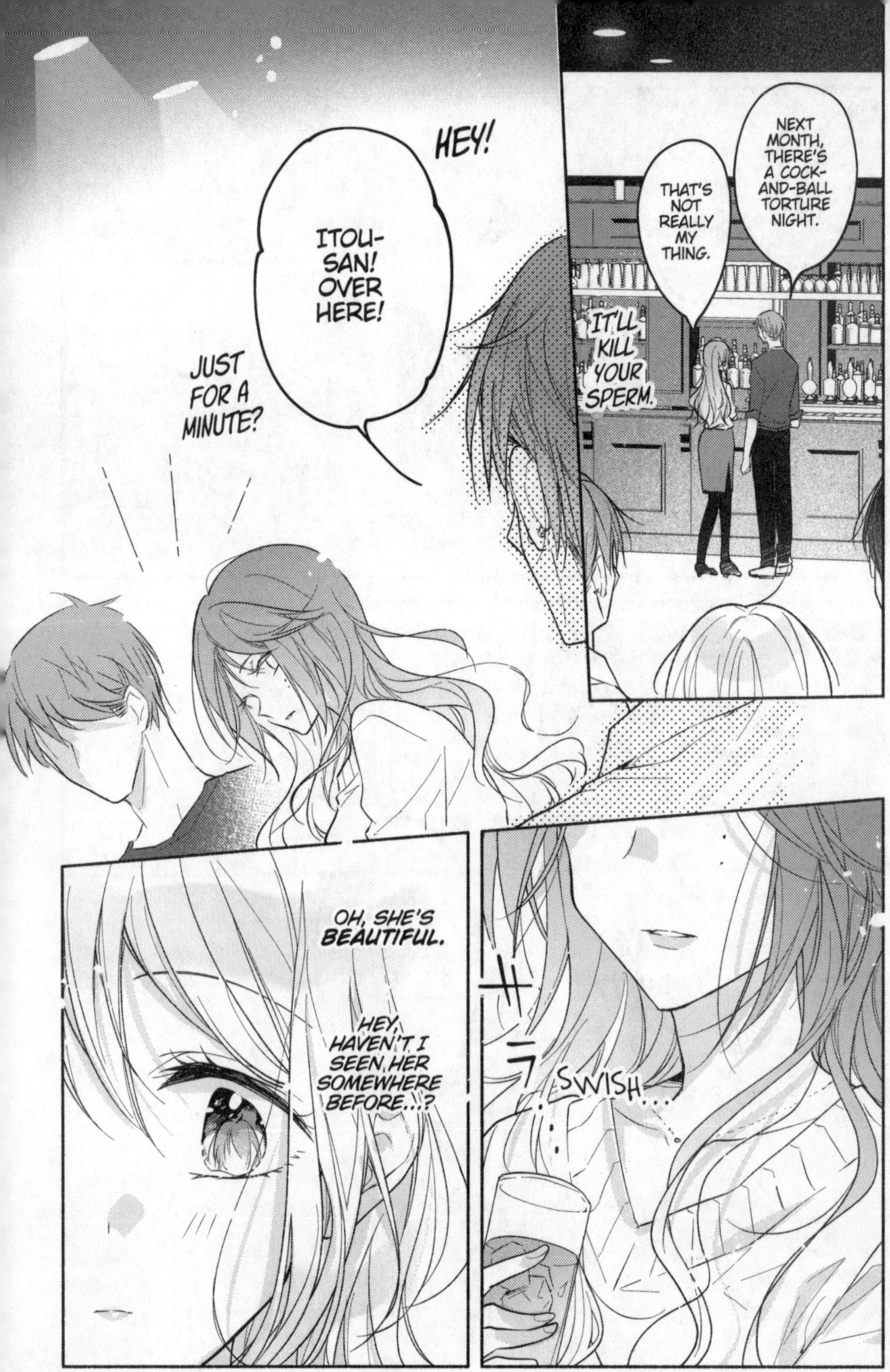
NEXT MONTH, THERE'S A COCK-AND-BALL TORTURE NIGHT.
THAT'S NOT REALLY MY THING.
IT'LL KILL YOUR SPERM.
HEY!
ITOU-SAN! OVER HERE!
JUST FOR A MINUTE?
SWISH...
OH, SHE'S **BEAUTIFUL.**
HEY, HAVEN'T I SEEN HER SOMEWHERE BEFORE...?

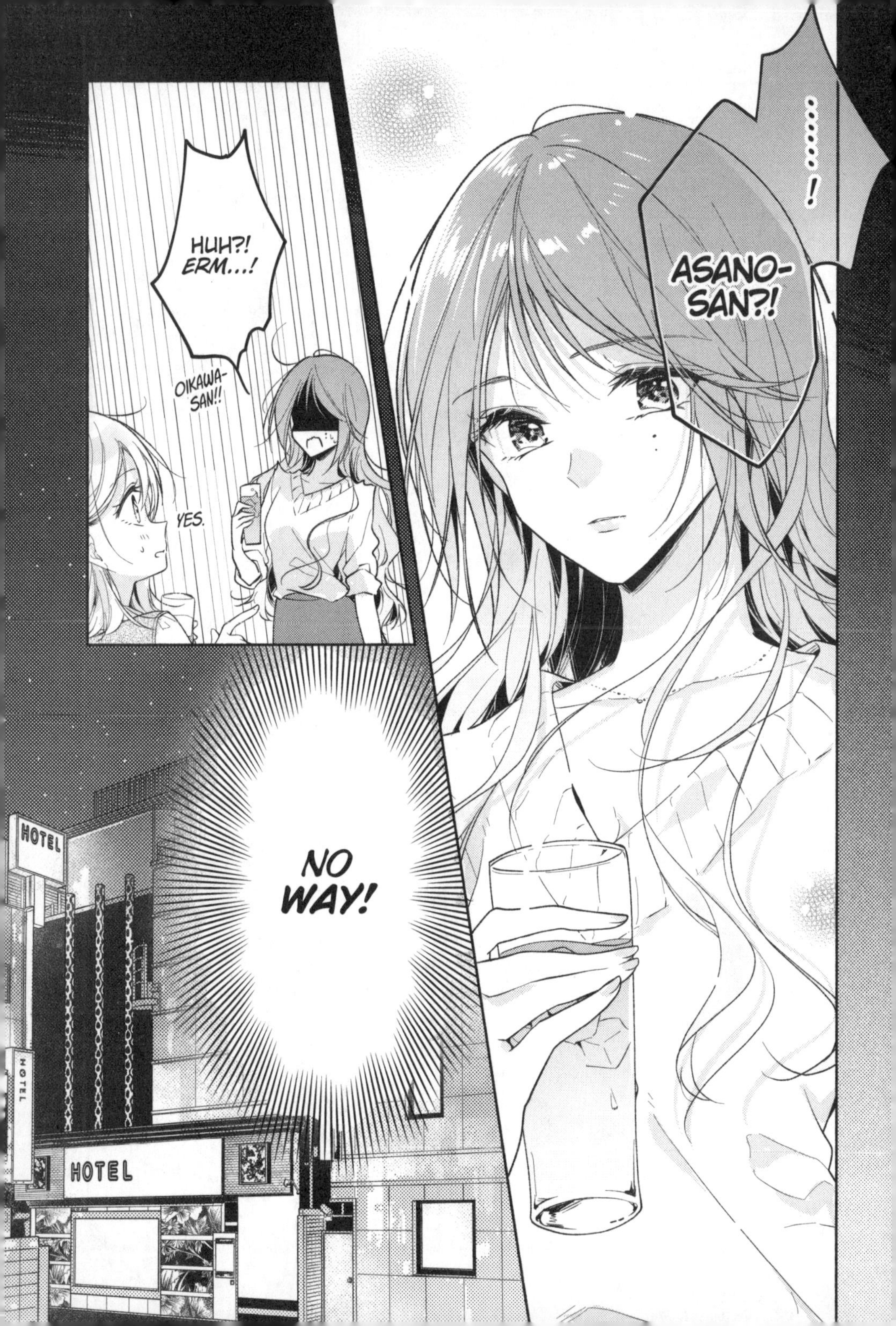
……!
ASANO-SAN?!
HUH?! ERM…!
OIKAWA-SAN!!
YES.
HOTEL
NO WAY!
HOTEL
HOTEL

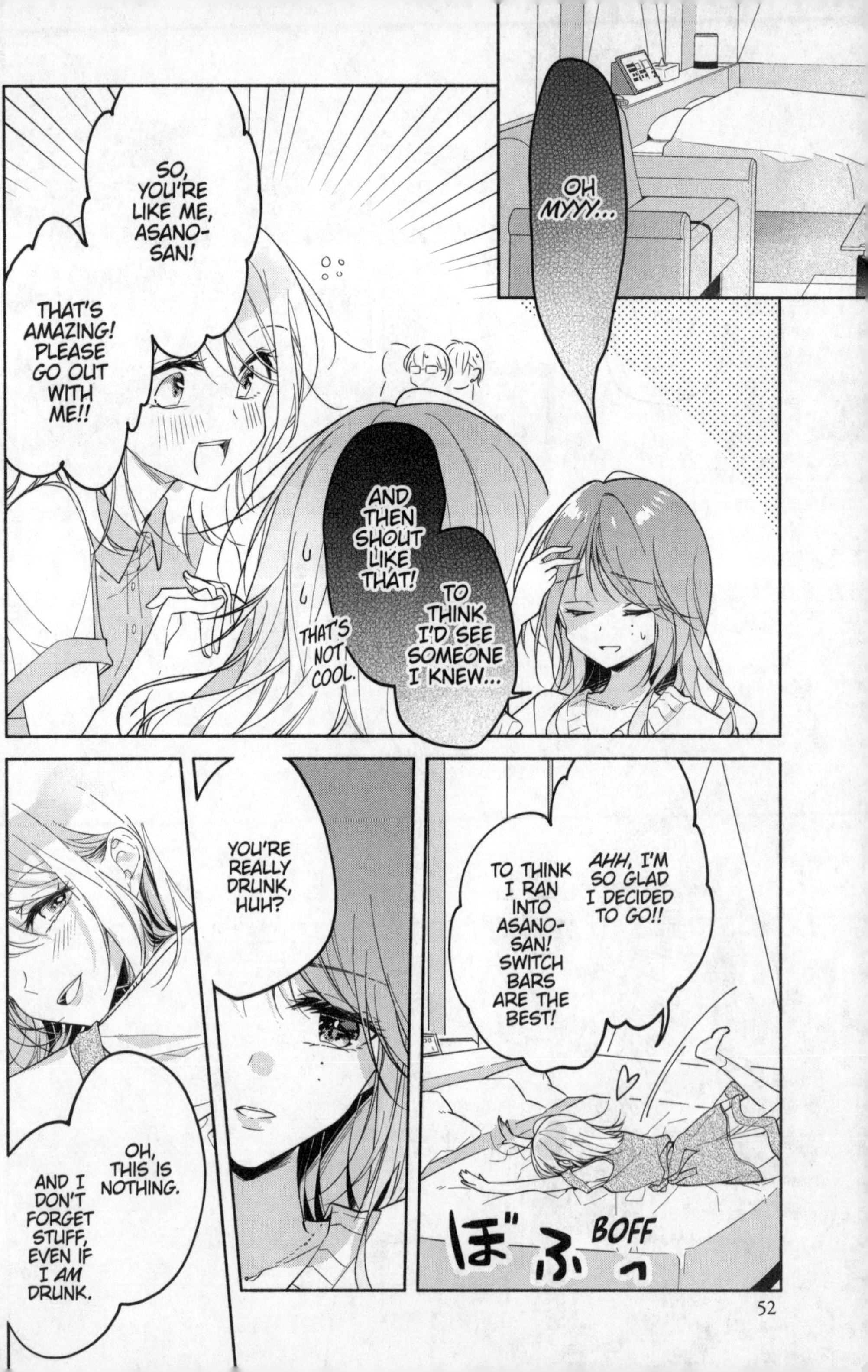
SO, YOU'RE LIKE ME, ASANO-SAN!
THAT'S AMAZING! PLEASE GO OUT WITH ME!!
OH MYYY...
TO THINK I'D SEE SOMEONE I KNEW...
AND THEN SHOUT LIKE THAT!
THAT'S NOT COOL.
AHH, I'M SO GLAD I DECIDED TO GO!!
TO THINK I RAN INTO ASANO-SAN! SWITCH BARS ARE THE BEST!
ぼふっ
BOFF
YOU'RE REALLY DRUNK, HUH?
OH, THIS IS NOTHING.
AND I DON'T FORGET STUFF, EVEN IF I *AM* DRUNK.

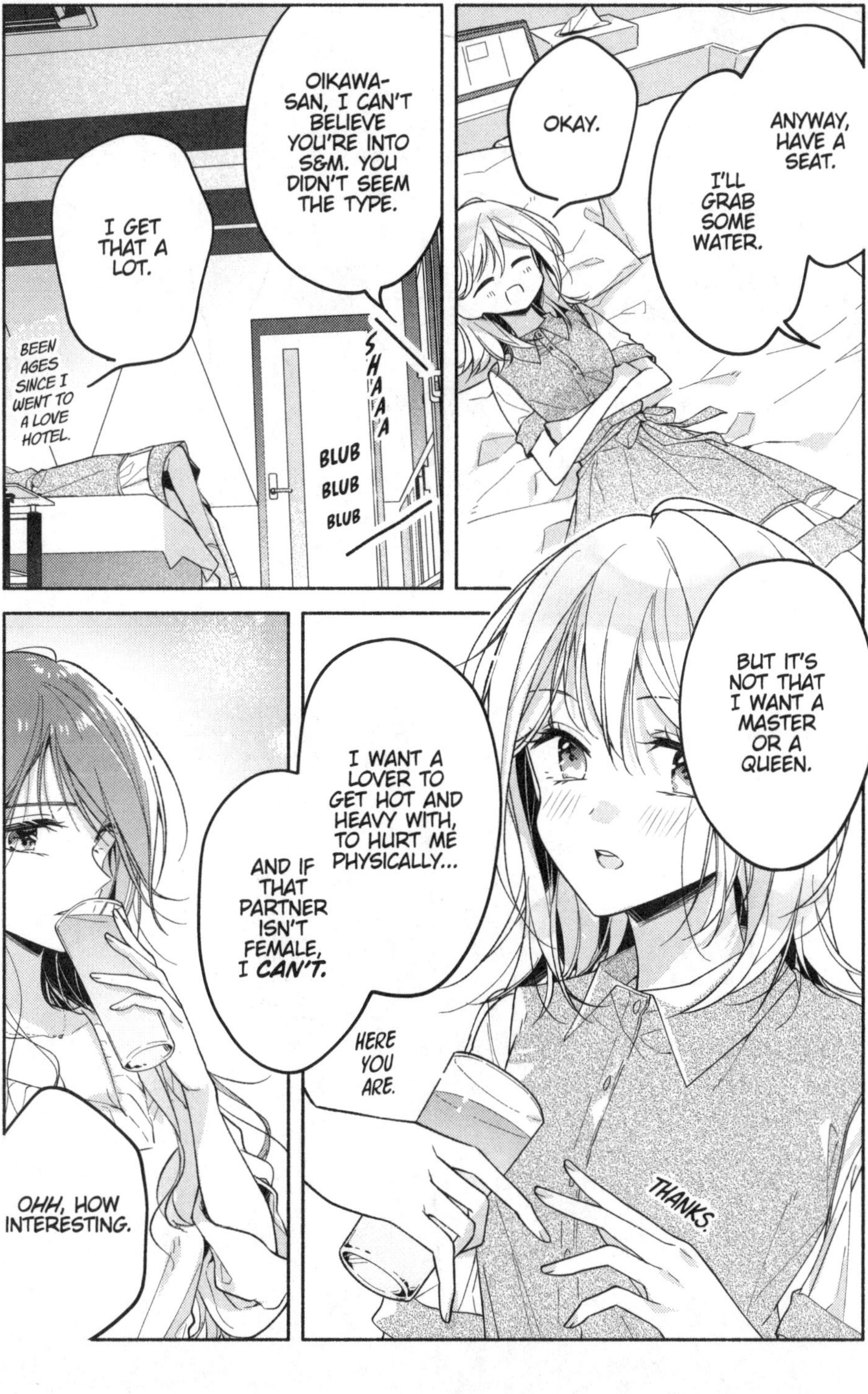
ANYWAY, HAVE A SEAT.
I'LL GRAB SOME WATER.
OKAY.
OIKAWA-SAN, I CAN'T BELIEVE YOU'RE INTO S&M. YOU DIDN'T SEEM THE TYPE.
I GET THAT A LOT.
BEEN AGES SINCE I WENT TO A LOVE HOTEL.
SHAAAA
BLUB BLUB BLUB
BUT IT'S NOT THAT I WANT A MASTER OR A QUEEN.
I WANT A LOVER TO GET HOT AND HEAVY WITH, TO HURT ME PHYSICALLY...
AND IF THAT PARTNER ISN'T FEMALE, I *CAN'T.*
HERE YOU ARE.
THANKS.
OHH, HOW INTERESTING.

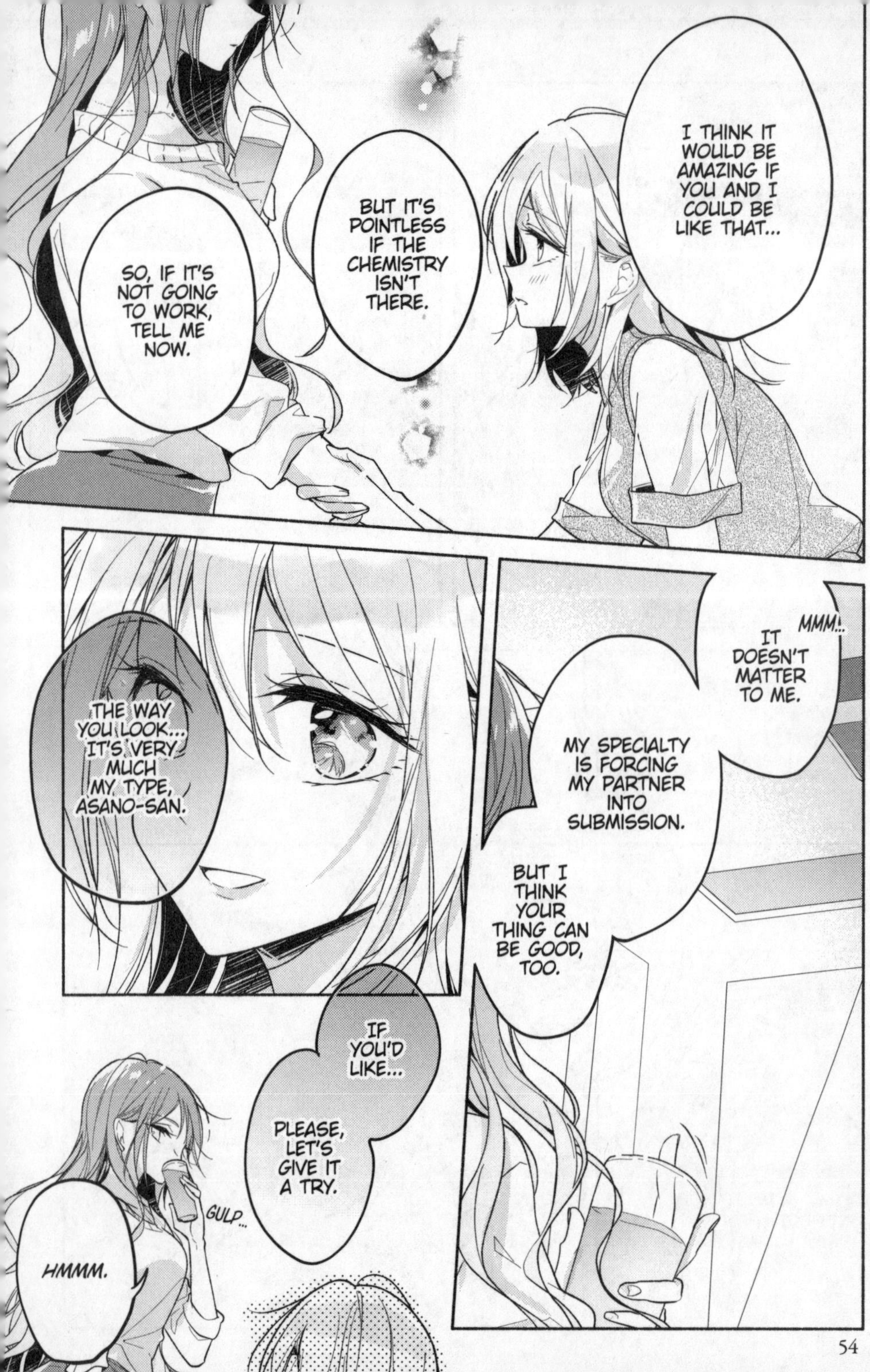
I THINK IT WOULD BE AMAZING IF YOU AND I COULD BE LIKE THAT...
BUT IT'S POINTLESS IF THE CHEMISTRY ISN'T THERE.
SO, IF IT'S NOT GOING TO WORK, TELL ME NOW.
MMM...
IT DOESN'T MATTER TO ME.
MY SPECIALTY IS FORCING MY PARTNER INTO SUBMISSION.
BUT I THINK YOUR THING CAN BE GOOD, TOO.
THE WAY YOU LOOK... IT'S VERY MUCH MY TYPE, ASANO-SAN.
IF YOU'D LIKE...
PLEASE, LET'S GIVE IT A TRY.
GULP...
HMMM.

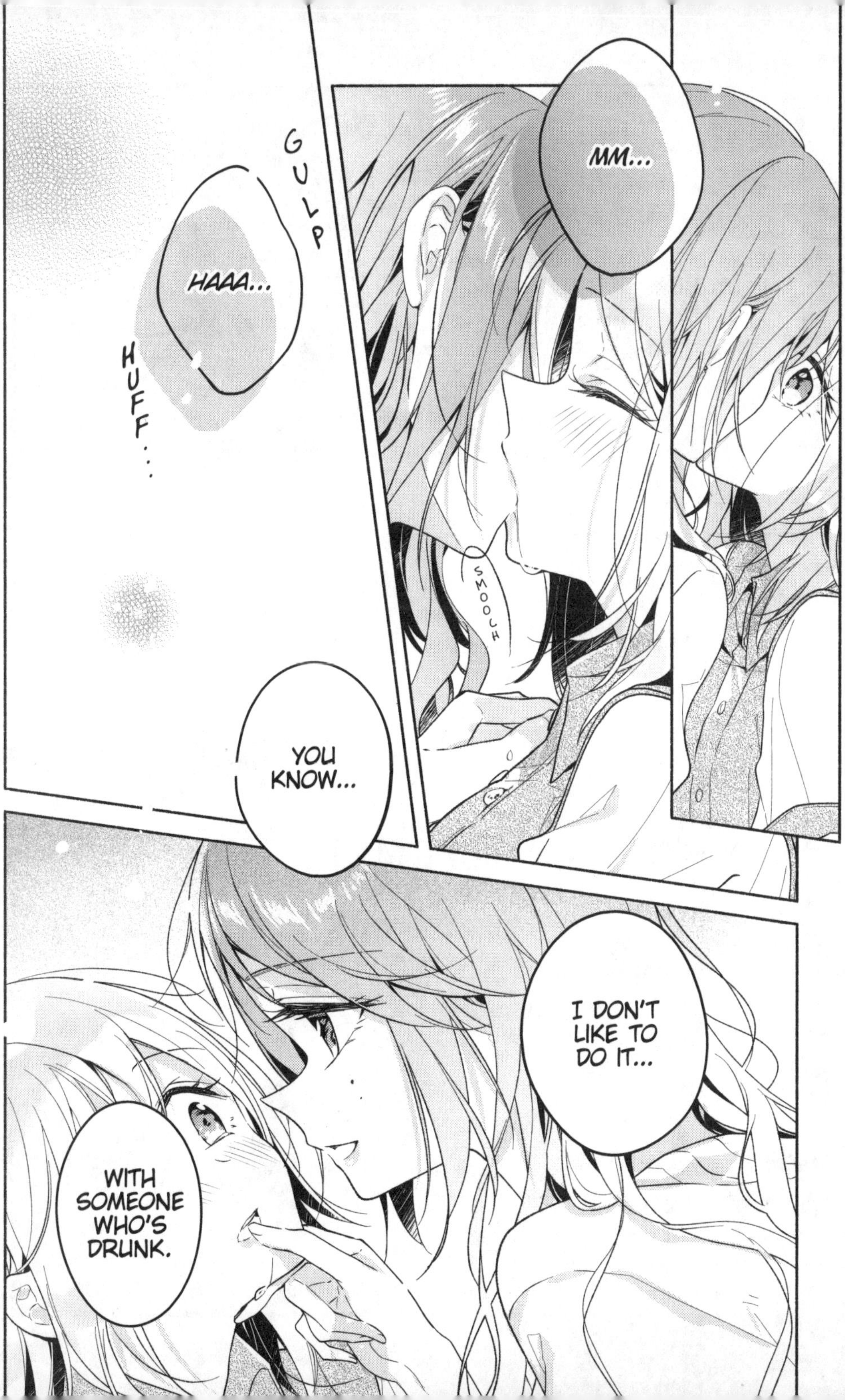
MM...
SMOOCH
GULP
HAAA...
HUFF...
YOU KNOW...
I DON'T LIKE TO DO IT...
WITH SOMEONE WHO'S DRUNK.

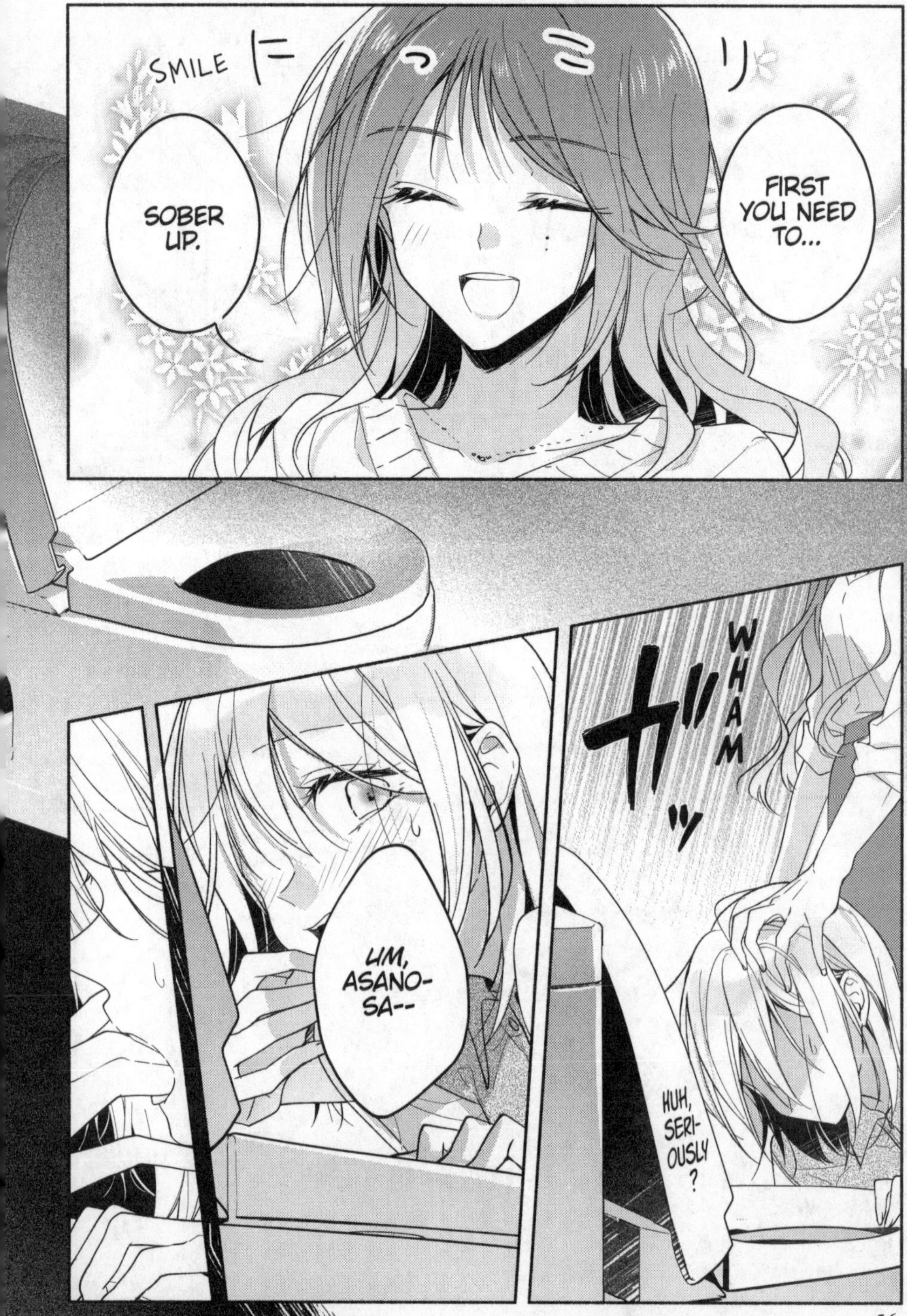
FIRST YOU NEED TO...
SOBER UP.
SMILE
ニッコリ
WHAM
ガッ
HUH, SERI-OUSLY?
UM, ASANO-SA--

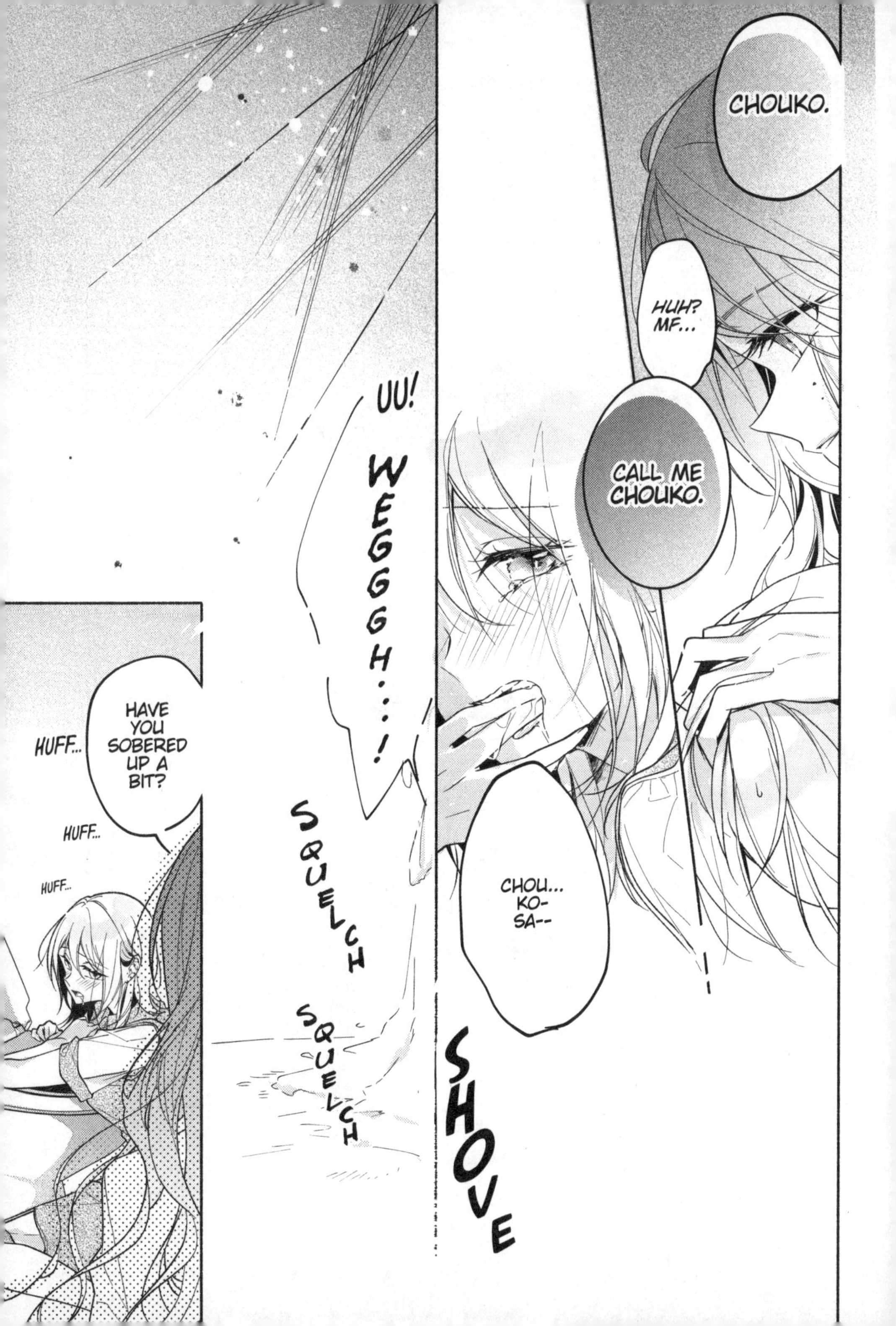
CHOUKO.
HUH? MF...
CALL ME CHOUKO.
CHOU... KO-SA--
SHOVE
UU!
WEGGGH...!
SQUELCH
SQUELCH
HAVE YOU SOBERED UP A BIT?
HUFF...
HUFF...
HUFF...

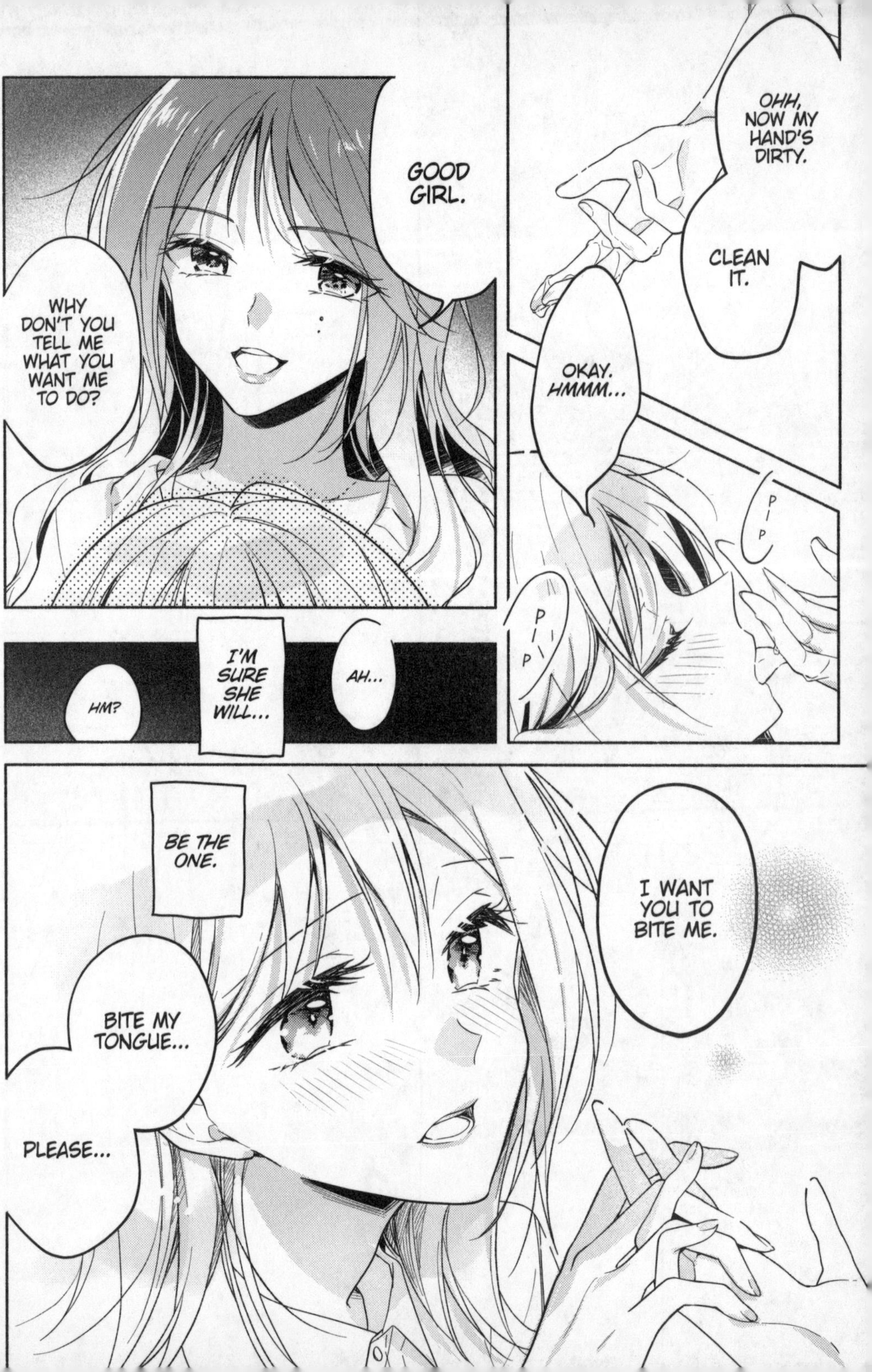
OHH, NOW MY HAND'S DIRTY.
CLEAN IT.
OKAY. HMMM...
PIP
PIP
GOOD GIRL.
WHY DON'T YOU TELL ME WHAT YOU WANT ME TO DO?
AH...
I'M SURE SHE WILL...
HM?
I WANT YOU TO BITE ME.
BE THE ONE.
BITE MY TONGUE...
PLEASE...

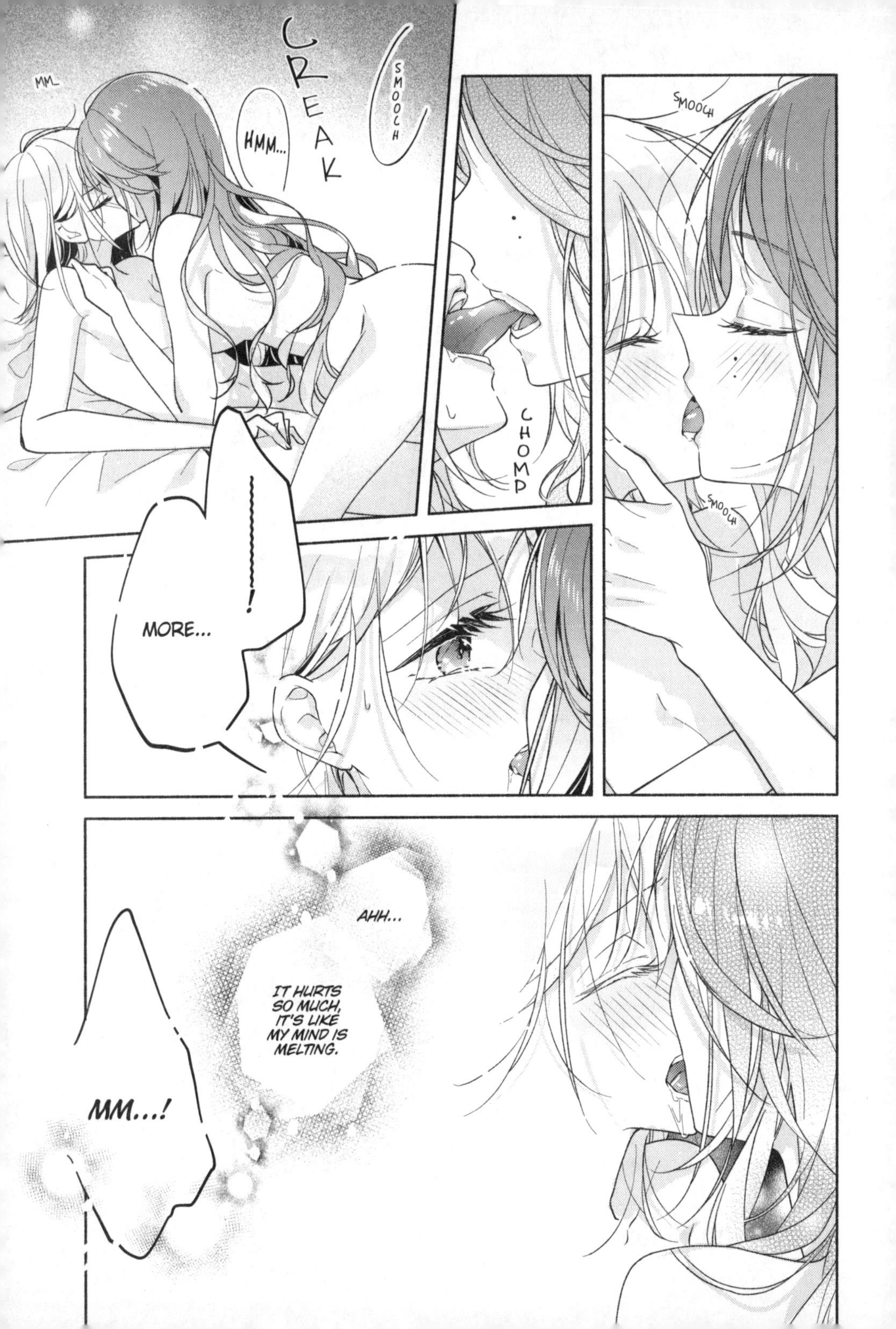
SMOOCH
SMOOCH
CHOMP
SMOOCH
CREAK
HMM...
MM..
——————!
MORE...
AHH...
IT HURTS SO MUCH, IT'S LIKE MY MIND IS MELTING.
MM...!

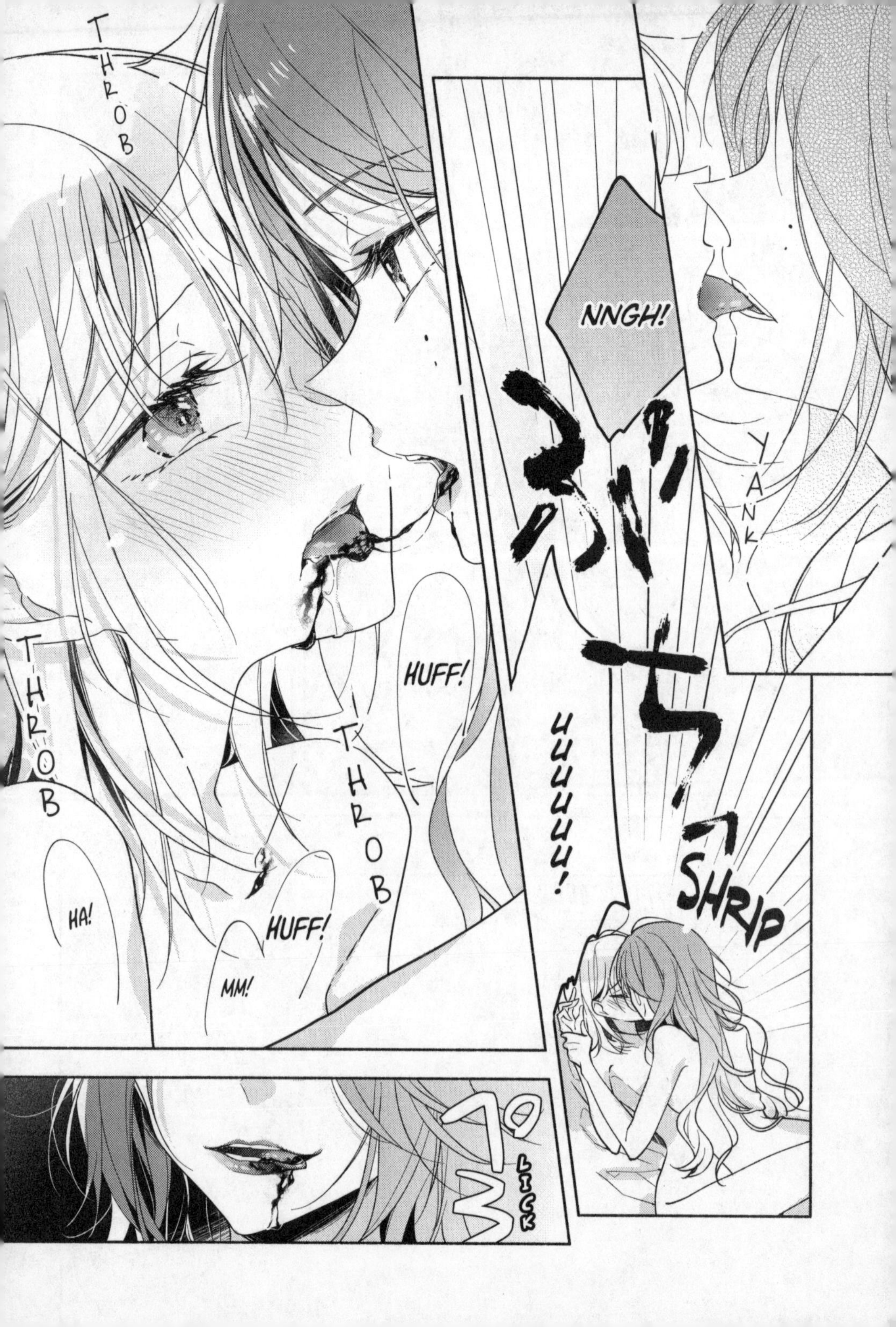
NNGH!
YANK
UUUUUUU!
SHRIP
THROB
THROB
HUFF!
THROB
HUFF!
HA!
MM!
LICK

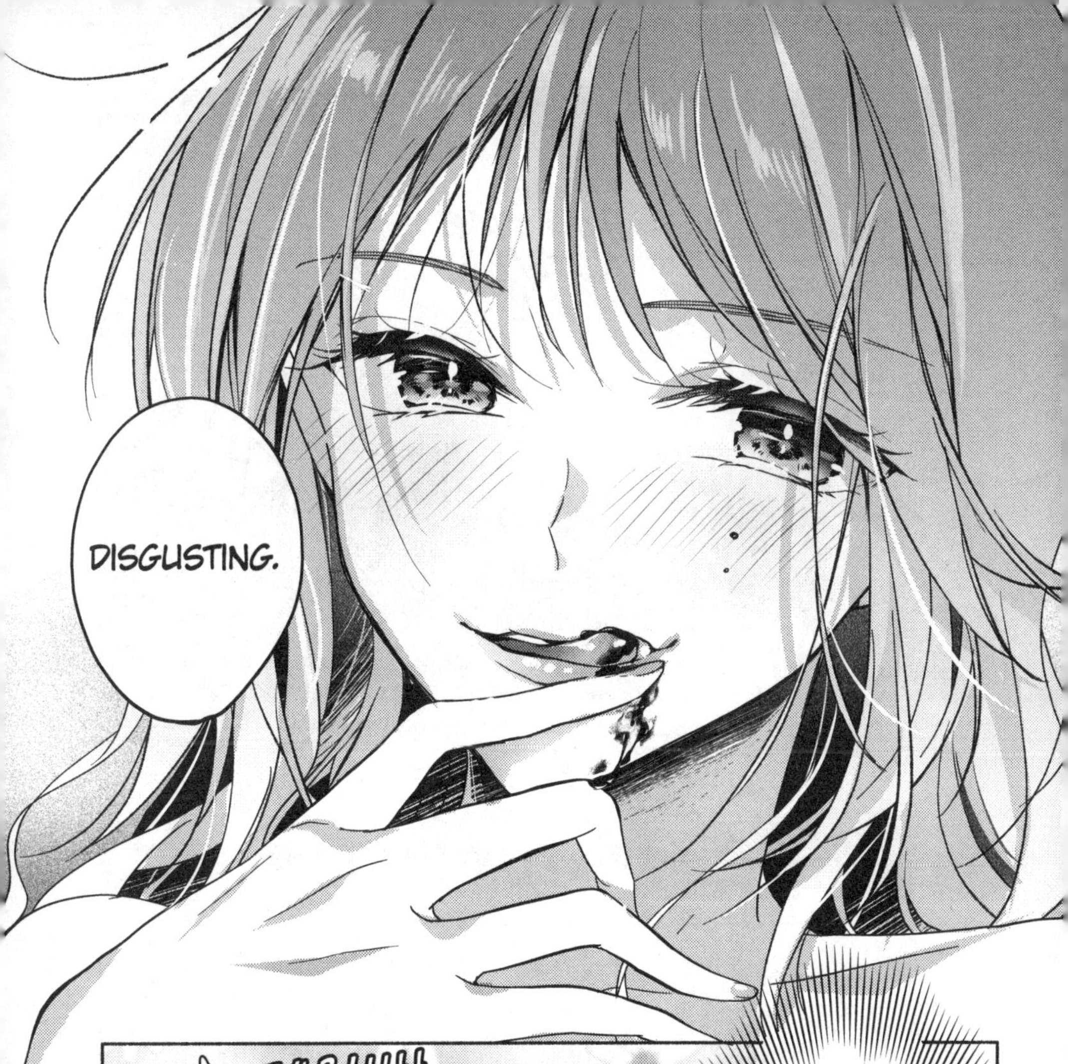
DISGUSTING.

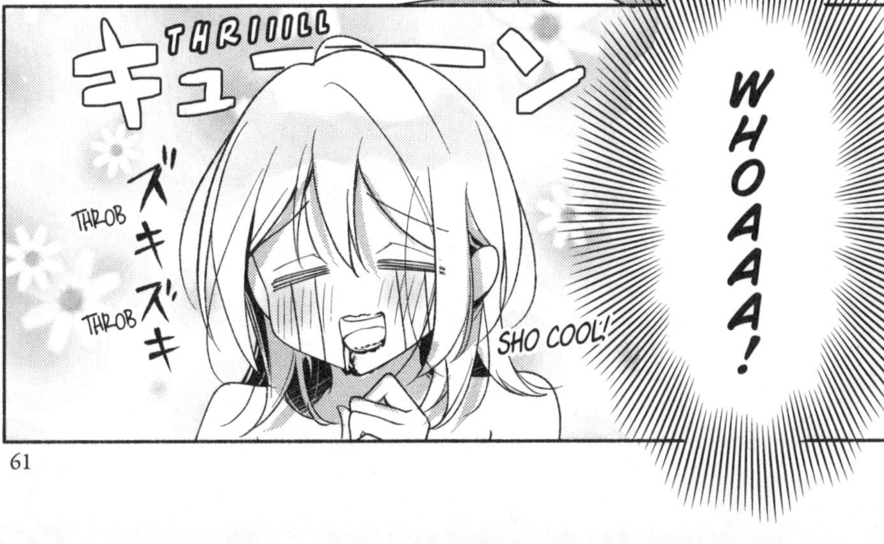
WHOAAA!
THRIIIILL
キューーン
SHO COOL!
THROB
ズキ
THROB
ズキ

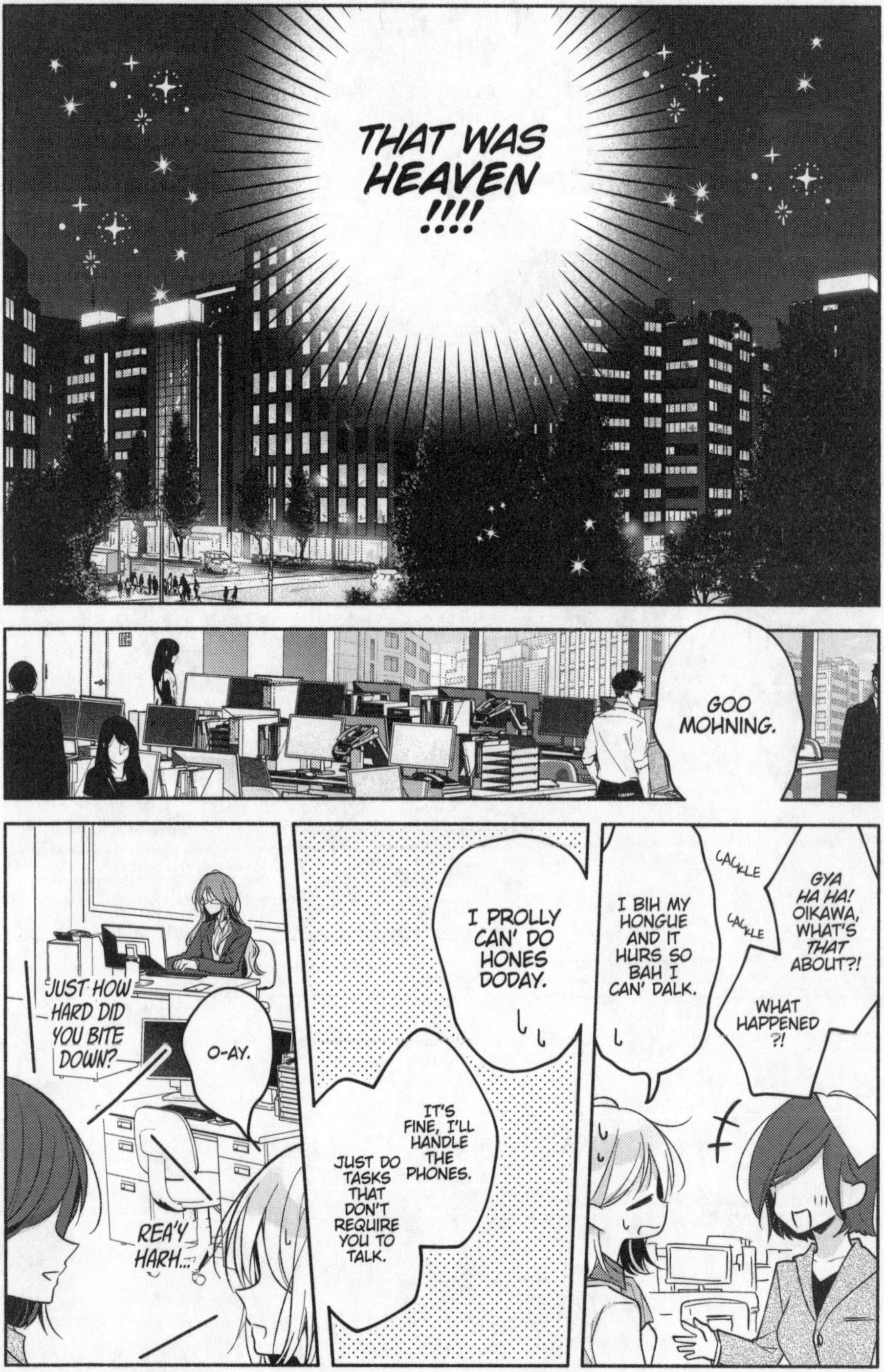
THAT WAS HEAVEN !!!!
GOO MOHNING.
GYA HA HA! OIKAWA, WHAT'S THAT ABOUT?!
CACKLE
CACKLE
WHAT HAPPENED ?!
I BIH MY HONGUE AND IT HURS SO BAH I CAN' DALK.
I PROLLY CAN' DO HONES DODAY.
IT'S FINE, I'LL HANDLE THE PHONES.
JUST DO TASKS THAT DON'T REQUIRE YOU TO TALK.
O-AY.
JUST HOW HARD DID YOU BITE DOWN?
REA'Y HARH...

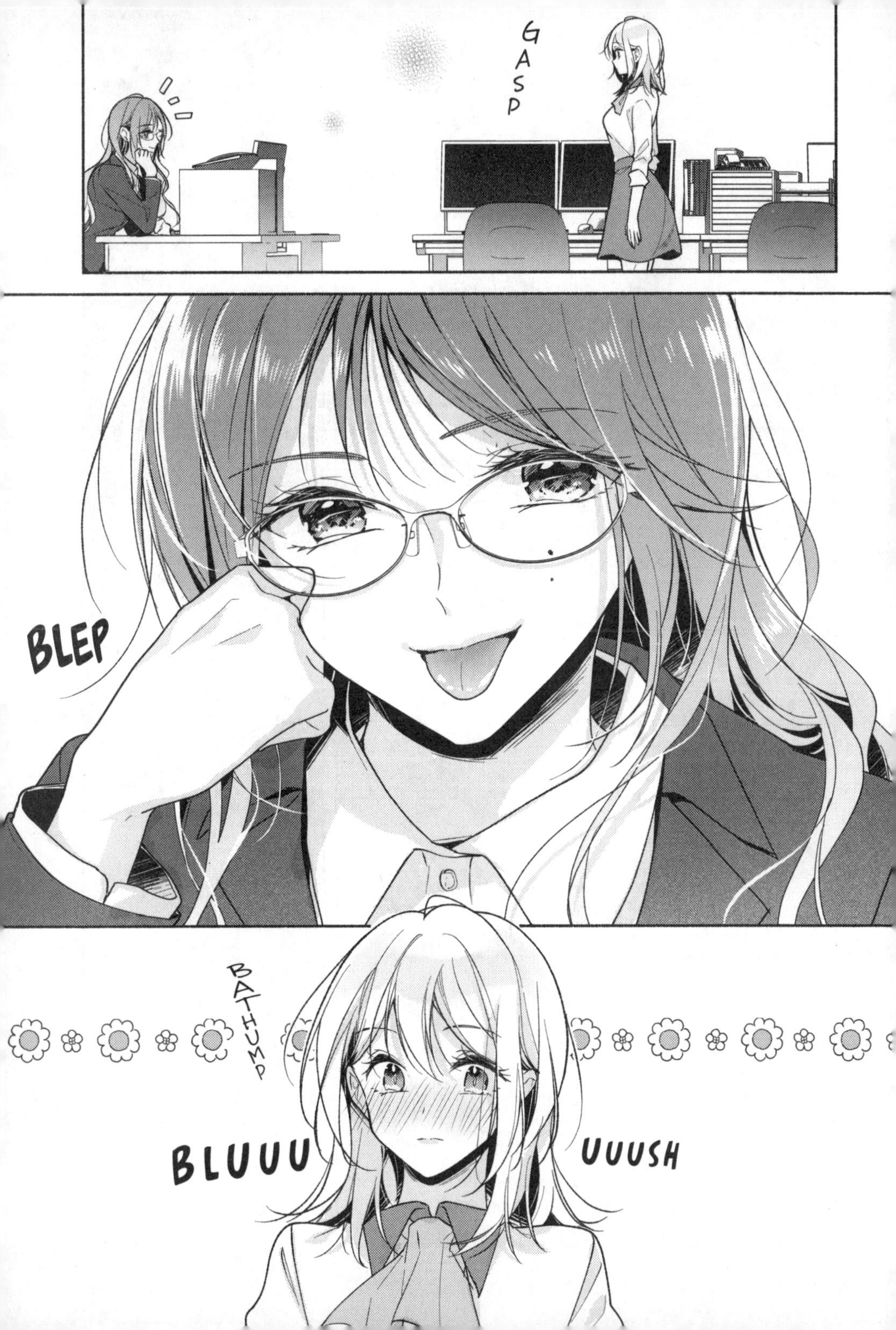
GASP
BLEP
BATHUMP
BLUUU
UUUSH

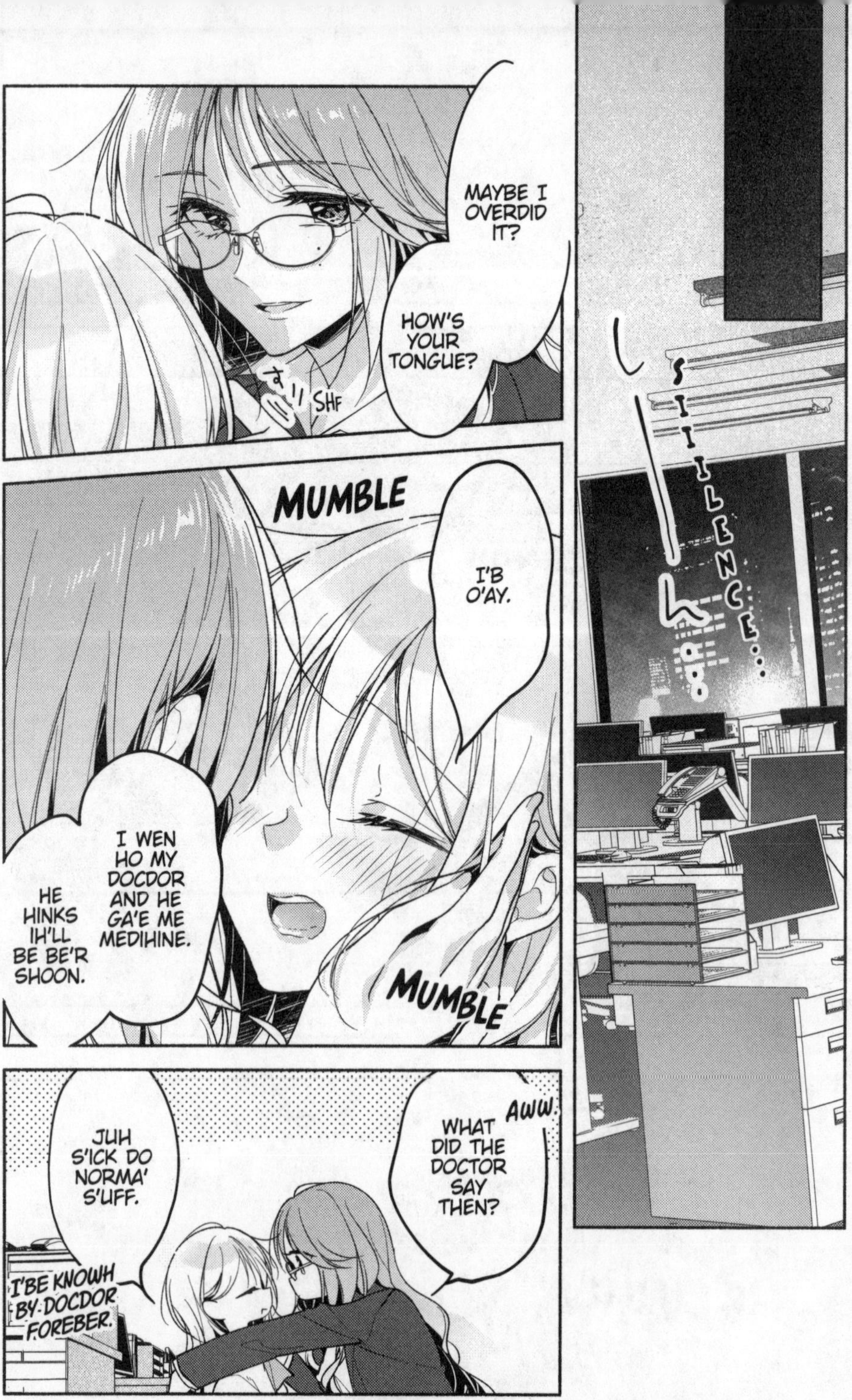

しーん
SIIILENCE...
MAYBE I OVERDID IT?
HOW'S YOUR TONGUE?
SHF
MUMBLE
I'B O'AY.
I WEN HO MY DOCDOR AND HE GA'E ME MEDIHINE.
HE HINKS IH'LL BE BE'R SHOON.
MUMBLE
AWW.
WHAT DID THE DOCTOR SAY THEN?
JUH S'ICK DO NORMA' S'UFF.
I'BE KNOWH BY DOCDOR FOREBER.

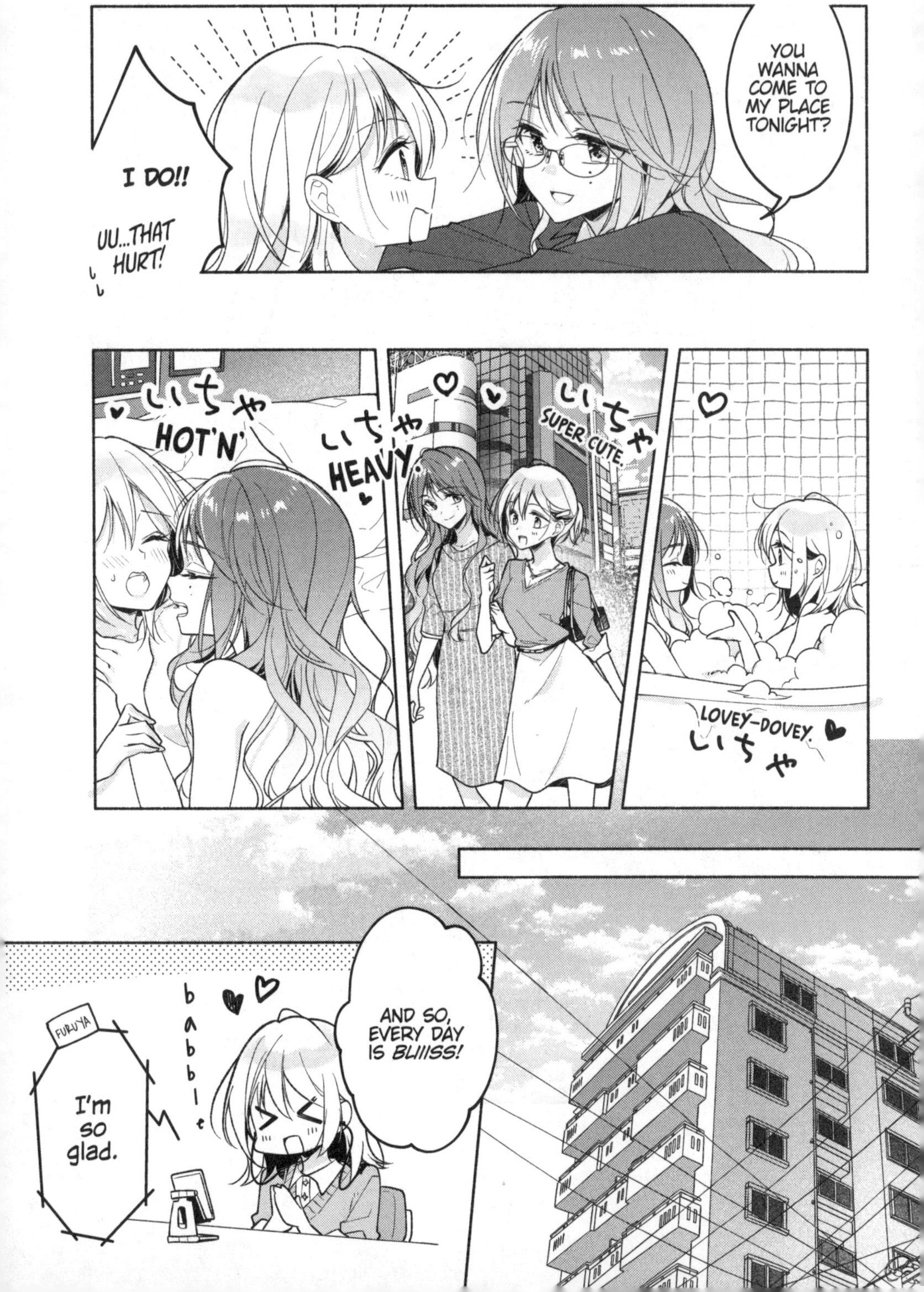
YOU WANNA COME TO MY PLACE TONIGHT?
I DO!!
UU...THAT HURT!
いちゃ SUPER CUTE.
LOVEY-DOVEY. いちゃ
いちゃ
いちゃ HOT'N'
いちゃ HEAVY.
AND SO, EVERY DAY IS *BLIIISS!*
babble
FURUYA
I'm so glad.

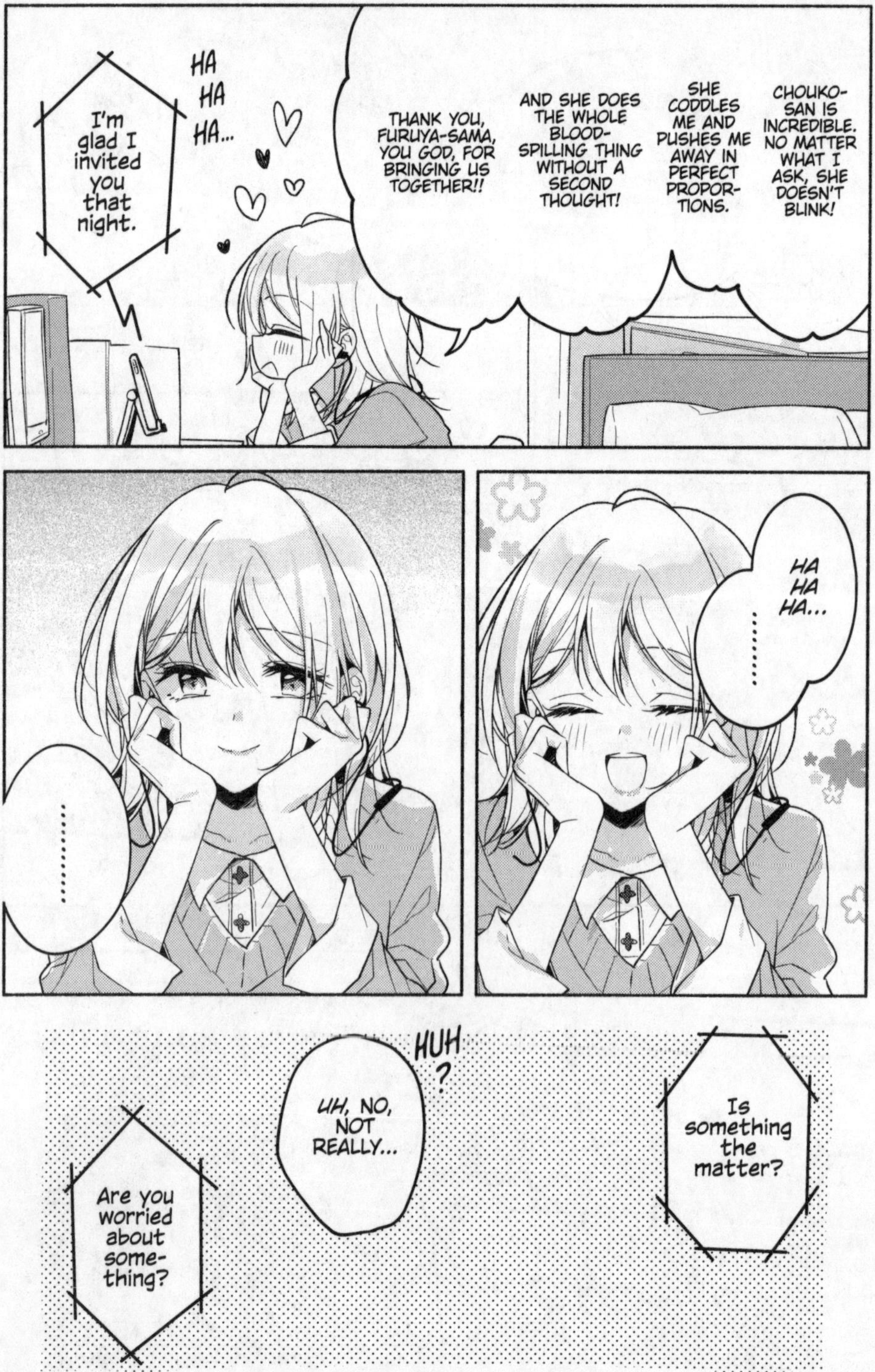
CHOUKO-SAN IS INCREDIBLE. NO MATTER WHAT I ASK, SHE DOESN'T BLINK!
SHE CODDLES ME AND PUSHES ME AWAY IN PERFECT PROPORTIONS.
AND SHE DOES THE WHOLE BLOOD-SPILLING THING WITHOUT A SECOND THOUGHT!
THANK YOU, FURUYA-SAMA, YOU GOD, FOR BRINGING US TOGETHER!!
HA HA HA...
I'm glad I invited you that night.
HA HA HA......
......
Is something the matter?
HUH?
UH, NO, NOT REALLY...
Are you worried about something?

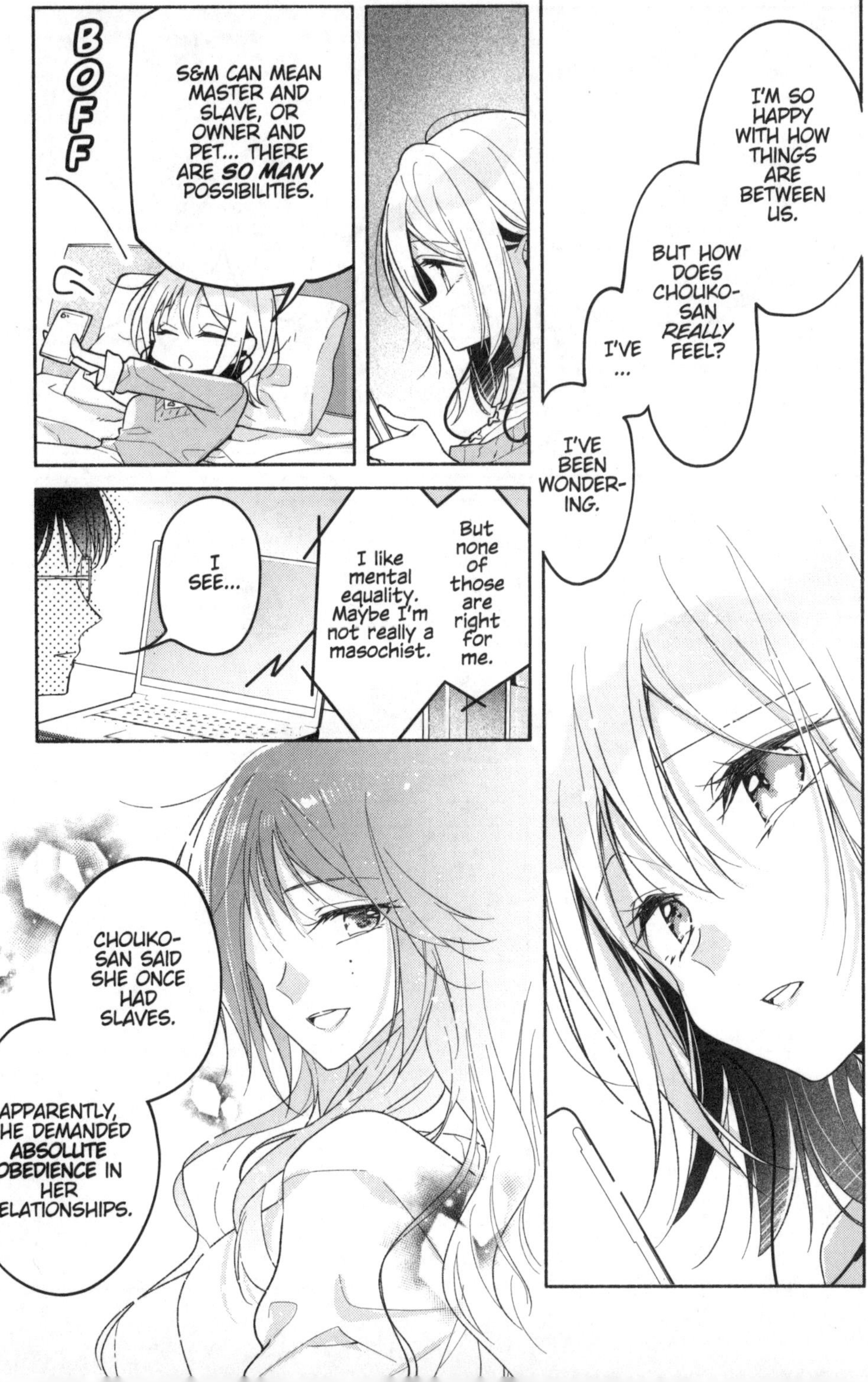
I'M SO HAPPY WITH HOW THINGS ARE BETWEEN US.
BUT HOW DOES CHOUKO-SAN *REALLY* FEEL?
I'VE ...
I'VE BEEN WONDER-ING.
BOFF
S&M CAN MEAN MASTER AND SLAVE, OR OWNER AND PET... THERE ARE ***SO MANY*** POSSIBILITIES.
But none of those are right for me.
I like mental equality. Maybe I'm not really a masochist.
I SEE...
CHOUKO-SAN SAID SHE ONCE HAD SLAVES.
APPARENTLY, SHE DEMANDED **ABSOLUTE OBEDIENCE** IN HER RELATIONSHIPS.

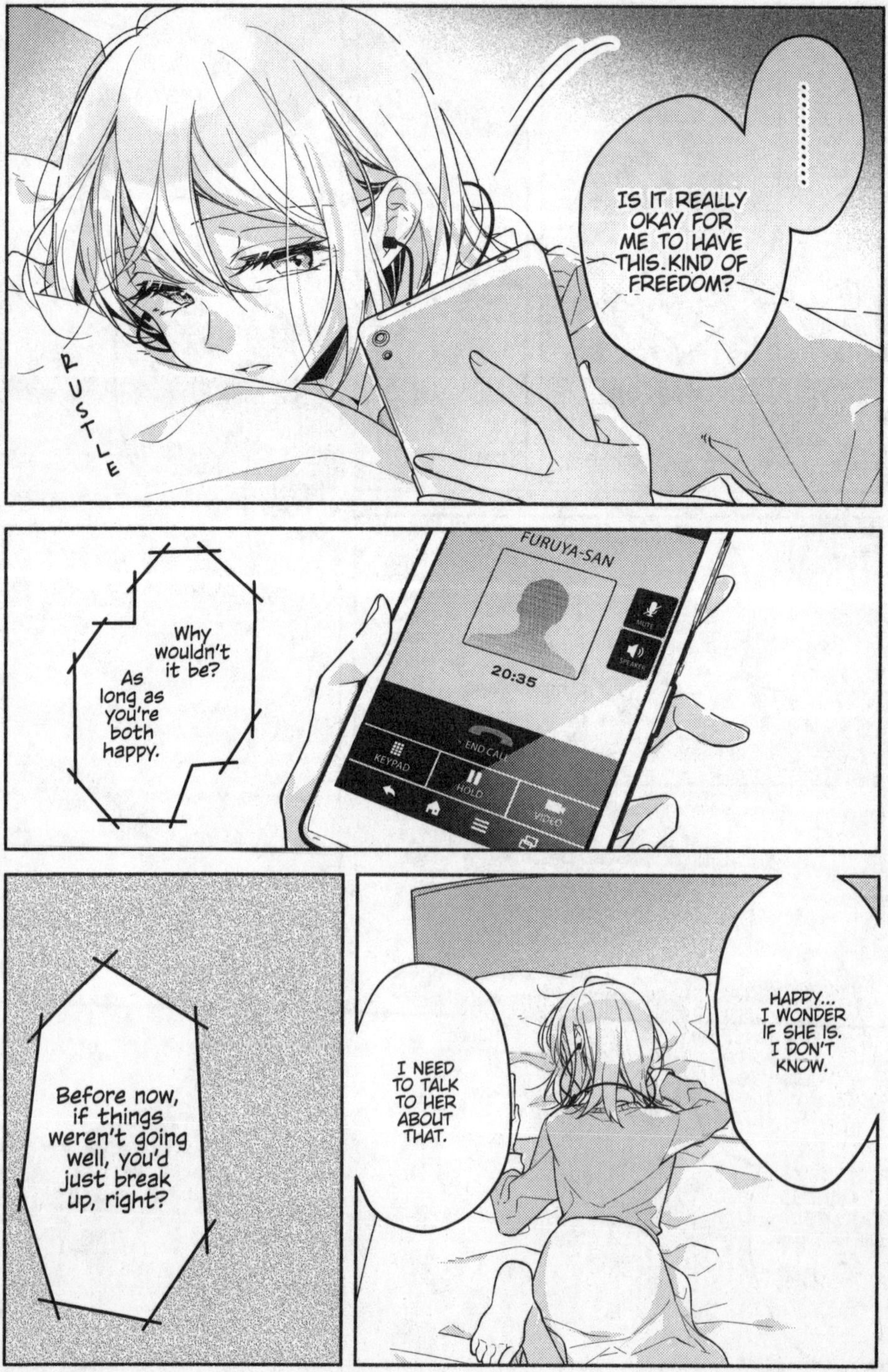
……
IS IT REALLY OKAY FOR ME TO HAVE THIS KIND OF FREEDOM?
RUSTLE
FURUYA-SAN
MUTE
SPEAKER
20:35
END CALL
KEYPAD
HOLD
VIDEO
Why wouldn't it be? As long as you're both happy.
HAPPY... I WONDER IF SHE IS. I DON'T KNOW.
I NEED TO TALK TO HER ABOUT THAT.
Before now, if things weren't going well, you'd just break up, right?

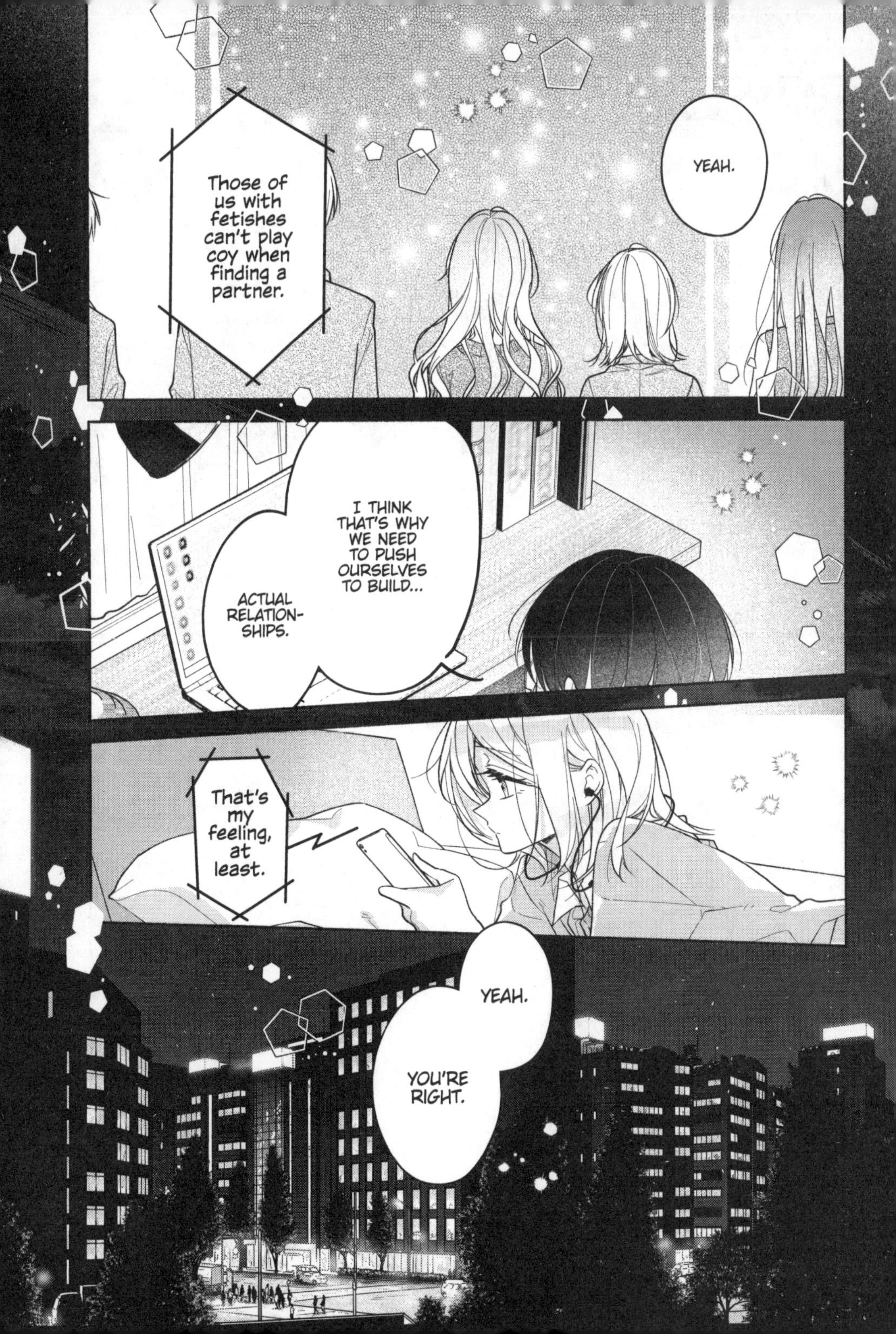
YEAH.
Those of us with fetishes can't play coy when finding a partner.
I THINK THAT'S WHY WE NEED TO PUSH OURSELVES TO BUILD...
ACTUAL RELATION-SHIPS.
That's my feeling, at least.
YEAH.
YOU'RE RIGHT.

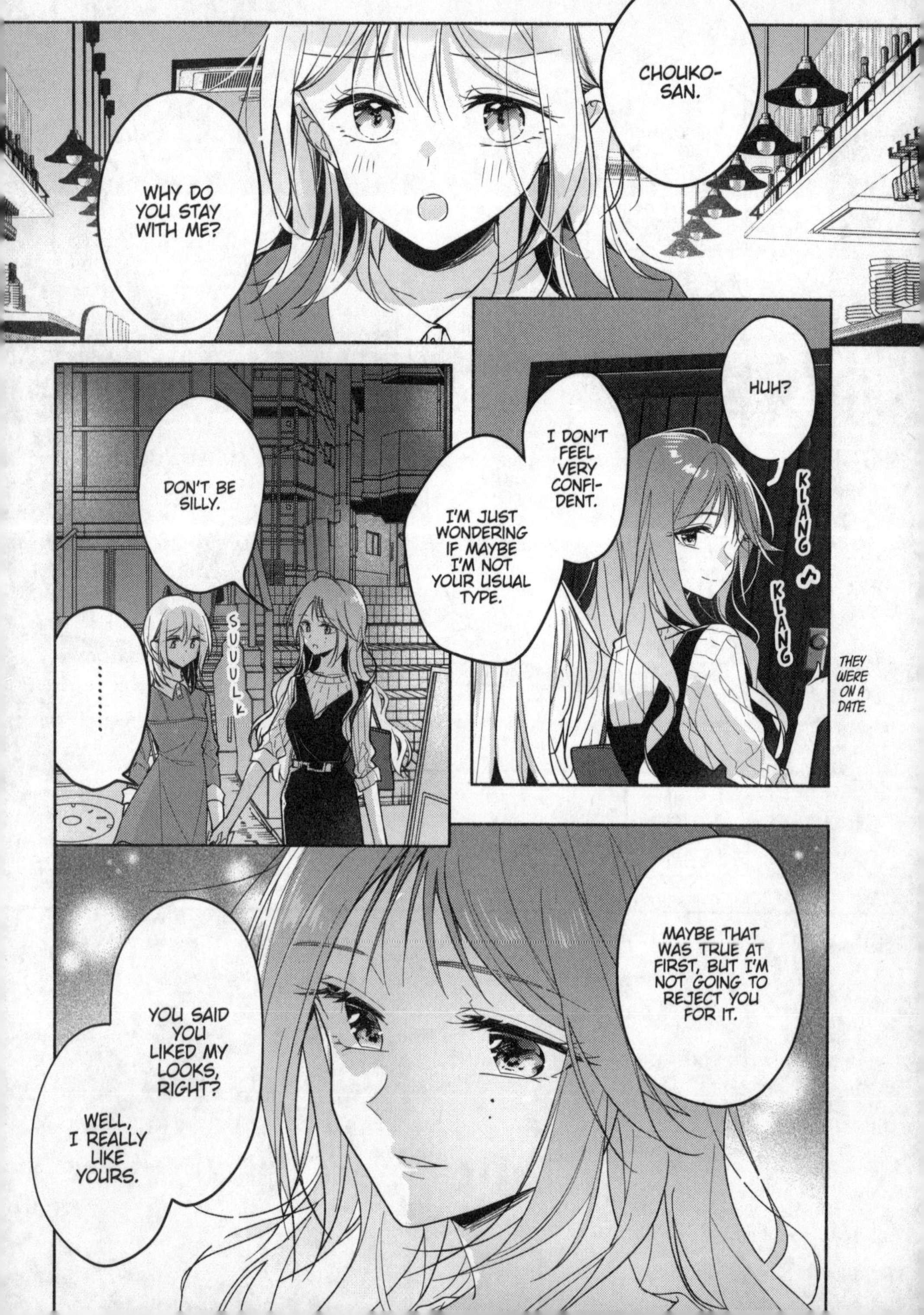
CHOUKO-SAN.
WHY DO YOU STAY WITH ME?
HUH?
KLANG KLANG
I DON'T FEEL VERY CONFIDENT.
I'M JUST WONDERING IF MAYBE I'M NOT YOUR USUAL TYPE.
THEY WERE ON A DATE.
DON'T BE SILLY.
SUUULK
......
MAYBE THAT WAS TRUE AT FIRST, BUT I'M NOT GOING TO REJECT YOU FOR IT.
YOU SAID YOU LIKED MY LOOKS, RIGHT?
WELL, I REALLY LIKE YOURS.

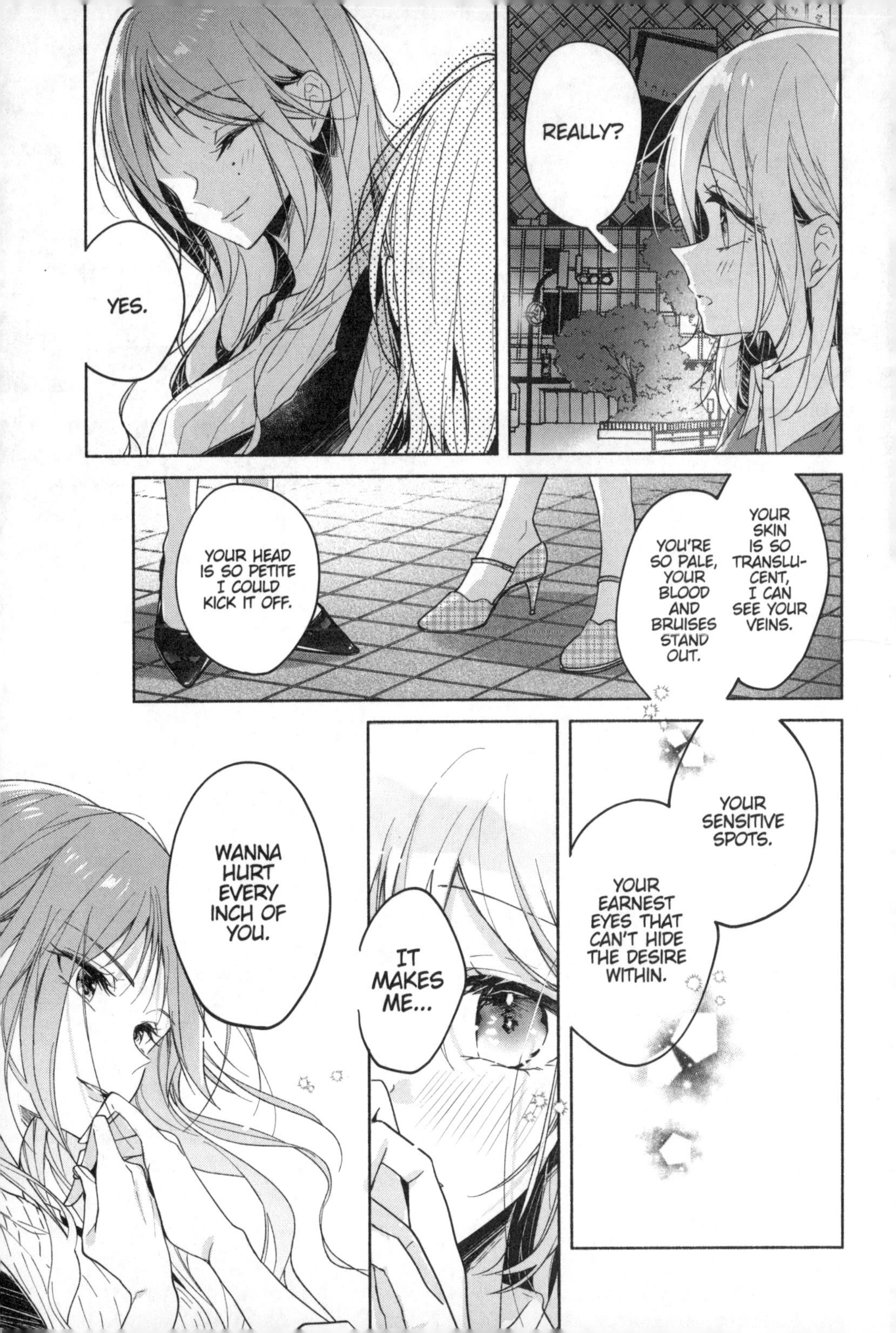
REALLY?
YES.
YOUR SKIN IS SO TRANSLU-CENT, I CAN SEE YOUR VEINS.
YOU'RE SO PALE, YOUR BLOOD AND BRUISES STAND OUT.
YOUR HEAD IS SO PETITE I COULD KICK IT OFF.
YOUR SENSITIVE SPOTS.
YOUR EARNEST EYES THAT CAN'T HIDE THE DESIRE WITHIN.
IT MAKES ME...
WANNA HURT EVERY INCH OF YOU.

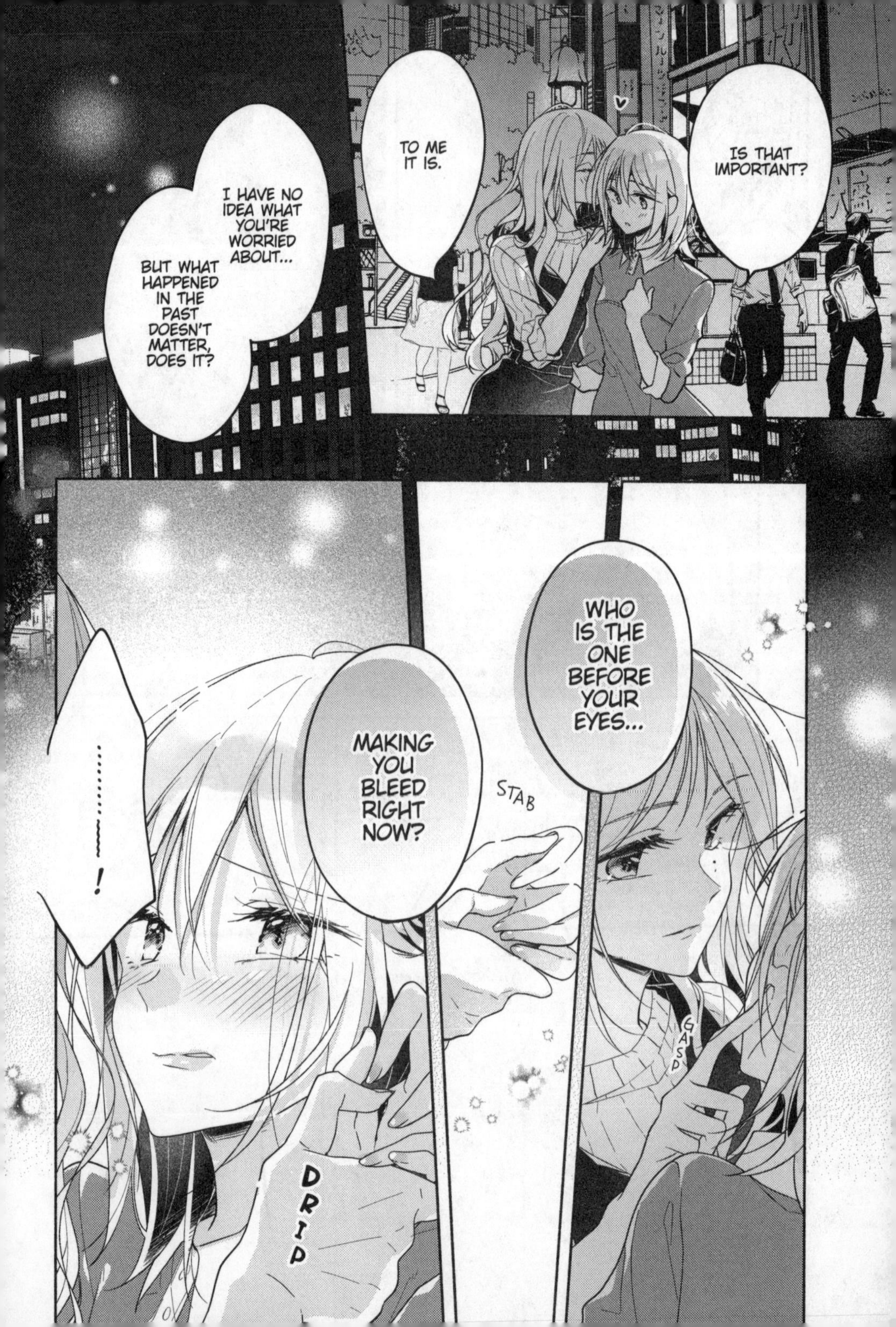
IS THAT IMPORTANT?
TO ME IT IS.
I HAVE NO IDEA WHAT YOU'RE WORRIED ABOUT...
BUT WHAT HAPPENED IN THE PAST DOESN'T MATTER, DOES IT?
WHO IS THE ONE BEFORE YOUR EYES...
GASP
STAB
MAKING YOU BLEED RIGHT NOW?
......!
DRIP

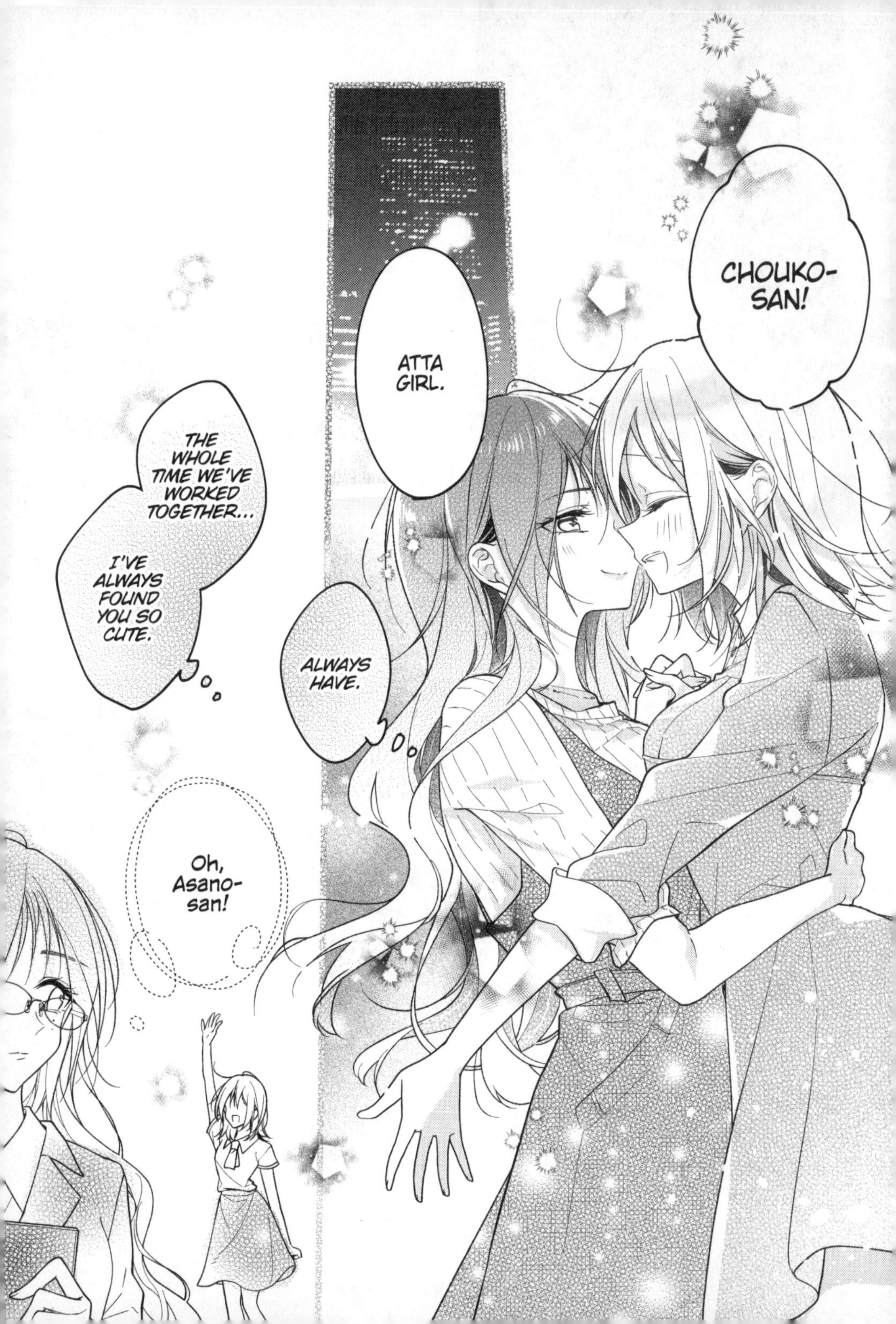
CHOUKO-SAN!
ATTA GIRL.
THE WHOLE TIME WE'VE WORKED TOGETHER...
I'VE ALWAYS FOUND YOU SO CUTE.
ALWAYS HAVE.
Oh, Asano-san!

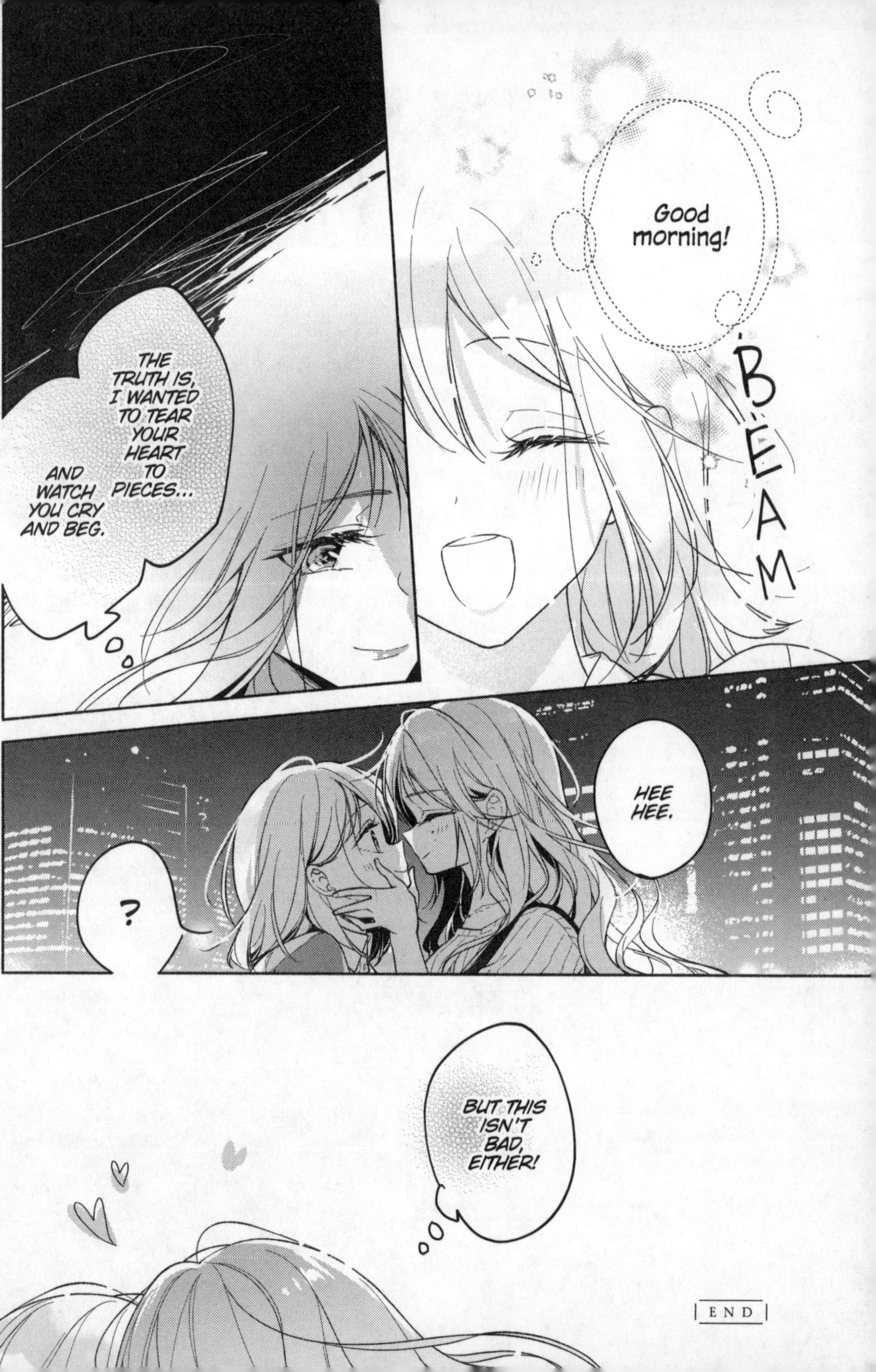
Good morning!
BEAM
THE TRUTH IS, I WANTED TO TEAR YOUR HEART TO PIECES...
AND WATCH YOU CRY AND BEG.
HEE HEE.
?
BUT THIS ISN'T BAD, EITHER!

END

Silky

Cats and Sugar Bowls

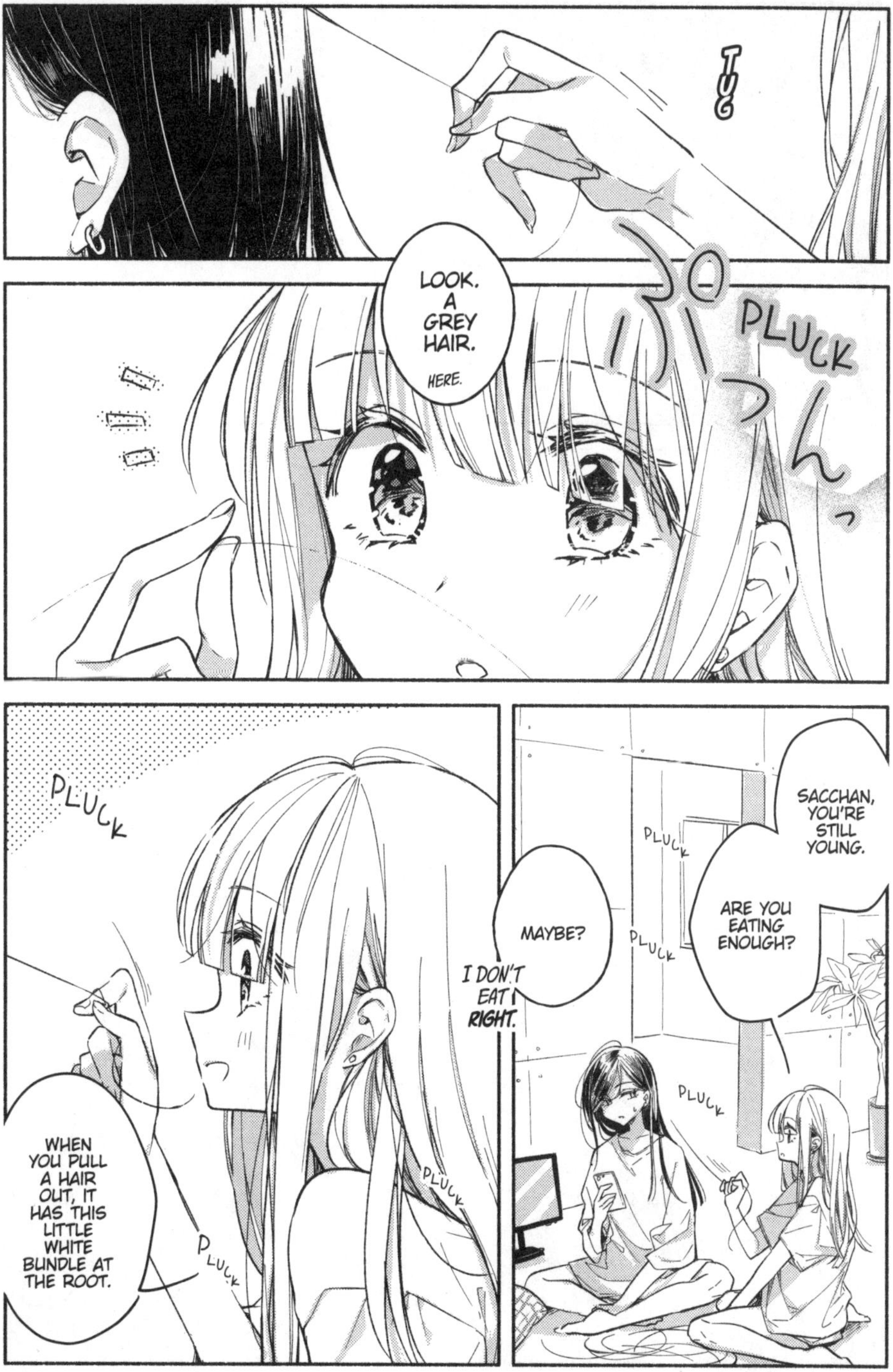
TUG
LOOK. A GREY HAIR.
HERE.
PLUCK
SACCHAN, YOU'RE STILL YOUNG.
ARE YOU EATING ENOUGH?
PLUCK
MAYBE?
PLUCK
I DON'T EAT RIGHT.
PLUCK
PLUCK
WHEN YOU PULL A HAIR OUT, IT HAS THIS LITTLE WHITE BUNDLE AT THE ROOT.
PLUCK
PLUCK

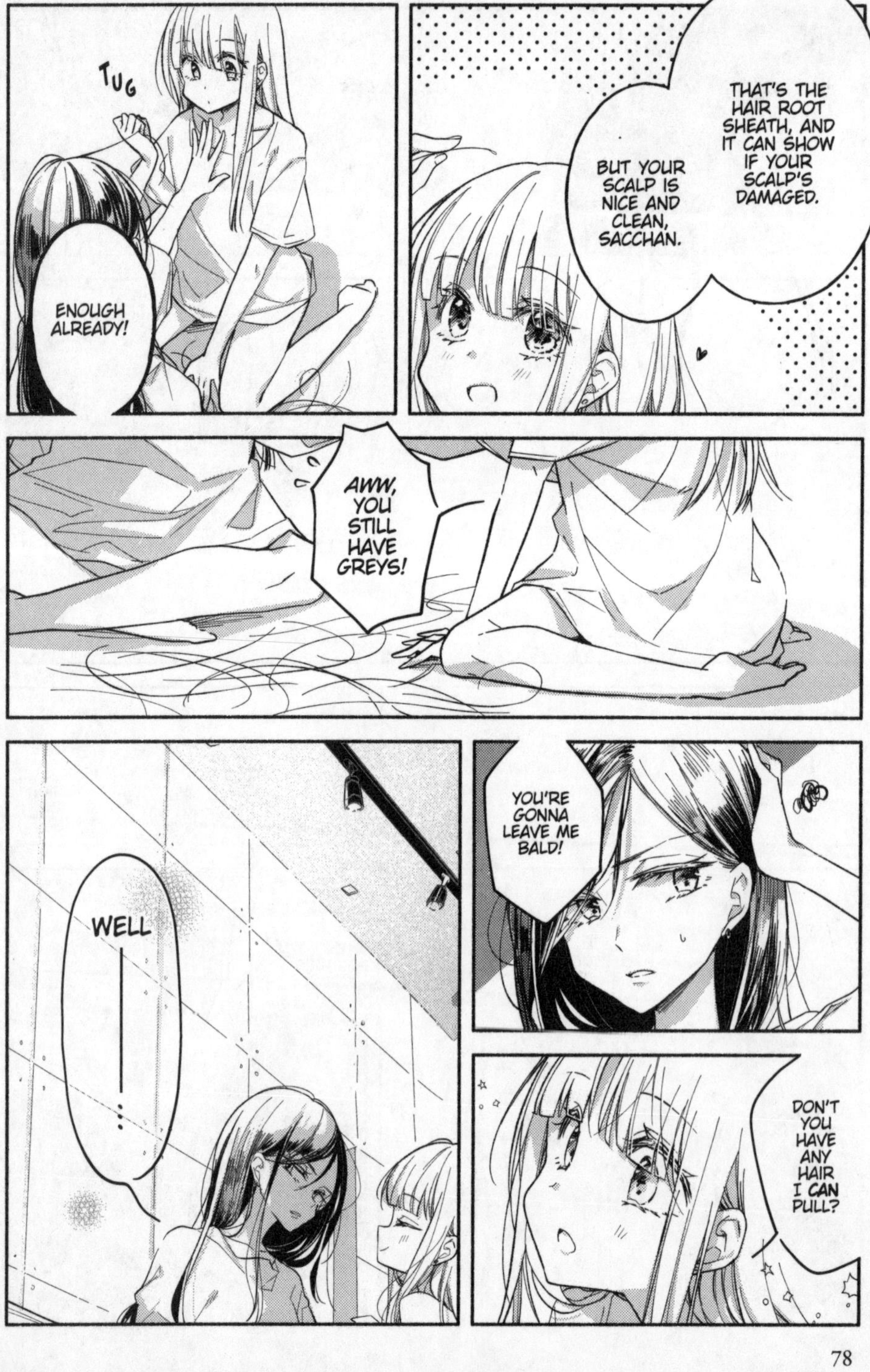
THAT'S THE HAIR ROOT SHEATH, AND IT CAN SHOW IF YOUR SCALP'S DAMAGED.
BUT YOUR SCALP IS NICE AND CLEAN, SACCHAN.
TUG
ENOUGH ALREADY!
AWW, YOU STILL HAVE GREYS!
YOU'RE GONNA LEAVE ME BALD!
DON'T YOU HAVE ANY HAIR I CAN PULL?
WELL —…

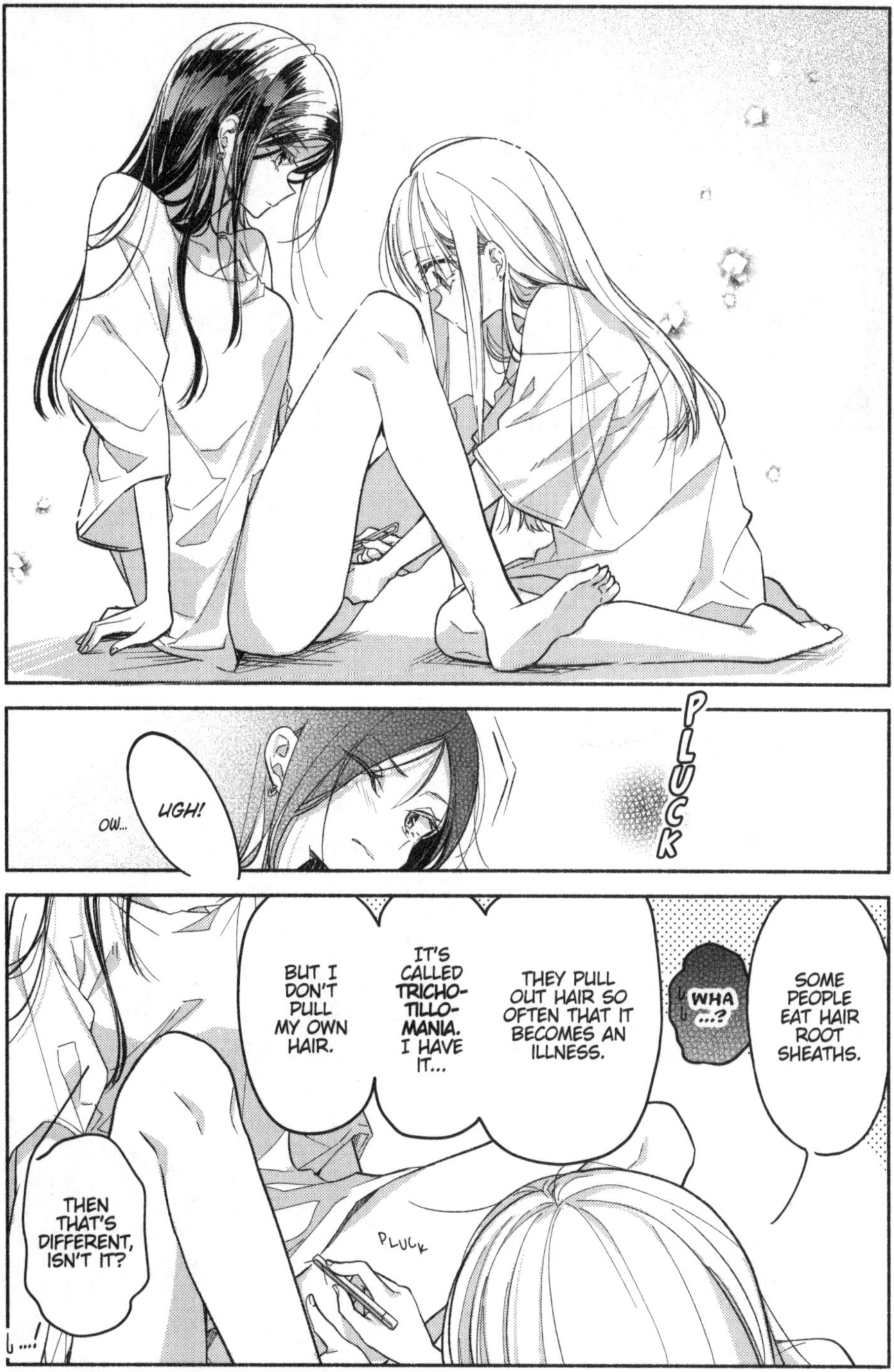
PLUCK
UGH!
OW...
SOME PEOPLE EAT HAIR ROOT SHEATHS.
WHA...?
THEY PULL OUT HAIR SO OFTEN THAT IT BECOMES AN ILLNESS.
IT'S CALLED TRICHO-TILLO-MANIA. I HAVE IT...
BUT I DON'T PULL MY OWN HAIR.
PLUCK
THEN THAT'S DIFFERENT, ISN'T IT?

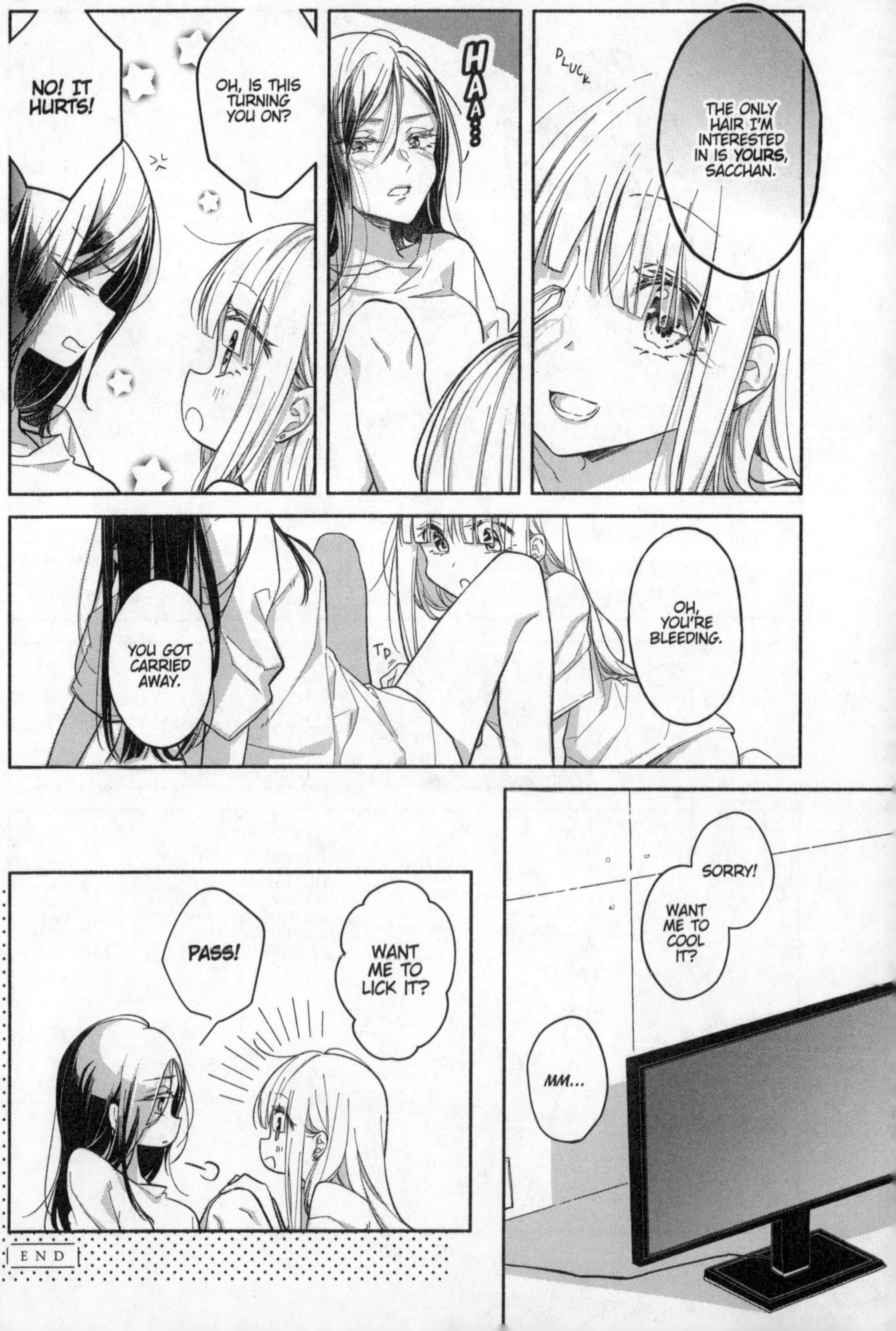
THE ONLY HAIR I'M INTERESTED IN IS YOURS, SACCHAN.
PLUCK
HAA...
OH, IS THIS TURNING YOU ON?
NO! IT HURTS!
OH, YOU'RE BLEEDING.
TP
YOU GOT CARRIED AWAY.
SORRY!
WANT ME TO COOL IT?
MM...
WANT ME TO LICK IT?
PASS!
END

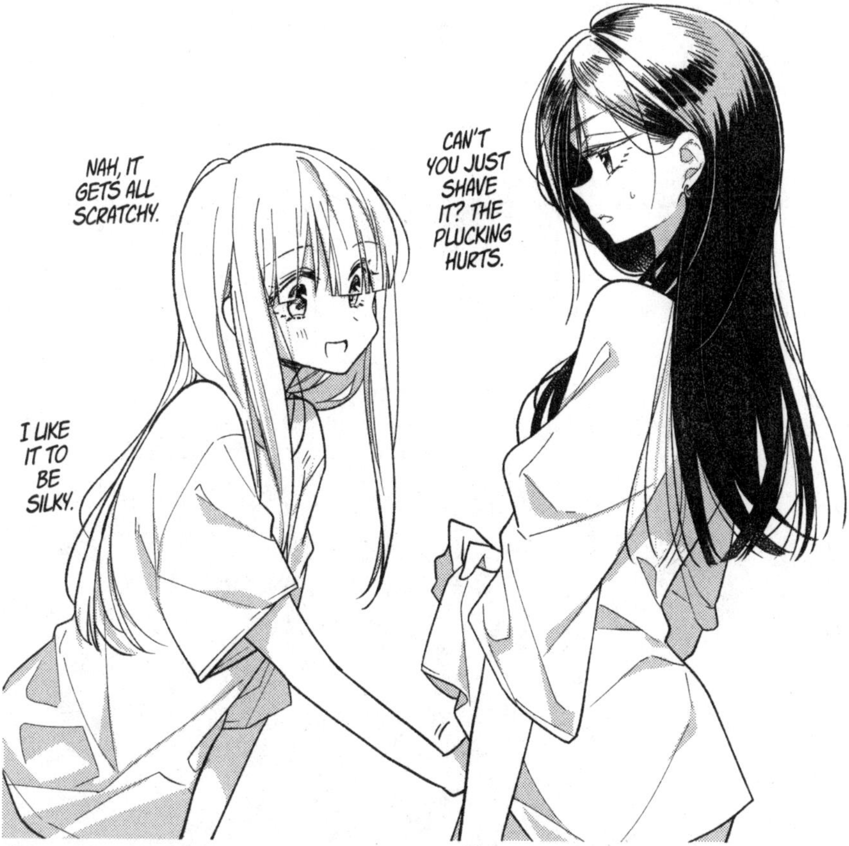
CAN'T YOU JUST SHAVE IT? THE PLUCKING HURTS.
NAH, IT GETS ALL SCRATCHY.
I LIKE IT TO BE SILKY.

Cats and Sugar Bowls

My Childhood Friend

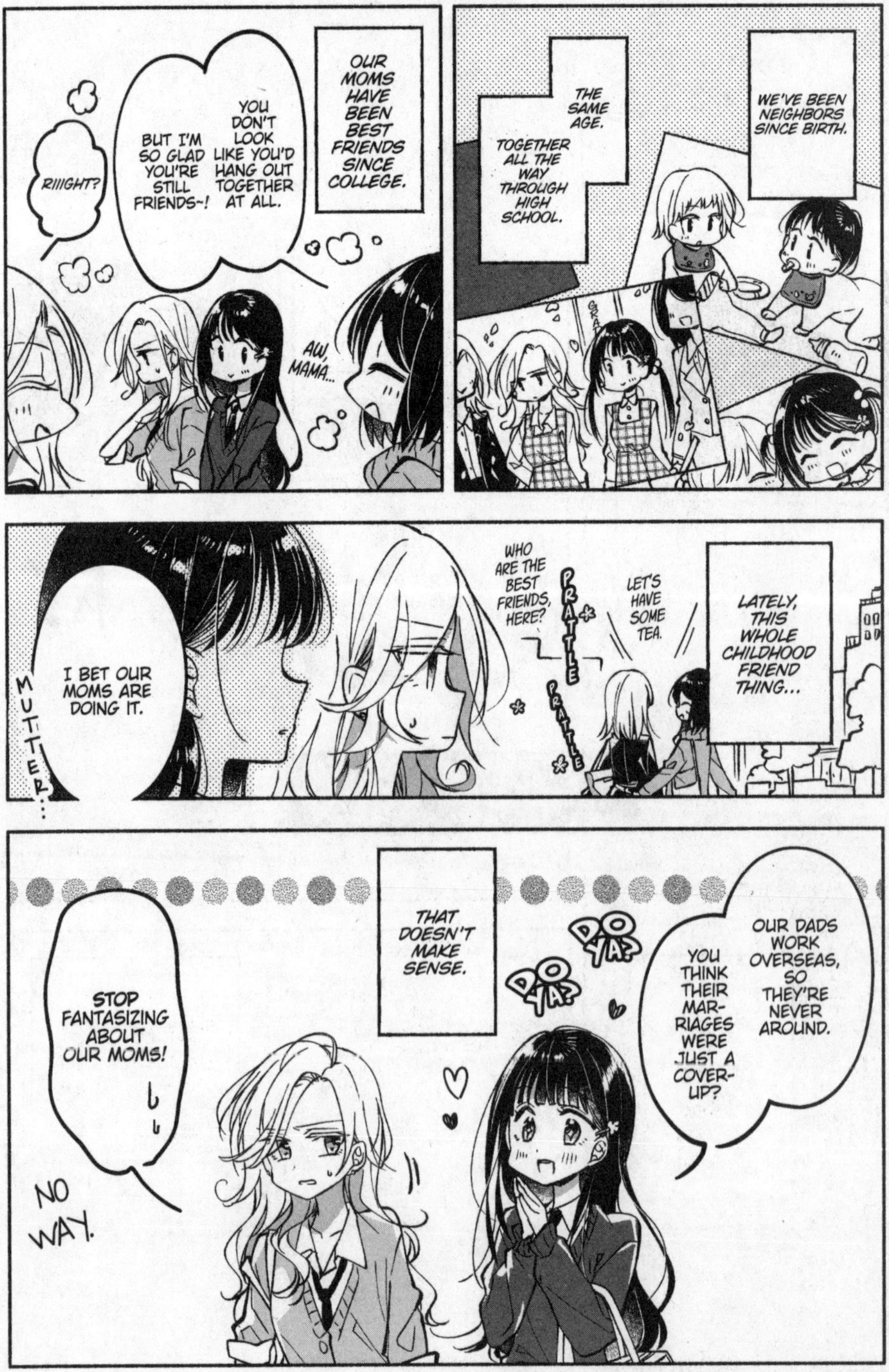
WE'VE BEEN NEIGHBORS SINCE BIRTH.
THE SAME AGE.
TOGETHER ALL THE WAY THROUGH HIGH SCHOOL.
OUR MOMS HAVE BEEN BEST FRIENDS SINCE COLLEGE.
YOU DON'T LOOK LIKE YOU'D HANG OUT TOGETHER AT ALL.
BUT I'M SO GLAD YOU'RE STILL FRIENDS~!
RIIIGHT?
AW, MAMA...
LATELY, THIS WHOLE CHILDHOOD FRIEND THING...
LET'S HAVE SOME TEA.
WHO ARE THE BEST FRIENDS, HERE?
PRATTLE
PRATTLE
I BET OUR MOMS ARE DOING IT.
MUTTER...
OUR DADS WORK OVERSEAS, SO THEY'RE NEVER AROUND.
YOU THINK THEIR MAR-RIAGES WERE JUST A COVER-UP?
DO YA?
DO YA?
THAT DOESN'T MAKE SENSE.
STOP FANTASIZING ABOUT OUR MOMS!
NO WAY.

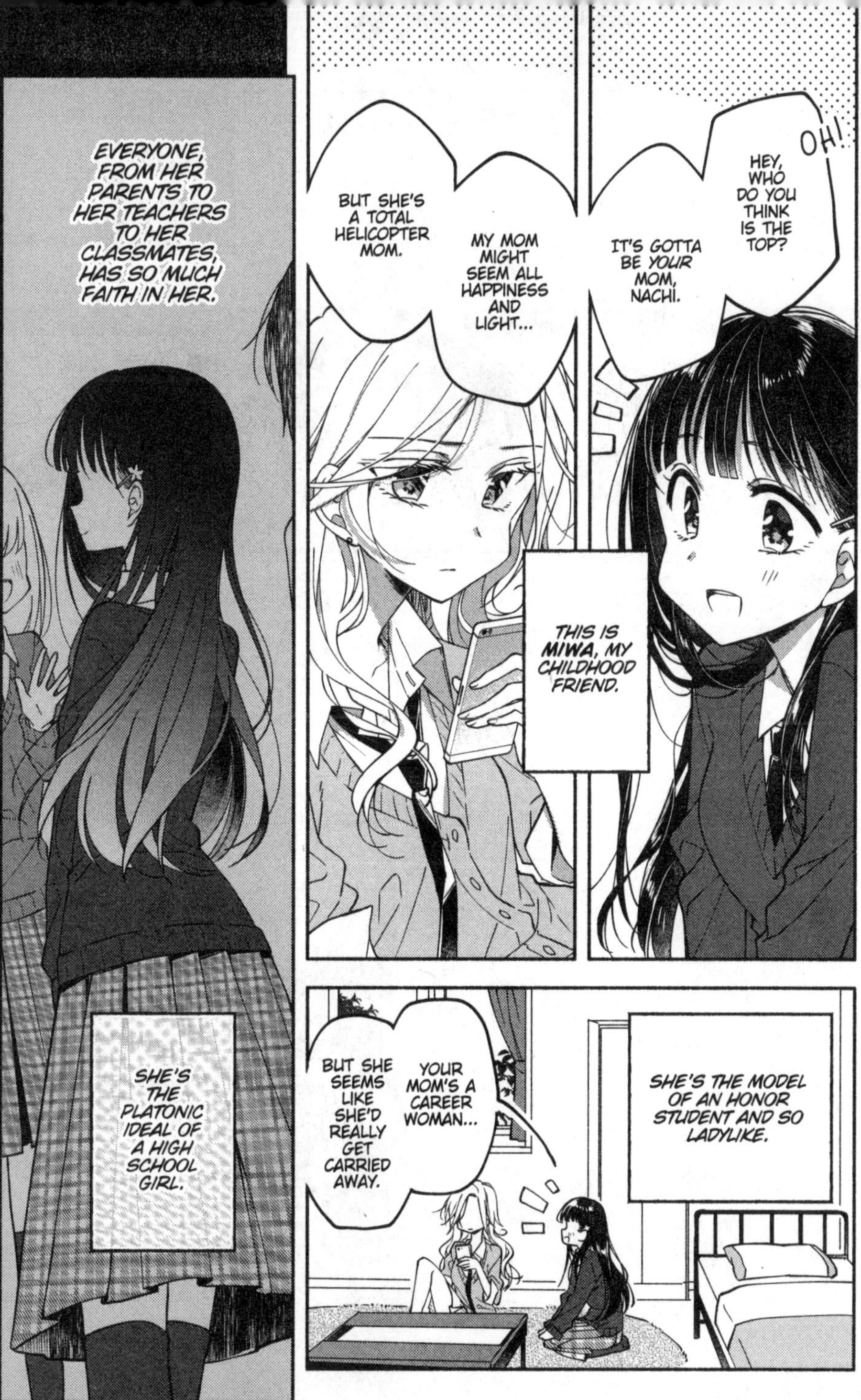
OH!
HEY, WHO DO YOU THINK IS THE TOP?
IT'S GOTTA BE YOUR MOM, NACHI.
MY MOM MIGHT SEEM ALL HAPPINESS AND LIGHT...
BUT SHE'S A TOTAL HELICOPTER MOM.
THIS IS MIWA, MY CHILDHOOD FRIEND.
SHE'S THE MODEL OF AN HONOR STUDENT AND SO LADYLIKE.
YOUR MOM'S A CAREER WOMAN...
BUT SHE SEEMS LIKE SHE'D REALLY GET CARRIED AWAY.
EVERYONE, FROM HER PARENTS TO HER TEACHERS TO HER CLASSMATES, HAS SO MUCH FAITH IN HER.
SHE'S THE PLATONIC IDEAL OF A HIGH SCHOOL GIRL.

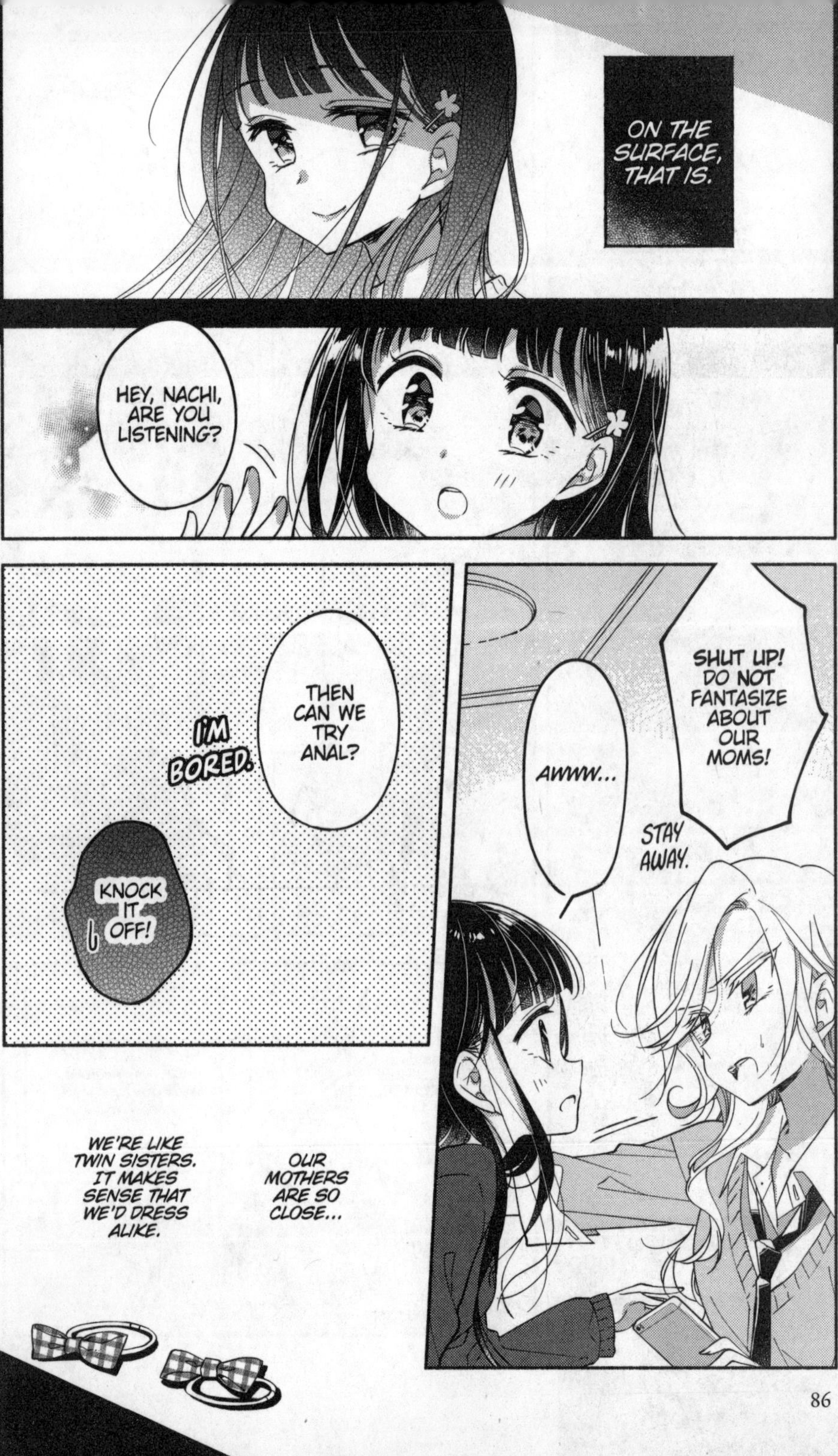
ON THE SURFACE, THAT IS.
HEY, NACHI, ARE YOU LISTENING?
SHUT UP! DO NOT FANTASIZE ABOUT OUR MOMS!
AWWW...
STAY AWAY.
THEN CAN WE TRY ANAL?
I'M BORED.
KNOCK IT OFF!
OUR MOTHERS ARE SO CLOSE...
WE'RE LIKE TWIN SISTERS. IT MAKES SENSE THAT WE'D DRESS ALIKE.

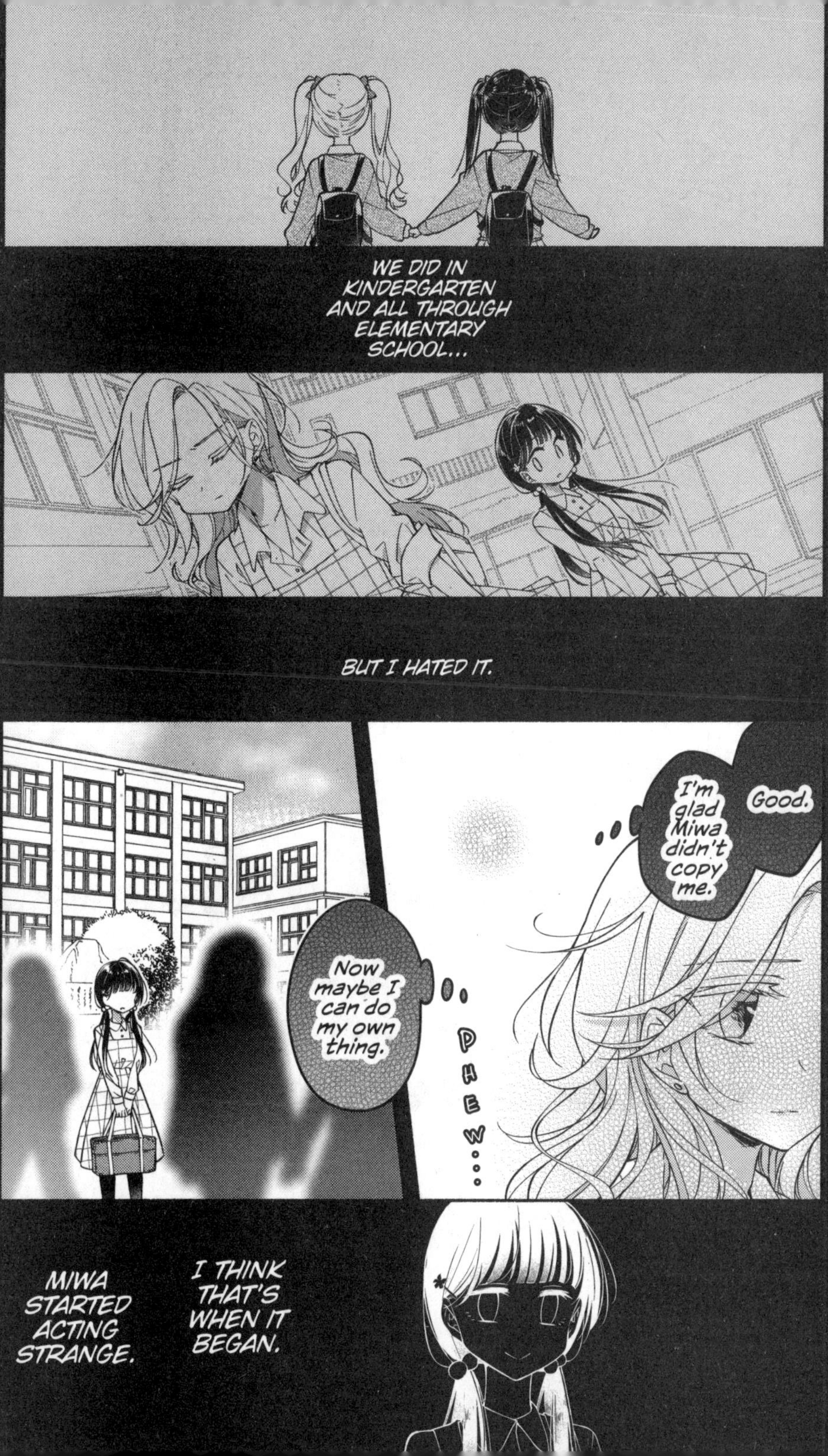
WE DID IN KINDERGARTEN AND ALL THROUGH ELEMENTARY SCHOOL...
BUT I HATED IT.
Good.
I'm glad Miwa didn't copy me.
PHEW...
Now maybe I can do my own thing.
I THINK THAT'S WHEN IT BEGAN.
MIWA STARTED ACTING STRANGE.

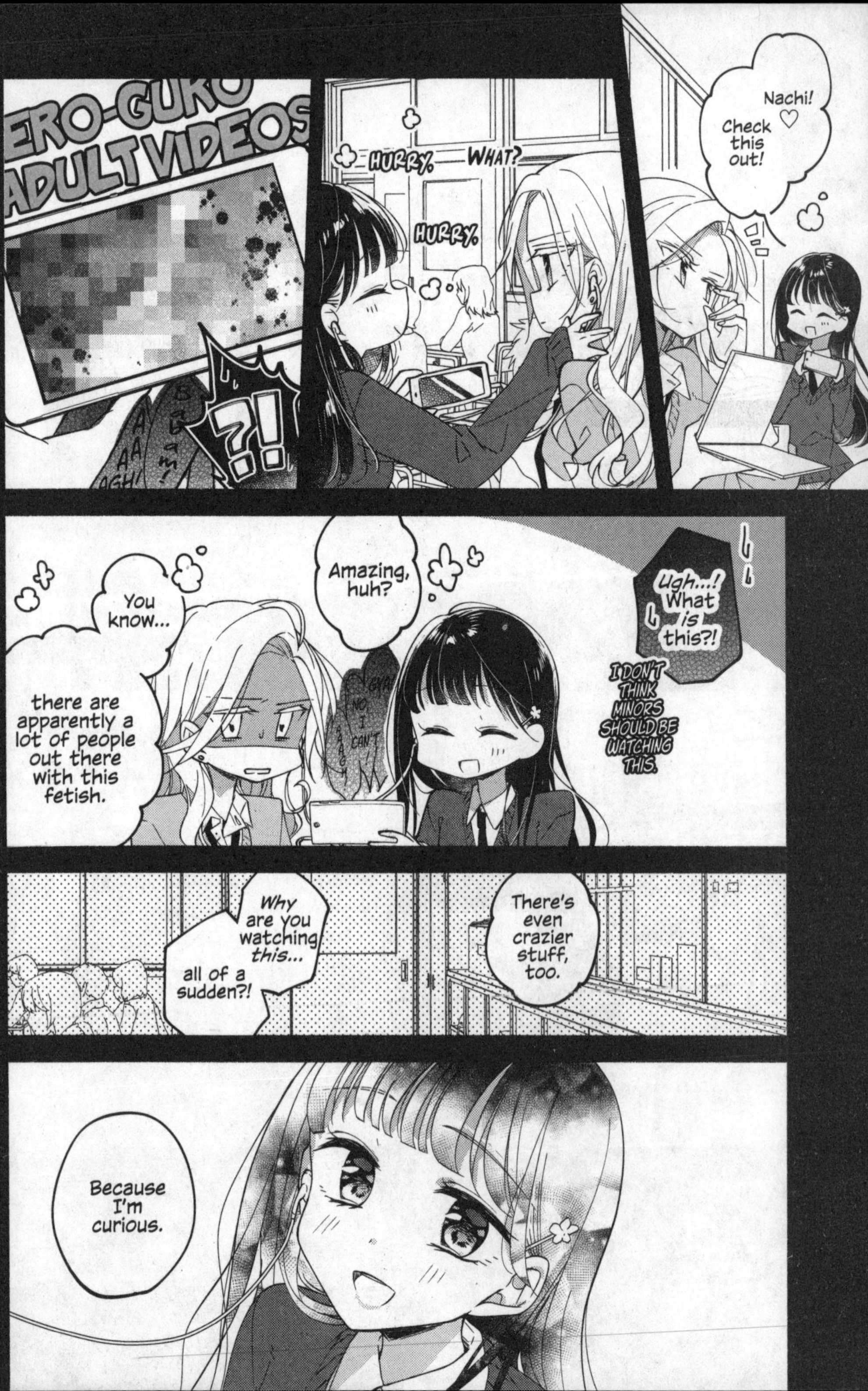
Nachi! ♡ Check this out!
WHAT?
HURRY. HURRY.
ERO-GURO ADULT VIDEOS
?!
Babam!
AAAAGH!
Ugh...! What is this?!
I DON'T THINK MINORS SHOULD BE WATCHING THIS.
Amazing, huh?
GYA! NO I CAN'T AAAGH
You know...
there are apparently a lot of people out there with this fetish.
There's even crazier stuff, too.
Why are you watching this...
all of a sudden?!
Because I'm curious.

AREN'T WE SUPPOSED TO BE STUDYING WORLD HISTORY?

CRUCIFIXION INVOLVES HAMMERING NAILS INTO THE HANDS, RIGHT? WONDER HOW THAT FEELS. IF YOU PULL THE NAILS OUT, HOW MUCH WOULD THE HANDS BLEED?

FASCINATED.

AND AFTER THAT...

I'M TIRED OF GIVING THEM ORDERS.

SIGH

I have three slaves, but being a dom isn't as exciting as I thought.

Where... do you find slaves?

I WANTED TO GET AWAY FROM MIWA SO BAD...

Places like Sk◯pe.

Oh, don't worry, I'm careful not to get doxxed.

I'M TOTALLY WORRIED.

BUT THEN I GOT WORRIED ABOUT JUST HOW FAR AWAY SHE WOULD GO.

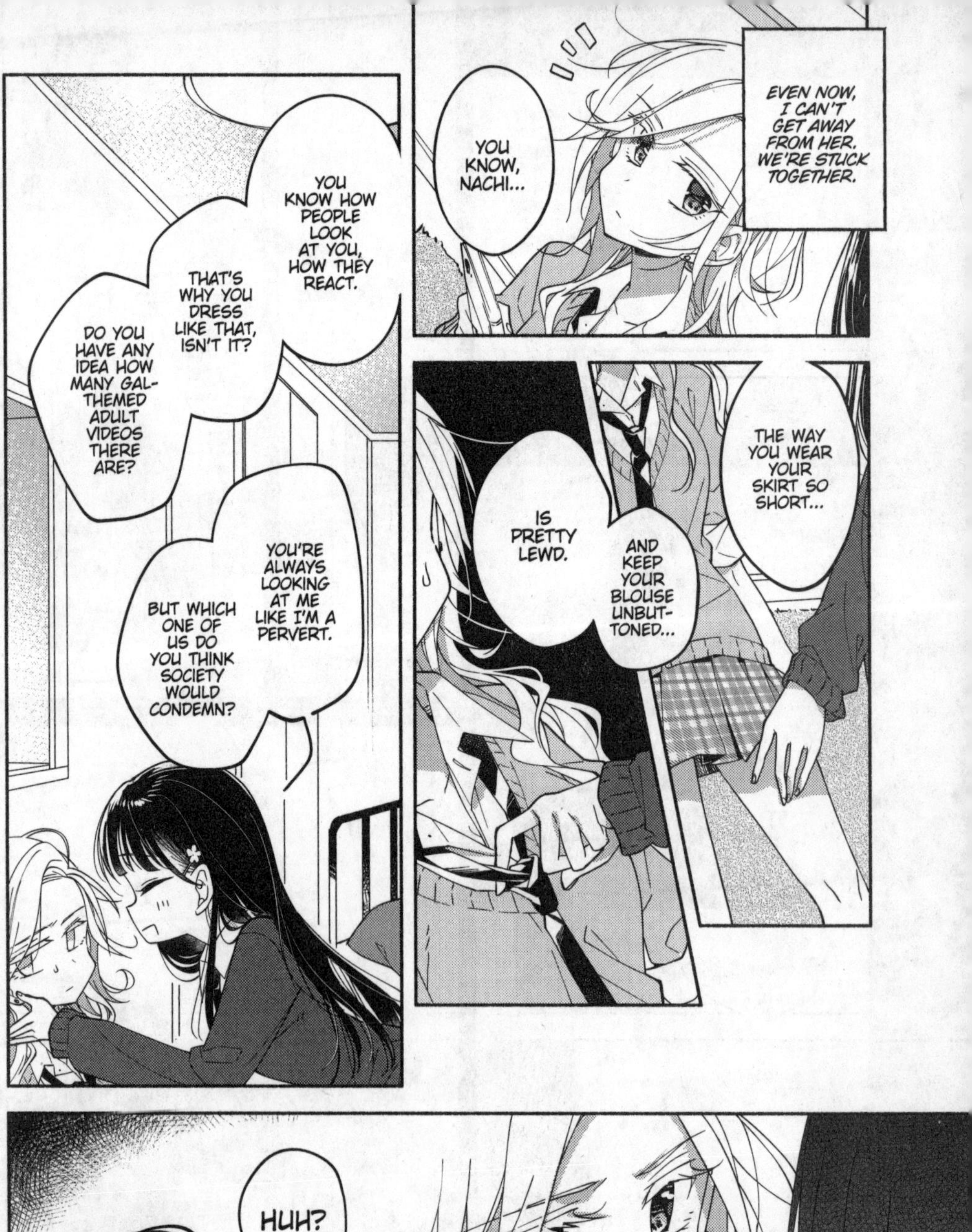
EVEN NOW, I CAN'T GET AWAY FROM HER. WE'RE STUCK TOGETHER.
YOU KNOW, NACHI...
THE WAY YOU WEAR YOUR SKIRT SO SHORT...
AND KEEP YOUR BLOUSE UNBUT-TONED...
IS PRETTY LEWD.
YOU KNOW HOW PEOPLE LOOK AT YOU, HOW THEY REACT.
THAT'S WHY YOU DRESS LIKE THAT, ISN'T IT?
DO YOU HAVE ANY IDEA HOW MANY GAL-THEMED ADULT VIDEOS THERE ARE?
YOU'RE ALWAYS LOOKING AT ME LIKE I'M A PERVERT.
BUT WHICH ONE OF US DO YOU THINK SOCIETY WOULD CONDEMN?
HUH?
IT'D DEFINITELY BE YOU.

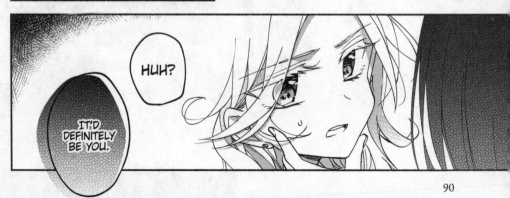

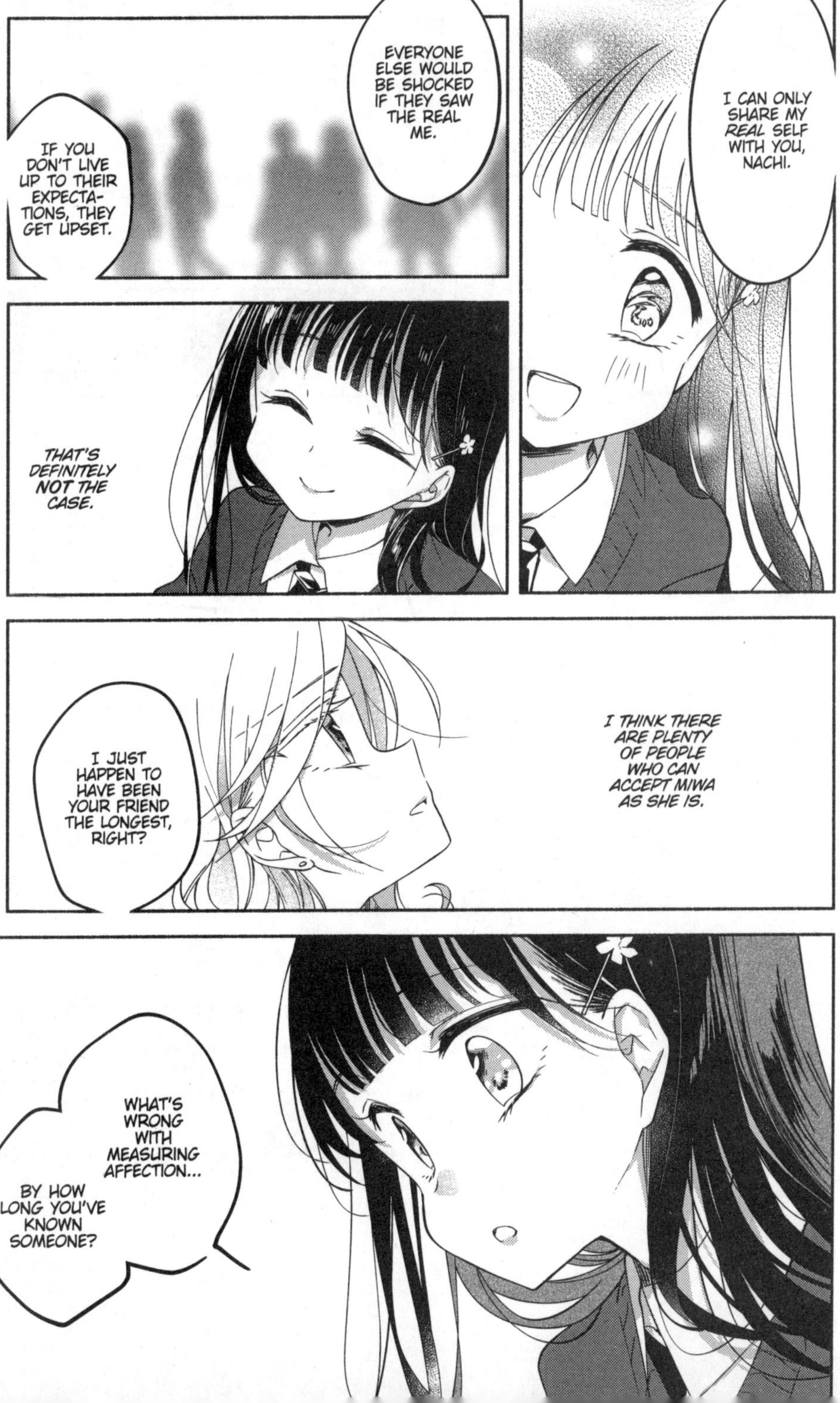
I CAN ONLY SHARE MY *REAL* SELF WITH YOU, NACHI.
EVERYONE ELSE WOULD BE SHOCKED IF THEY SAW THE REAL ME.
IF YOU DON'T LIVE UP TO THEIR EXPECTATIONS, THEY GET UPSET.
THAT'S DEFINITELY **NOT THE** *CASE.*
I THINK THERE ARE PLENTY OF PEOPLE WHO CAN ACCEPT MIWA AS SHE IS.
I JUST HAPPEN TO HAVE BEEN YOUR FRIEND THE LONGEST, RIGHT?
WHAT'S WRONG WITH MEASURING AFFECTION...
BY HOW LONG YOU'VE KNOWN SOMEONE?

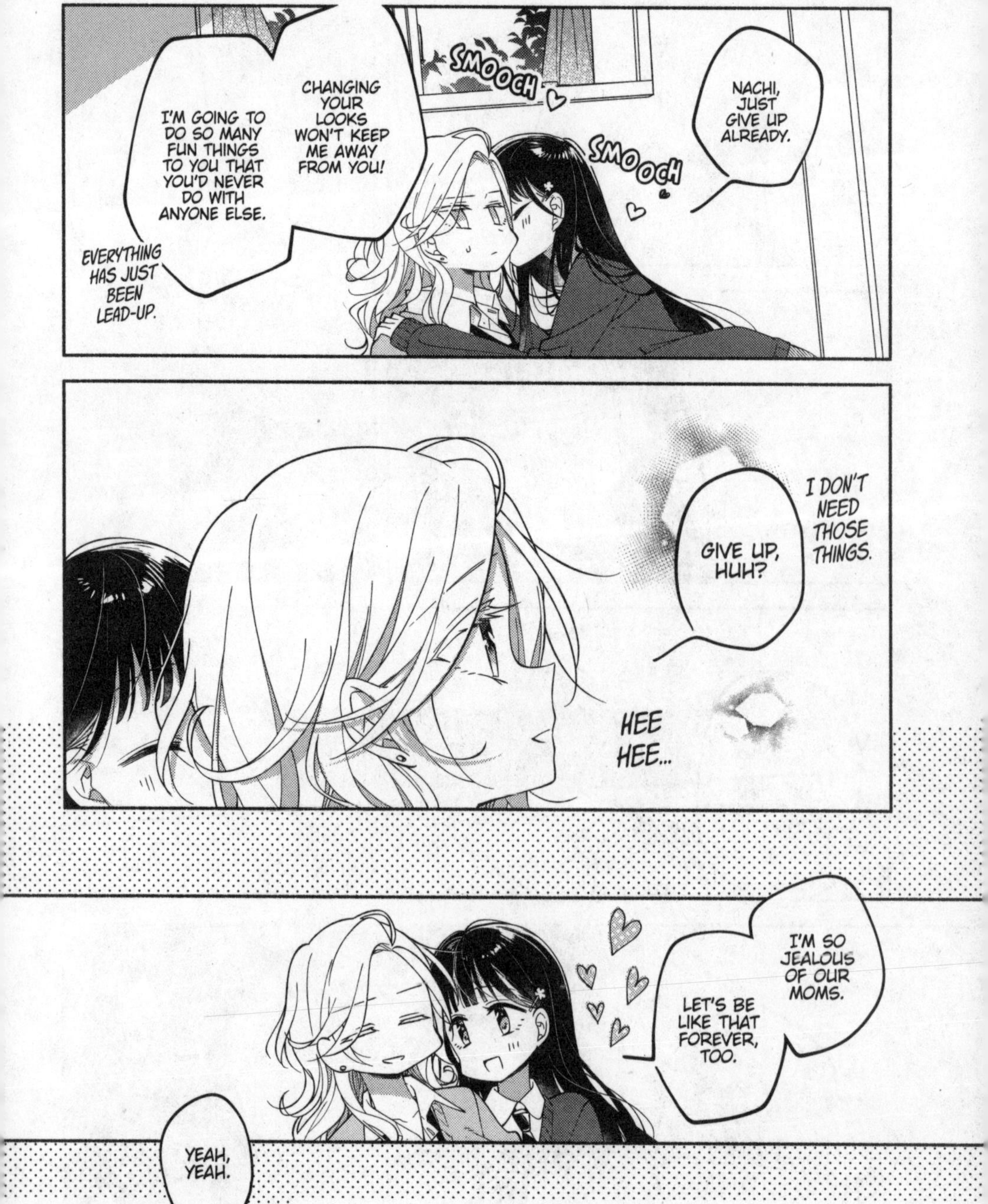
NACHI, JUST GIVE UP ALREADY.
SMOOCH
SMOOCH
CHANGING YOUR LOOKS WON'T KEEP ME AWAY FROM YOU!
I'M GOING TO DO SO MANY FUN THINGS TO YOU THAT YOU'D NEVER DO WITH ANYONE ELSE.
EVERYTHING HAS JUST BEEN LEAD-UP.
I DON'T NEED THOSE THINGS.
GIVE UP, HUH?
HEE HEE...
I'M SO JEALOUS OF OUR MOMS.
LET'S BE LIKE THAT FOREVER, TOO.
YEAH, YEAH.

END

One AM at the Laundromat

Cats and Sugar Bowls

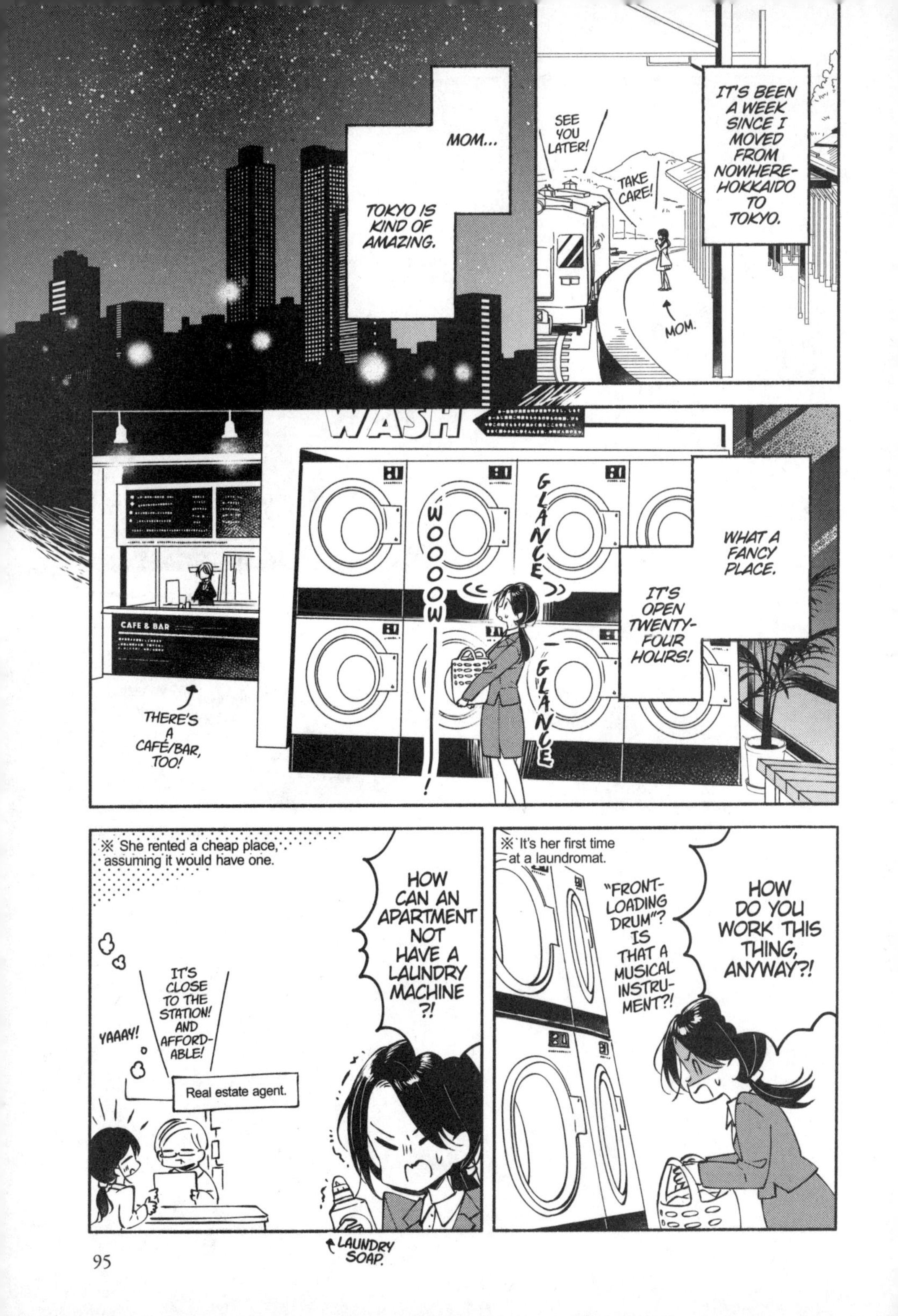
IT'S BEEN A WEEK SINCE I MOVED FROM NOWHERE-HOKKAIDO TO TOKYO.
SEE YOU LATER!
TAKE CARE!
MOM.
MOM...
TOKYO IS KIND OF AMAZING.
WASH
WHAT A FANCY PLACE.
IT'S OPEN TWENTY-FOUR HOURS!
GLANCE
GLANCE
WOOOOOW!
CAFE & BAR
THERE'S A CAFÉ/BAR, TOO!
※ It's her first time at a laundromat.
HOW DO YOU WORK THIS THING, ANYWAY?!
"FRONT-LOADING DRUM"? IS THAT A MUSICAL INSTRUMENT?!
※ She rented a cheap place, assuming it would have one.
HOW CAN AN APARTMENT NOT HAVE A LAUNDRY MACHINE?!
IT'S CLOSE TO THE STATION! AND AFFORDABLE!
YAAAY!
Real estate agent.
LAUNDRY SOAP.

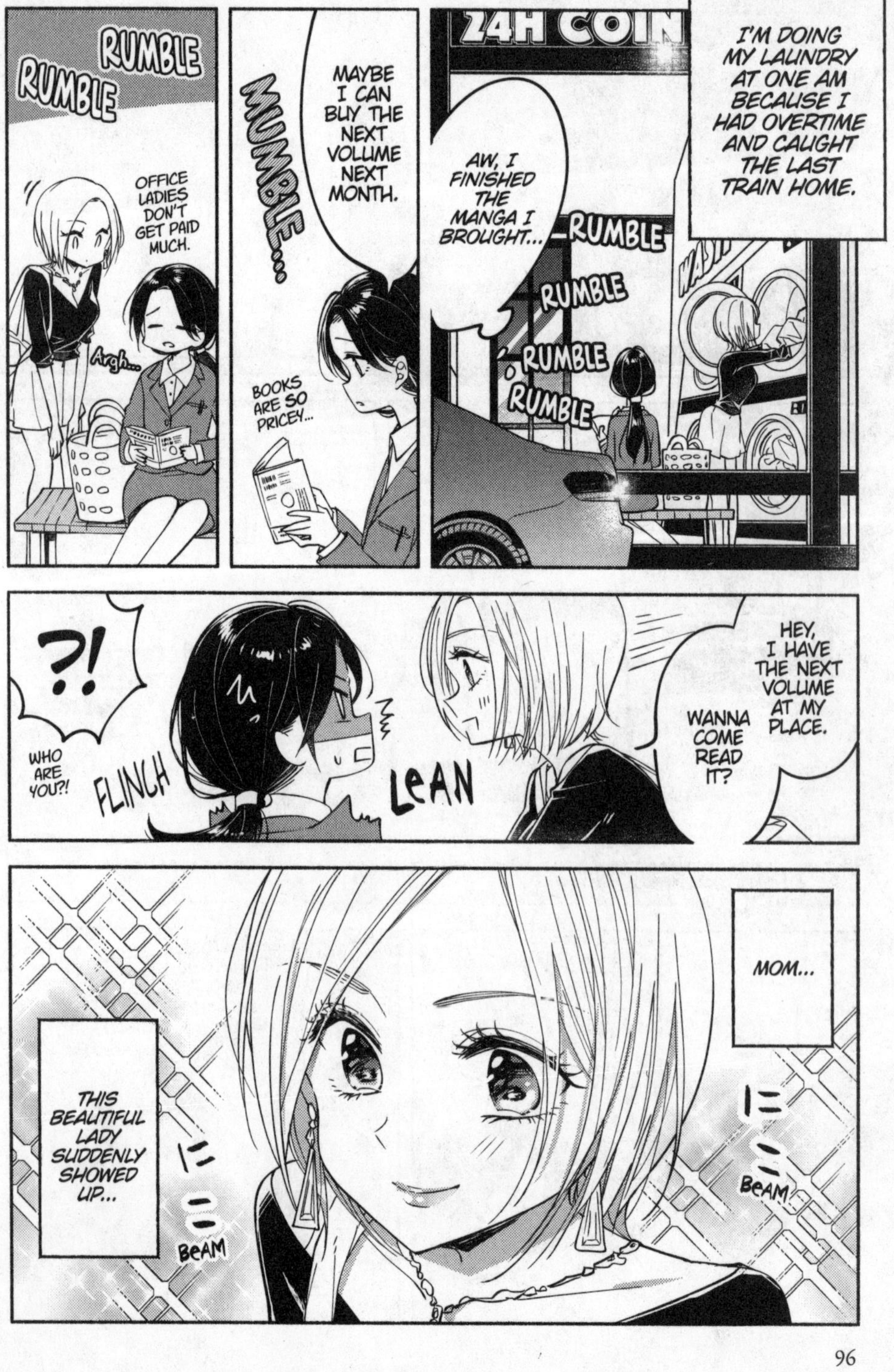
I'M DOING MY LAUNDRY AT ONE AM BECAUSE I HAD OVERTIME AND CAUGHT THE LAST TRAIN HOME.
24H COIN
AW, I FINISHED THE MANGA I BROUGHT...
RUMBLE
RUMBLE
RUMBLE
RUMBLE
MAYBE I CAN BUY THE NEXT VOLUME NEXT MONTH.
MUMBLE...
BOOKS ARE SO PRICEY...
RUMBLE
RUMBLE
OFFICE LADIES DON'T GET PAID MUCH.
Argh...
HEY, I HAVE THE NEXT VOLUME AT MY PLACE.
WANNA COME READ IT?
LEAN
?!
FLINCH
WHO ARE YOU?!
MOM...
にこ
BEAM
THIS BEAUTIFUL LADY SUDDENLY SHOWED UP...
にこ
BEAM

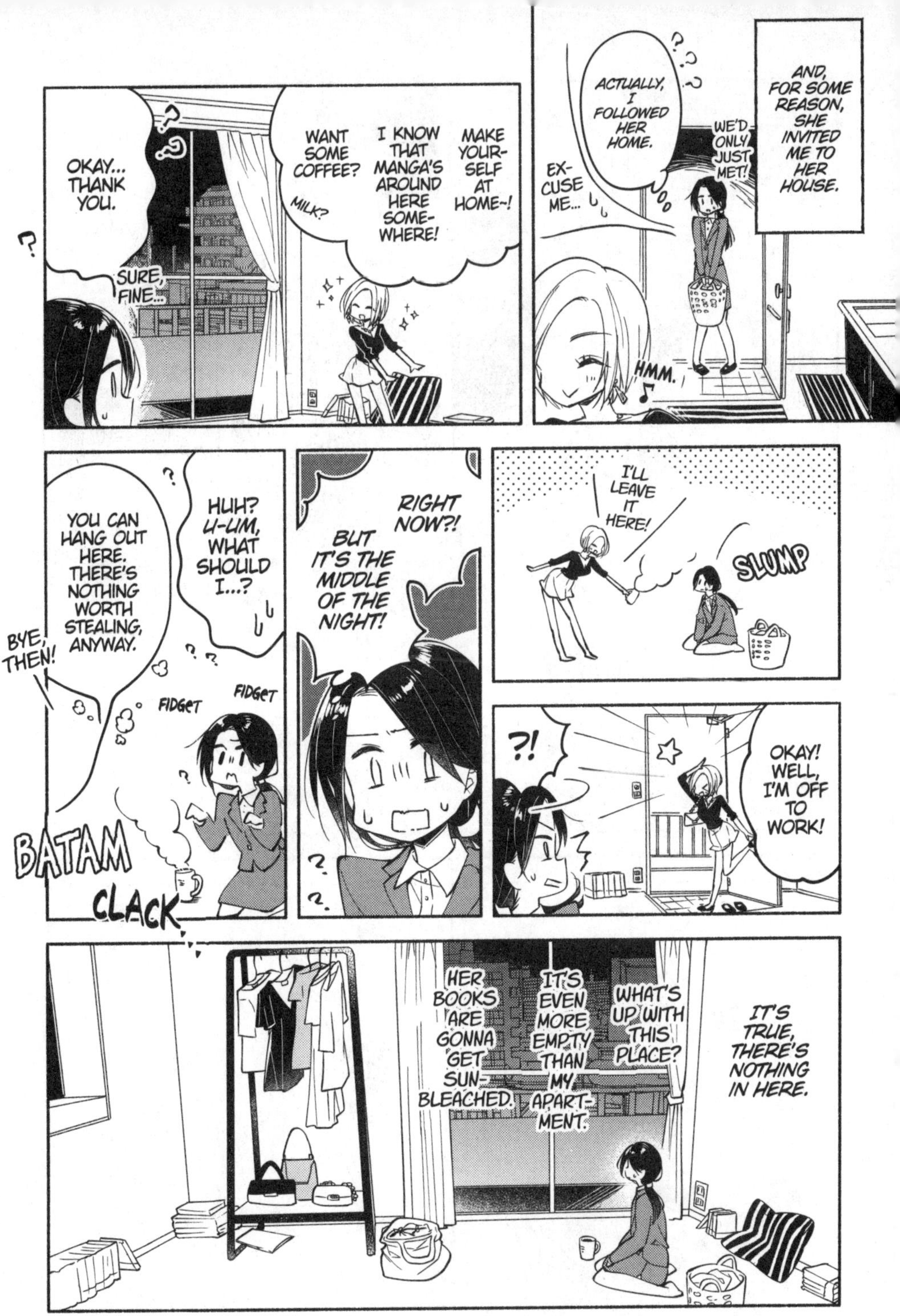
AND, FOR SOME REASON, SHE INVITED ME TO HER HOUSE.
ACTUALLY, I FOLLOWED HER HOME.
WE'D ONLY JUST MET!
EX-CUSE ME...
HMM.
MAKE YOUR-SELF AT HOME~!
I KNOW THAT MANGA'S AROUND HERE SOME-WHERE!
WANT SOME COFFEE?
MILK?
OKAY... THANK YOU.
SURE, FINE...
I'LL LEAVE IT HERE!
SLUMP
OKAY! WELL, I'M OFF TO WORK!
?!
RIGHT NOW?!
BUT IT'S THE MIDDLE OF THE NIGHT!
HUH? U-UM, WHAT SHOULD I...?
YOU CAN HANG OUT HERE. THERE'S NOTHING WORTH STEALING, ANYWAY.
BYE, THEN!
FIDGET
FIDGET
BATAM
CLACK
IT'S TRUE, THERE'S NOTHING IN HERE.
WHAT'S UP WITH THIS PLACE?
IT'S EVEN MORE EMPTY THAN MY APART-MENT.
HER BOOKS ARE GONNA GET SUN-BLEACHED.

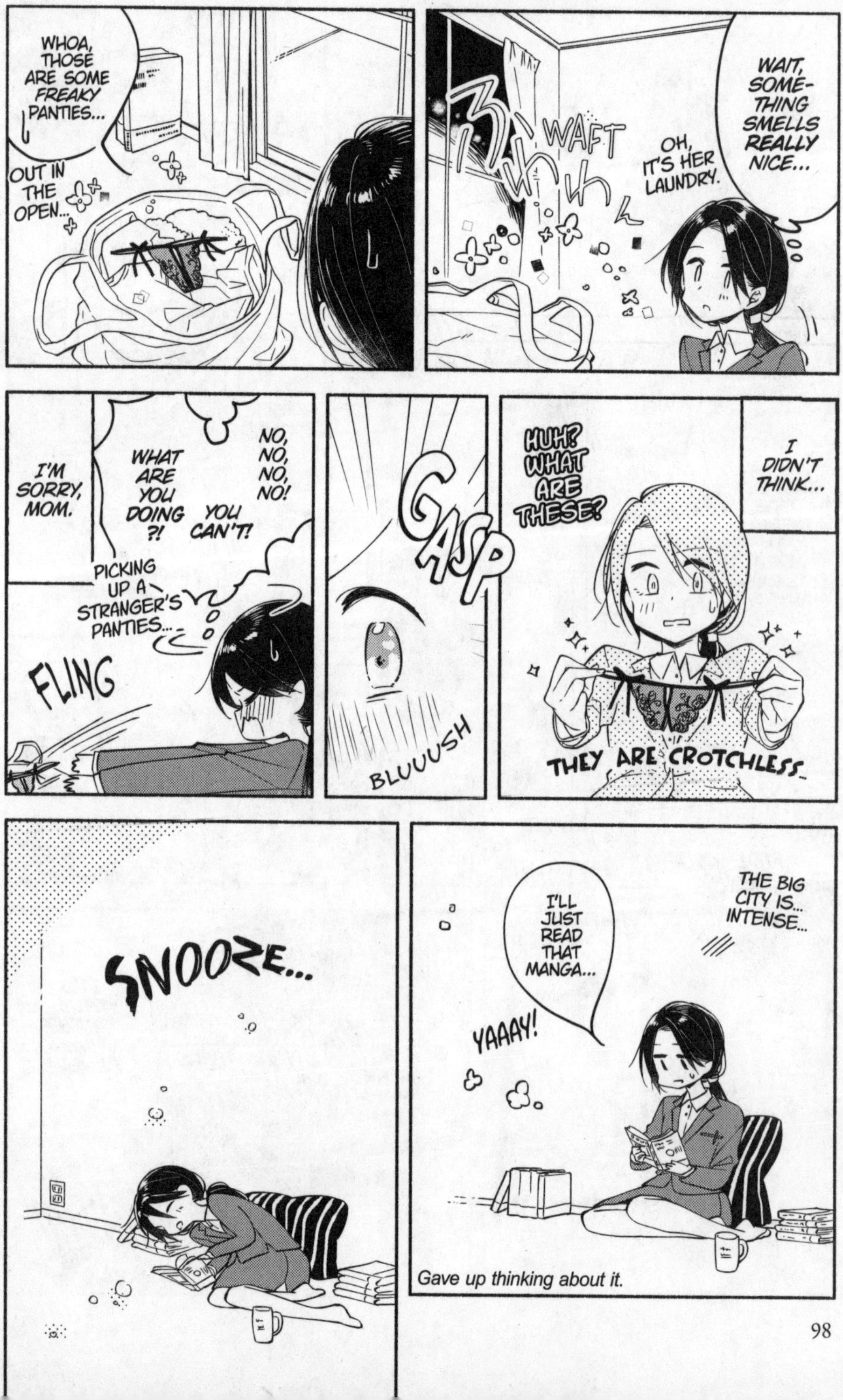
WAIT, SOMETHING SMELLS REALLY NICE...
OH, IT'S HER LAUNDRY.
WAFT
WHOA, THOSE ARE SOME FREAKY PANTIES...
OUT IN THE OPEN...
I DIDN'T THINK...
HUH? WHAT ARE THESE?
THEY ARE CROTCHLESS...
GASP
BLUUUSH
NO, NO, NO, NO!
YOU CAN'T!
WHAT ARE YOU DOING?!
I'M SORRY, MOM.
PICKING UP A STRANGER'S PANTIES...
FLING
THE BIG CITY IS... INTENSE...
I'LL JUST READ THAT MANGA...
YAAAY!
Gave up thinking about it.
SNOOZE...

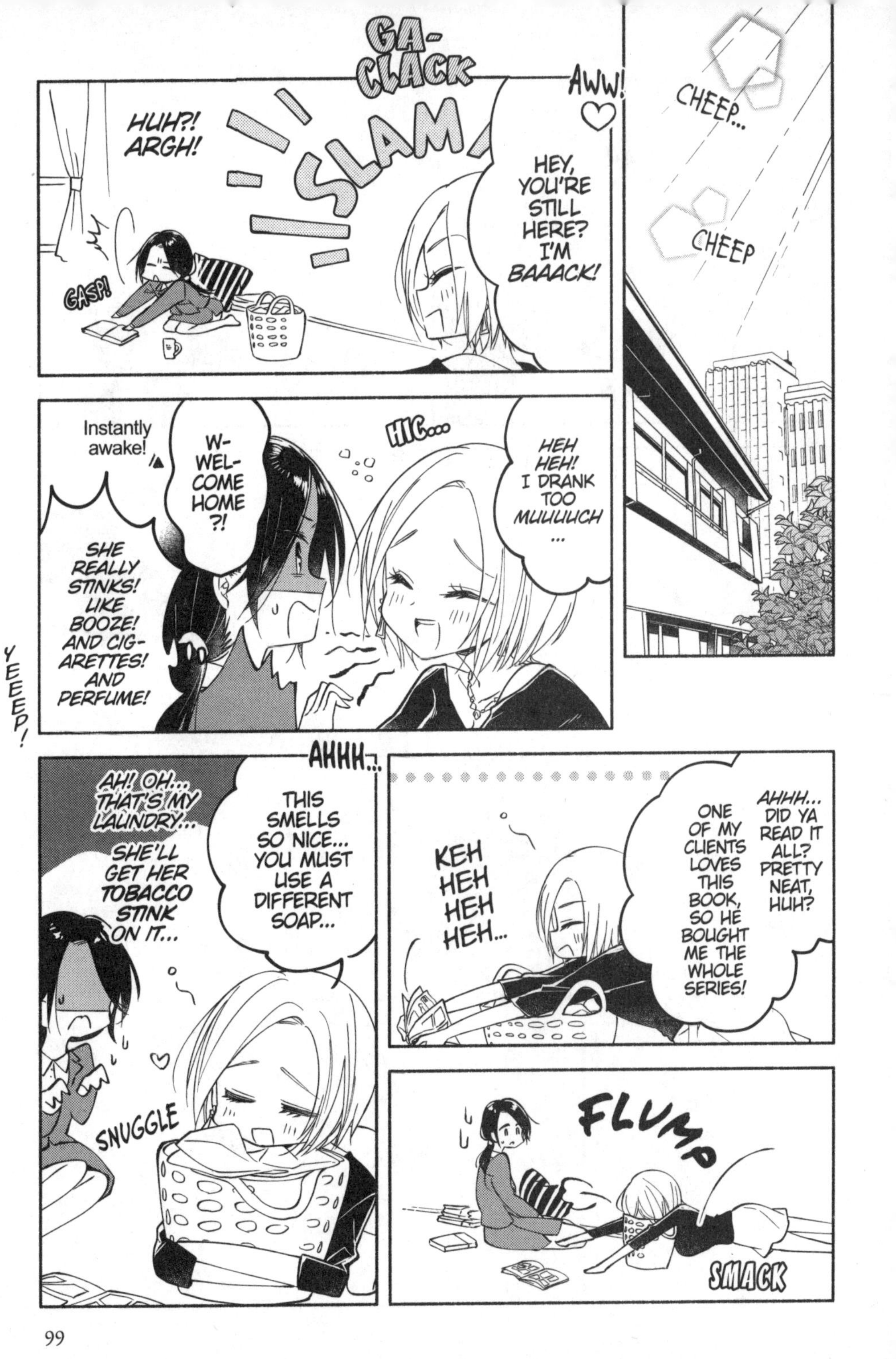
CHEEP...
CHEEP
AWW! ♡
GA-CLACK
SLAM
HEY, YOU'RE STILL HERE? I'M BAAACK!
HUH?! ARGH!
GASP!
HEH HEH! I DRANK TOO MUUUUCH ...
HIC...
W-WELCOME HOME?!
Instantly awake!
SHE REALLY STINKS! LIKE BOOZE! AND CIGARETTES! AND PERFUME!
YEEEP!
AHHH... DID YA READ IT ALL? PRETTY NEAT, HUH?
ONE OF MY CLIENTS LOVES THIS BOOK, SO HE BOUGHT ME THE WHOLE SERIES!
KEH HEH HEH HEH...
FLUMP
SMACK
AHHH...
THIS SMELLS SO NICE... YOU MUST USE A DIFFERENT SOAP...
AH! OH... THAT'S MY LAUNDRY...
SHE'LL GET HER TOBACCO STINK ON IT...
SNUGGLE

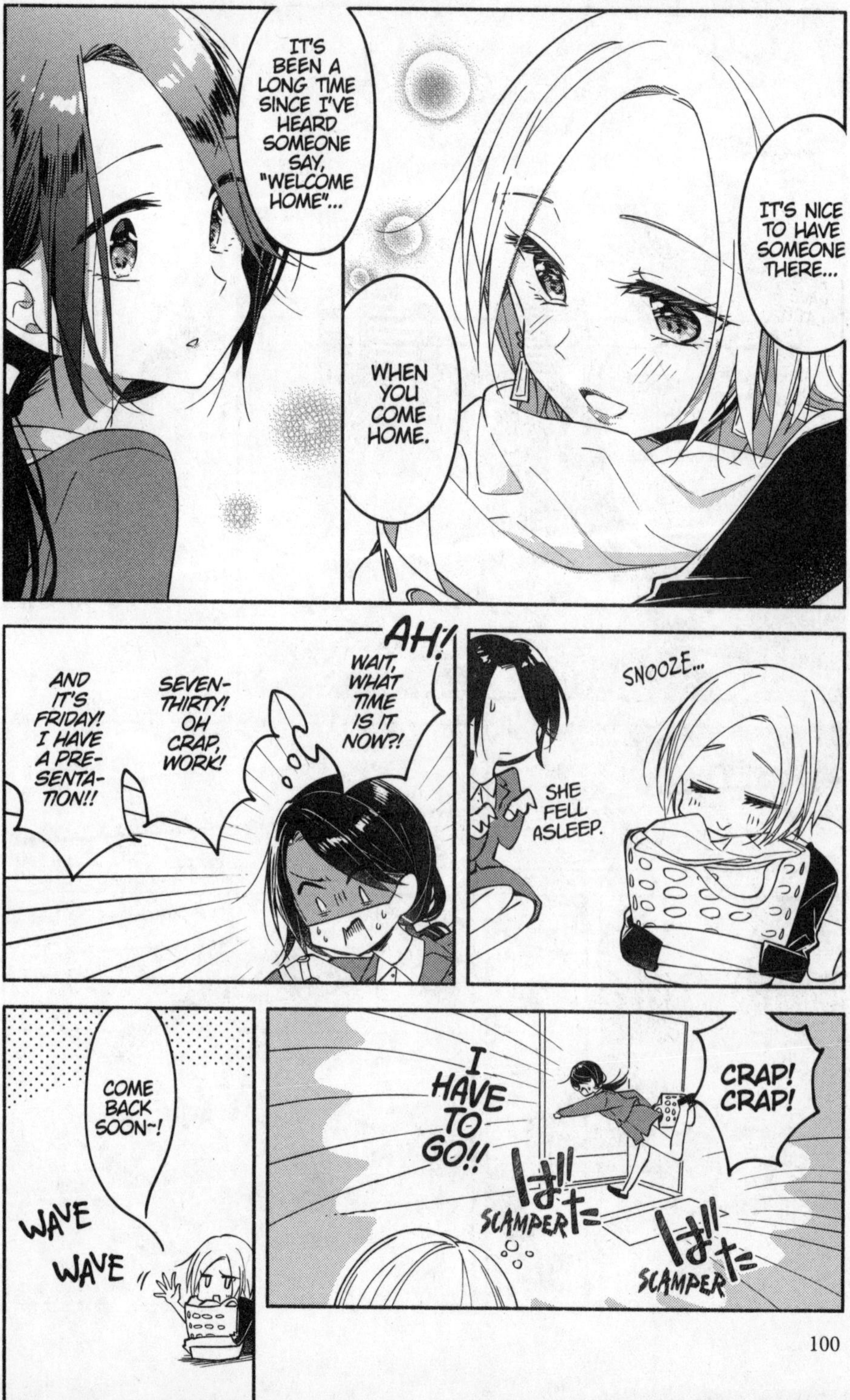
IT'S NICE TO HAVE SOMEONE THERE...
WHEN YOU COME HOME.
IT'S BEEN A LONG TIME SINCE I'VE HEARD SOMEONE SAY, "WELCOME HOME"...
SNOOZE...
SHE FELL ASLEEP.
AH!
WAIT, WHAT TIME IS IT NOW?!
SEVEN-THIRTY! OH CRAP, WORK!
AND IT'S FRIDAY! I HAVE A PRESENTATION!!
CRAP! CRAP!
I HAVE TO GO!!
ばた
SCAMPER
ばた
SCAMPER
COME BACK SOON~!
WAVE WAVE

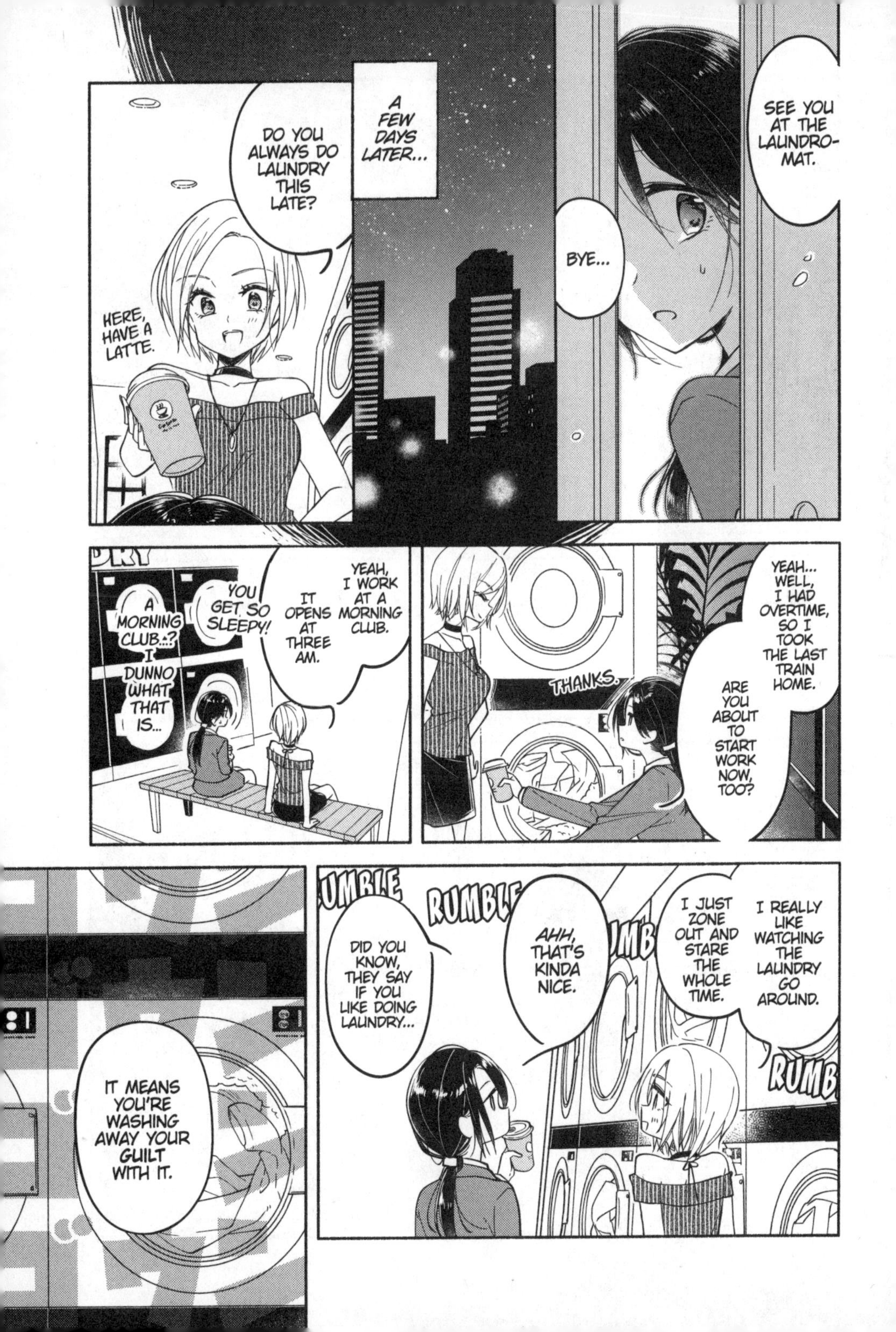
SEE YOU AT THE LAUNDRO-MAT.
BYE...
A FEW DAYS LATER...
DO YOU ALWAYS DO LAUNDRY THIS LATE?
HERE, HAVE A LATTE.
YEAH... WELL, I HAD OVERTIME, SO I TOOK THE LAST TRAIN HOME.
ARE YOU ABOUT TO START WORK NOW, TOO?
THANKS.
YEAH, I WORK AT A MORNING CLUB.
IT OPENS AT THREE AM.
YOU GET SO SLEEPY!
A MORNING CLUB...? I DUNNO WHAT THAT IS...
RUMB
UMB
RUMBLE
UMBLE
I REALLY LIKE WATCHING THE LAUNDRY GO AROUND.
I JUST ZONE OUT AND STARE THE WHOLE TIME.
AHH, THAT'S KINDA NICE.
DID YOU KNOW, THEY SAY IF YOU LIKE DOING LAUNDRY...
IT MEANS YOU'RE WASHING AWAY YOUR GUILT WITH IT.

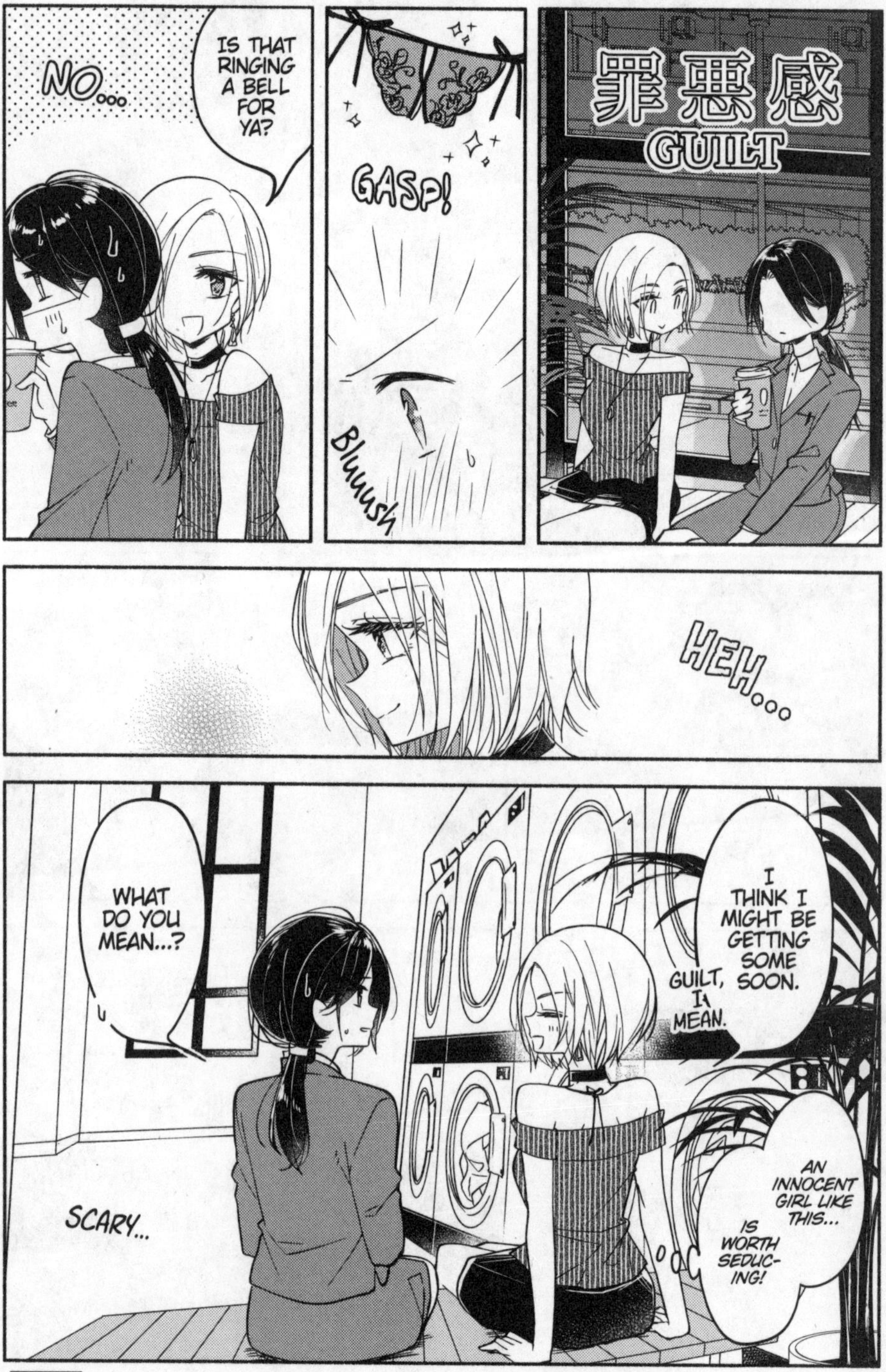
罪悪感
GUILT
GASP!
Bluuush
IS THAT RINGING A BELL FOR YA?
NO...
HEH...
I THINK I MIGHT BE GETTING SOME SOON.
GUILT, I MEAN.
WHAT DO YOU MEAN...?
AN INNOCENT GIRL LIKE THIS...
IS WORTH SEDUC-ING!
SCARY...

END

Killing Time
of the Butterfly

Cats and Sugar Bowls

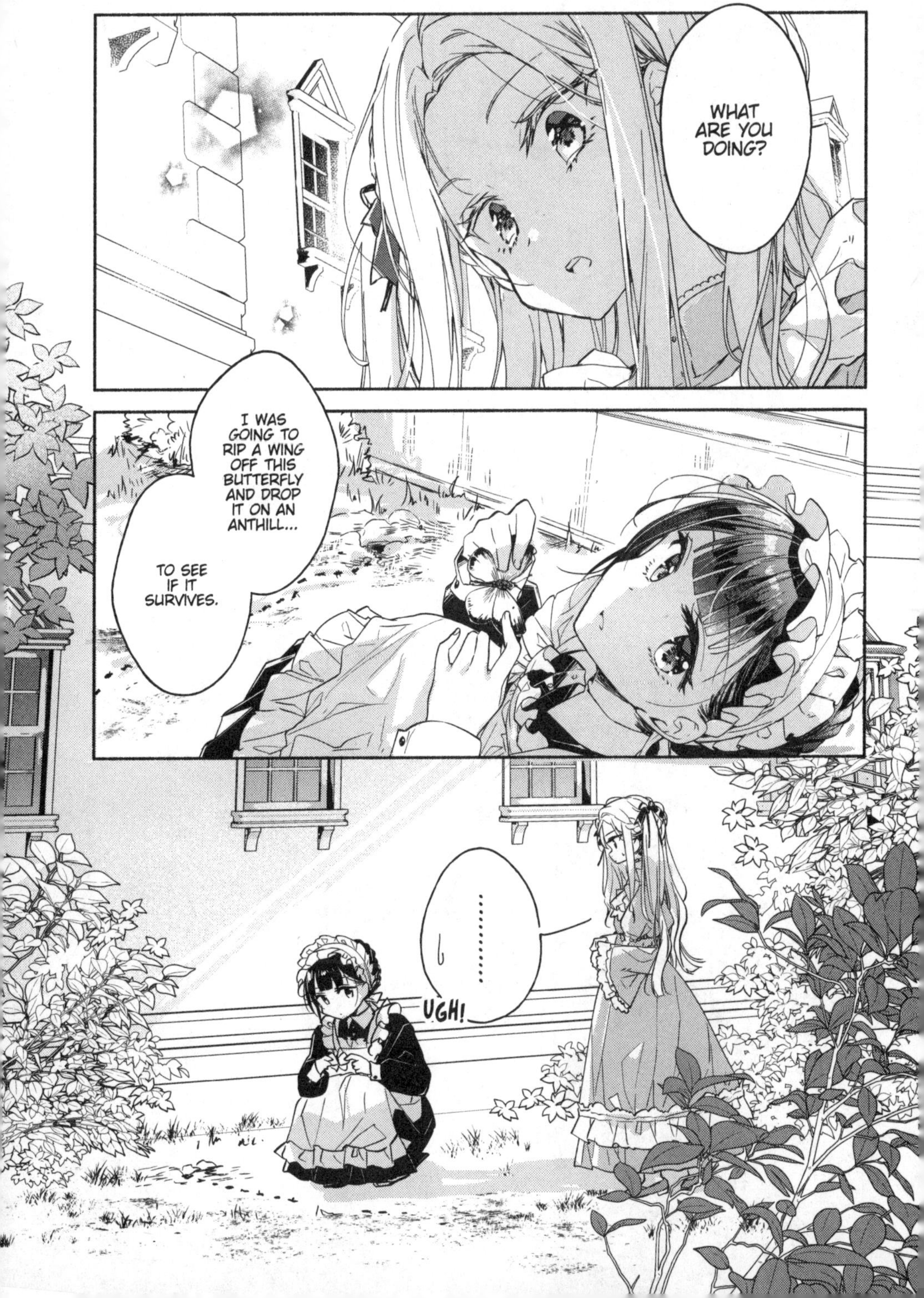
WHAT ARE YOU DOING?
I WAS GOING TO RIP A WING OFF THIS BUTTERFLY AND DROP IT ON AN ANTHILL...
TO SEE IF IT SURVIVES.
......
UGH!

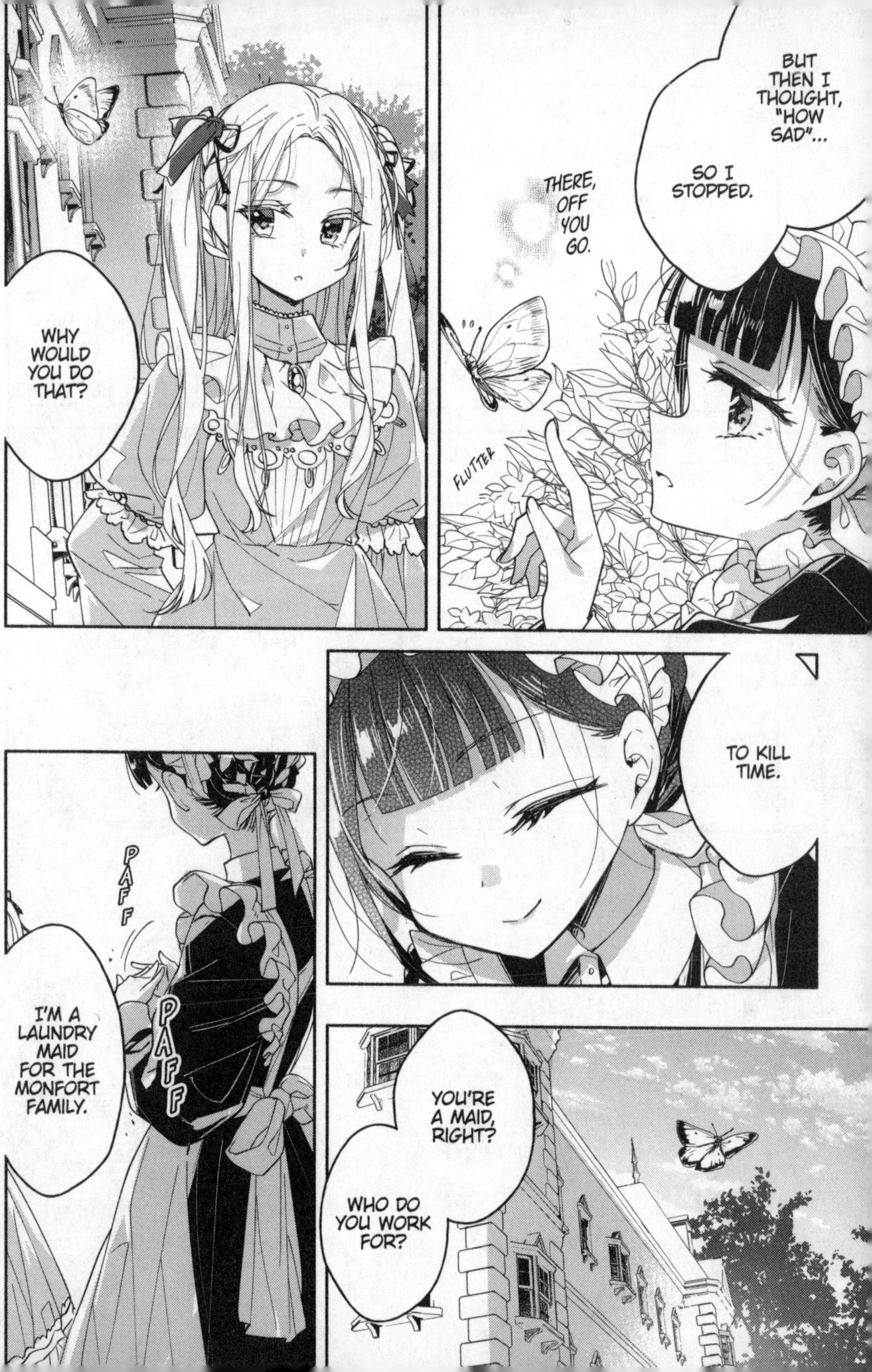
BUT THEN I THOUGHT, "HOW SAD"...
SO I STOPPED.
THERE, OFF YOU GO.
FLUTTER
WHY WOULD YOU DO THAT?
TO KILL TIME.
YOU'RE A MAID, RIGHT?
WHO DO YOU WORK FOR?
PAFF
PAFF
I'M A LAUNDRY MAID FOR THE MONFORT FAMILY.

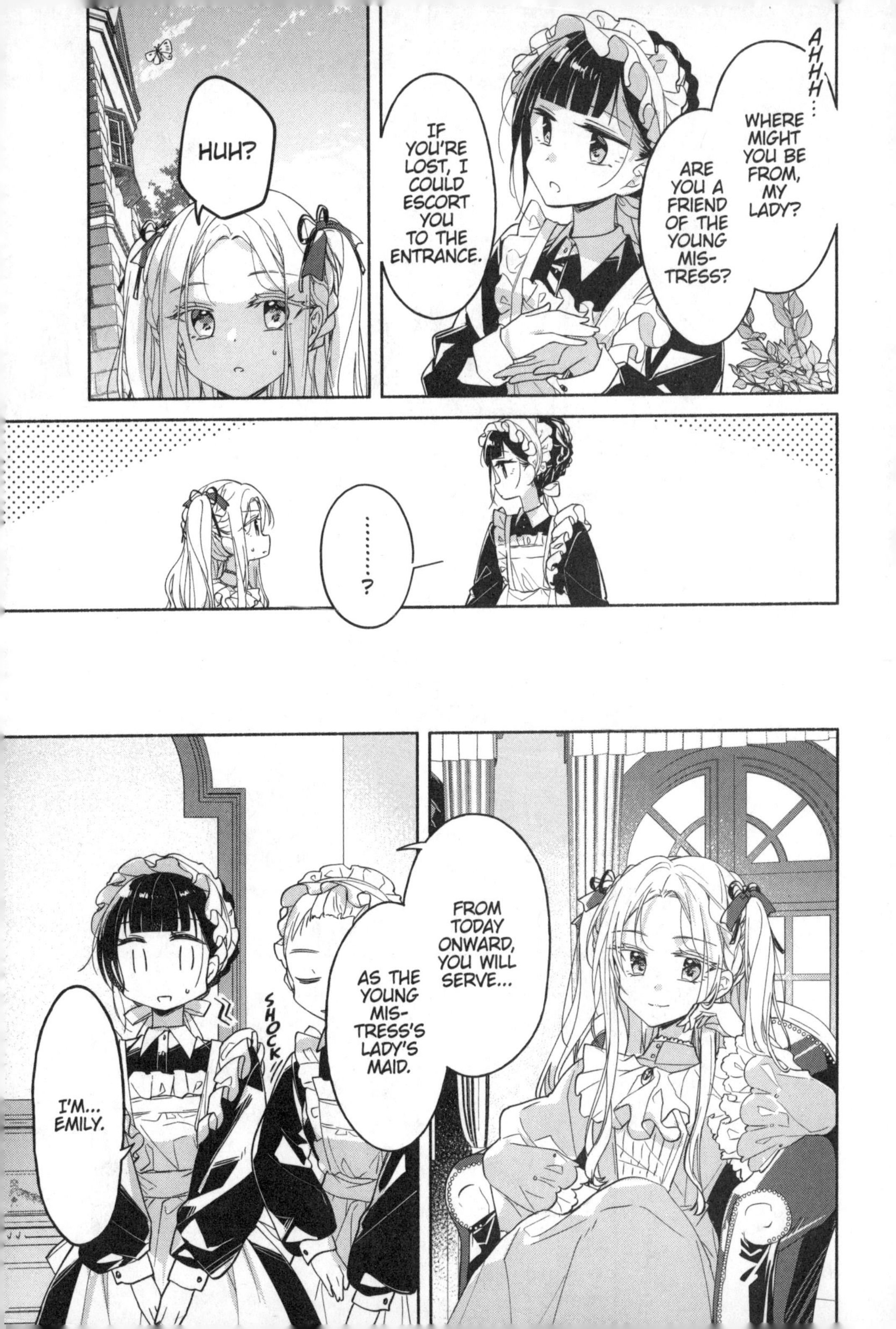
AHHH...
WHERE MIGHT YOU BE FROM, MY LADY?
ARE YOU A FRIEND OF THE YOUNG MIS-TRESS?
IF YOU'RE LOST, I COULD ESCORT YOU TO THE ENTRANCE.
HUH?
......?
FROM TODAY ONWARD, YOU WILL SERVE...
AS THE YOUNG MIS-TRESS'S LADY'S MAID.
SHOCK
I'M... EMILY.

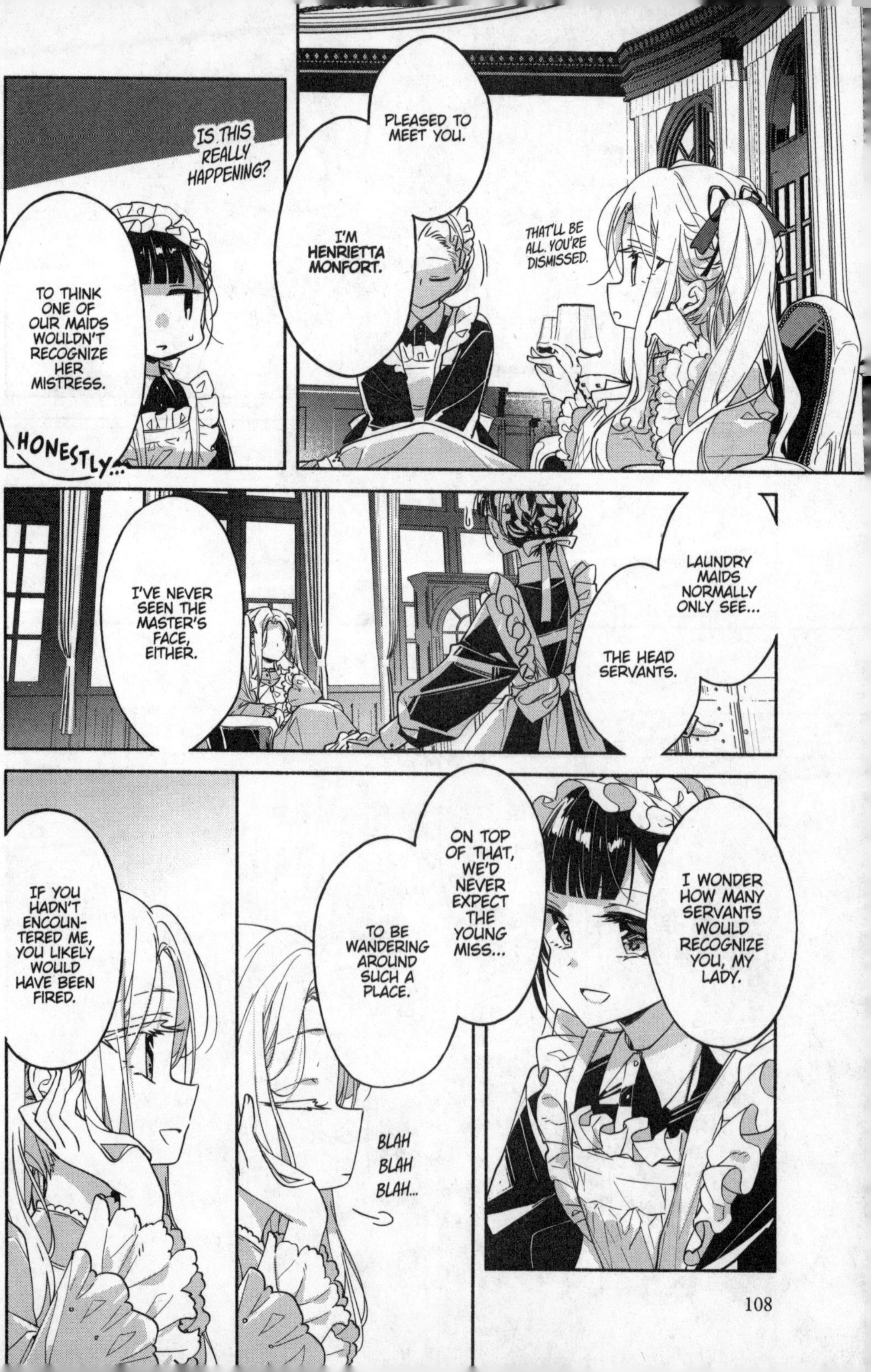

THAT'LL BE ALL. YOU'RE DISMISSED.
PLEASED TO MEET YOU.
I'M HENRIETTA MONFORT.
IS THIS REALLY HAPPENING?
TO THINK ONE OF OUR MAIDS WOULDN'T RECOGNIZE HER MISTRESS.
HONESTLY...
LAUNDRY MAIDS NORMALLY ONLY SEE...
THE HEAD SERVANTS.
I'VE NEVER SEEN THE MASTER'S FACE, EITHER.
I WONDER HOW MANY SERVANTS WOULD RECOGNIZE YOU, MY LADY.
ON TOP OF THAT, WE'D NEVER EXPECT THE YOUNG MISS...
TO BE WANDERING AROUND SUCH A PLACE.
BLAH BLAH BLAH...
IF YOU HADN'T ENCOUN-TERED ME, YOU LIKELY WOULD HAVE BEEN FIRED.

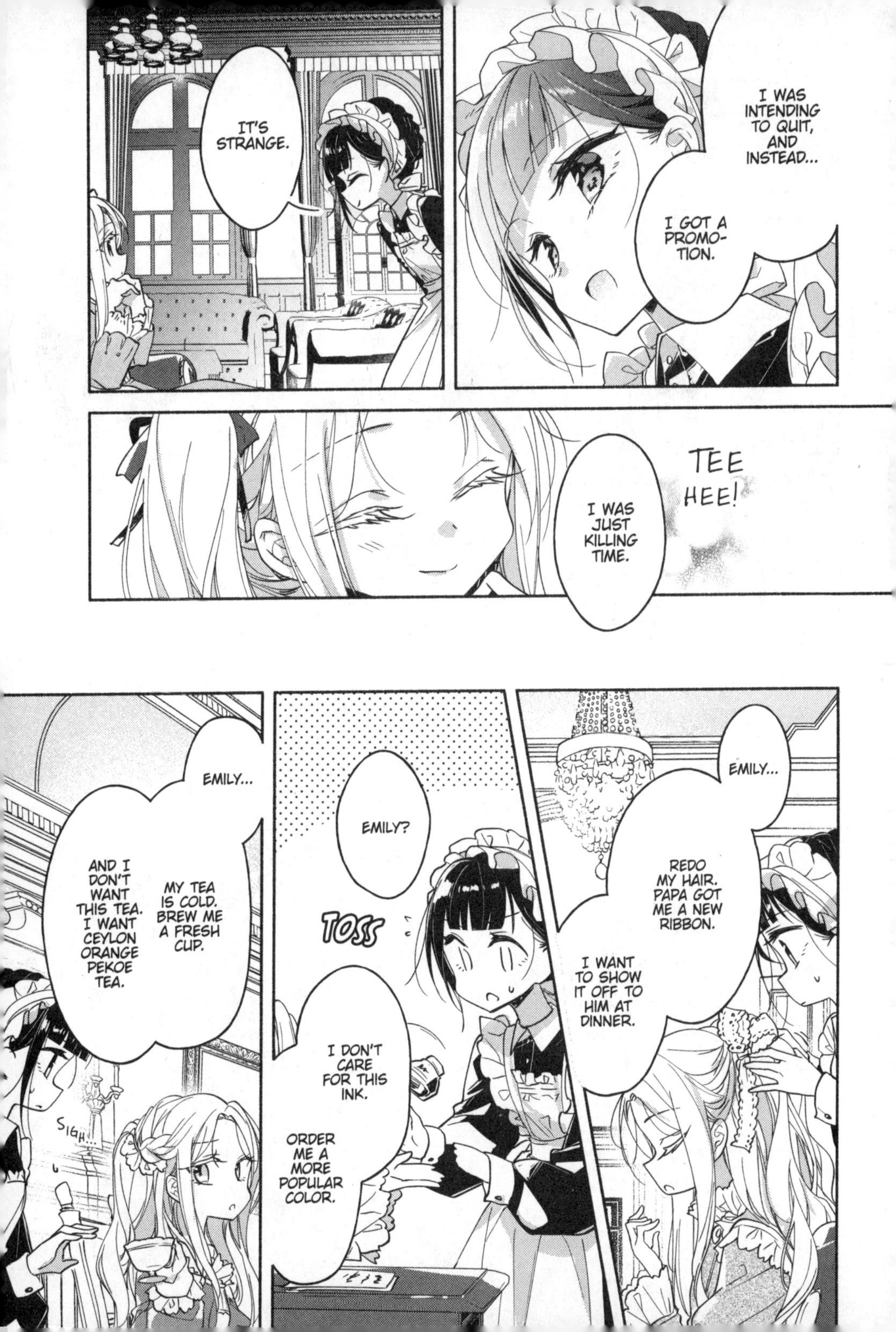
I WAS INTENDING TO QUIT, AND INSTEAD...
I GOT A PROMOTION.
IT'S STRANGE.
TEE HEE!
I WAS JUST KILLING TIME.
EMILY...
REDO MY HAIR. PAPA GOT ME A NEW RIBBON.
I WANT TO SHOW IT OFF TO HIM AT DINNER.
EMILY?
TOSS
I DON'T CARE FOR THIS INK.
ORDER ME A MORE POPULAR COLOR.
EMILY...
MY TEA IS COLD. BREW ME A FRESH CUP.
AND I DON'T WANT THIS TEA. I WANT CEYLON ORANGE PEKOE TEA.
SIGH...

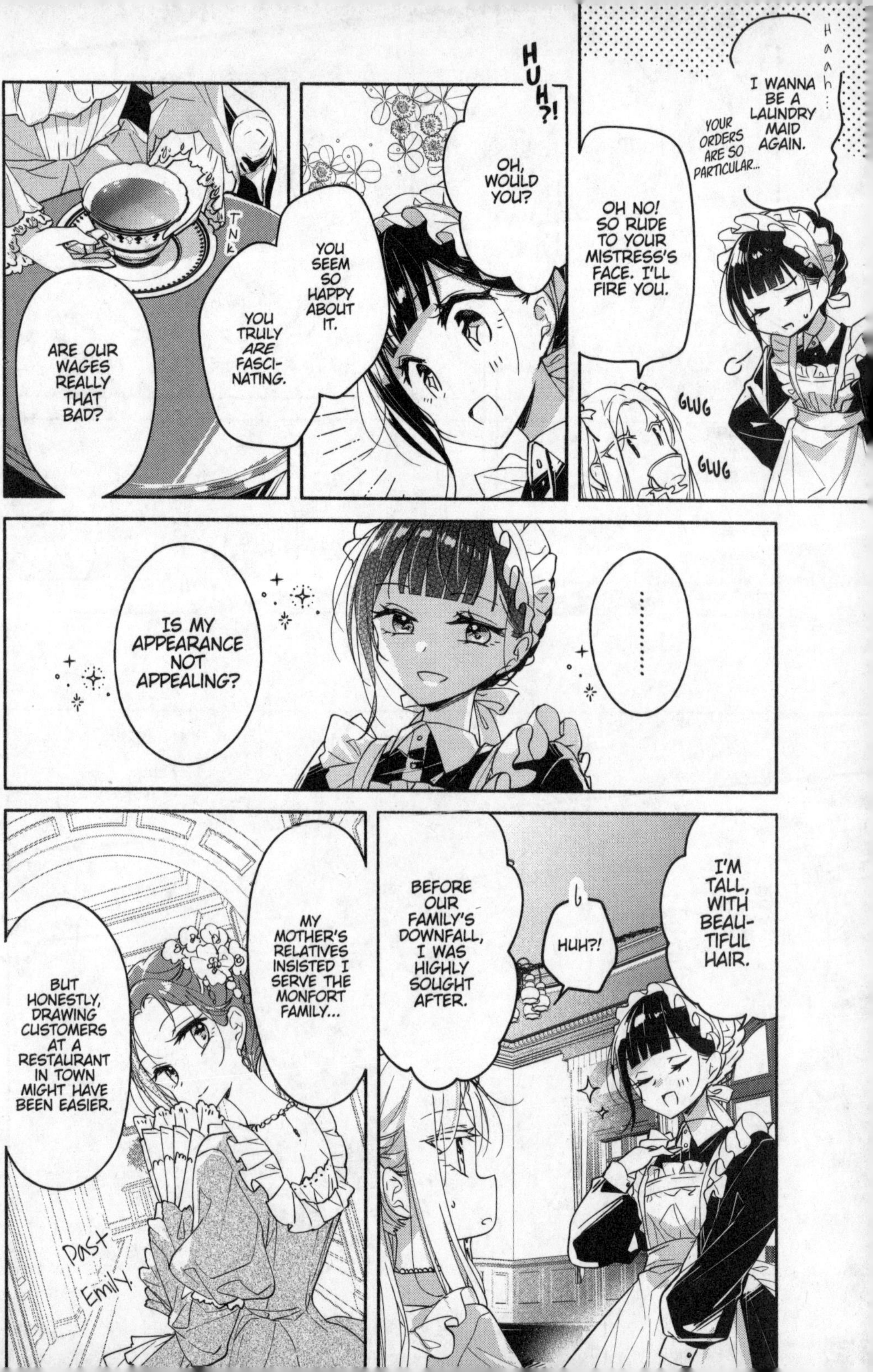
Haaah...
I WANNA BE A LAUNDRY MAID AGAIN.
YOUR ORDERS ARE SO PARTICULAR...
OH NO! SO RUDE TO YOUR MISTRESS'S FACE. I'LL FIRE YOU.
GLUG
GLUG
HUH?!
OH, WOULD YOU?
YOU SEEM SO HAPPY ABOUT IT.
YOU TRULY *ARE* FASCINATING.
TNK
ARE OUR WAGES REALLY THAT BAD?
....
IS MY APPEARANCE NOT APPEALING?
I'M TALL, WITH BEAUTIFUL HAIR.
HUH?!
BEFORE OUR FAMILY'S DOWNFALL, I WAS HIGHLY SOUGHT AFTER.
MY MOTHER'S RELATIVES INSISTED I SERVE THE MONFORT FAMILY...
BUT HONESTLY, DRAWING CUSTOMERS AT A RESTAURANT IN TOWN MIGHT HAVE BEEN EASIER.
Past Emily.

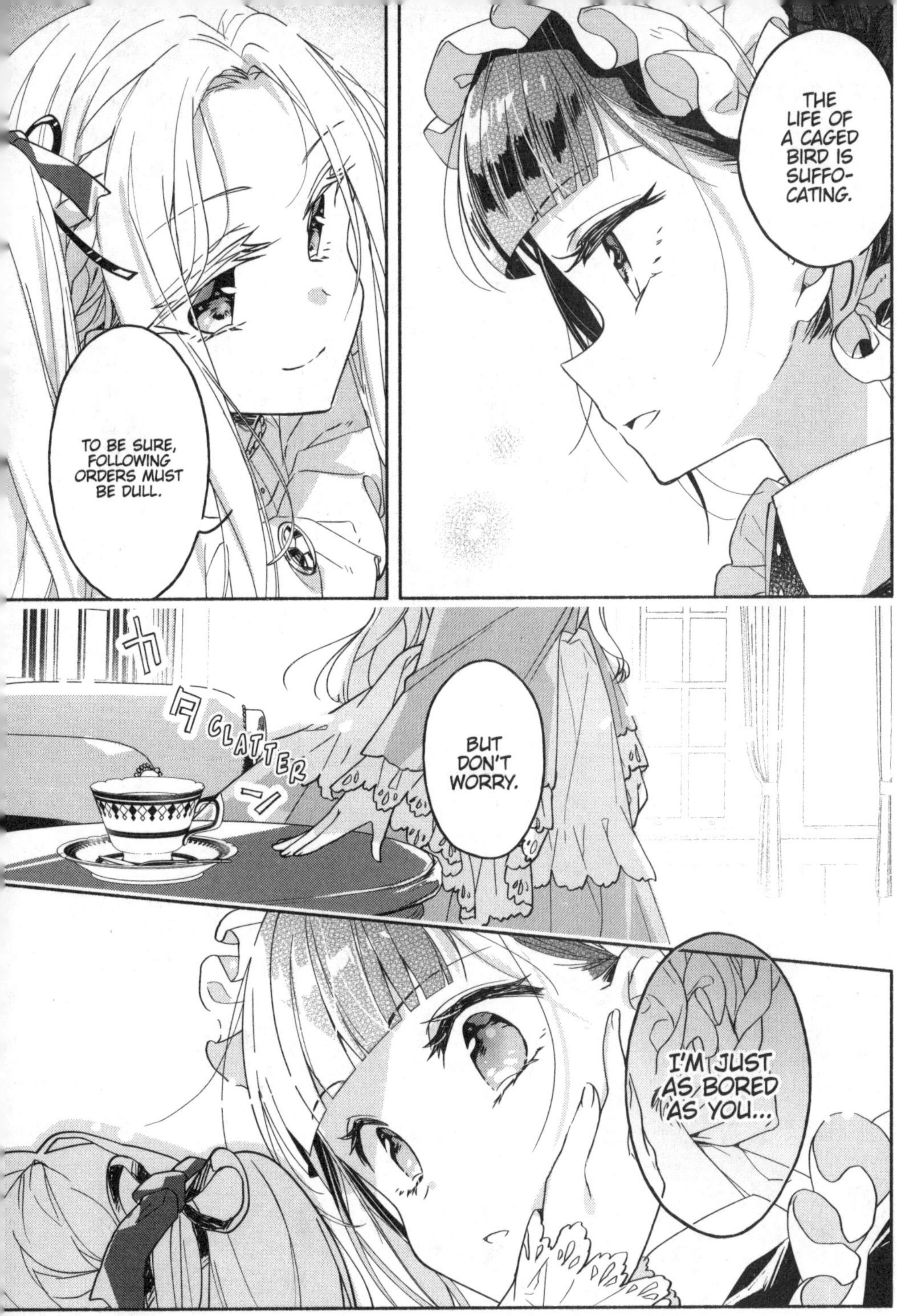
THE LIFE OF A CAGED BIRD IS SUFFOCATING.
TO BE SURE, FOLLOWING ORDERS MUST BE DULL.
BUT DON'T WORRY.
CLATTER
I'M JUST AS BORED AS YOU...

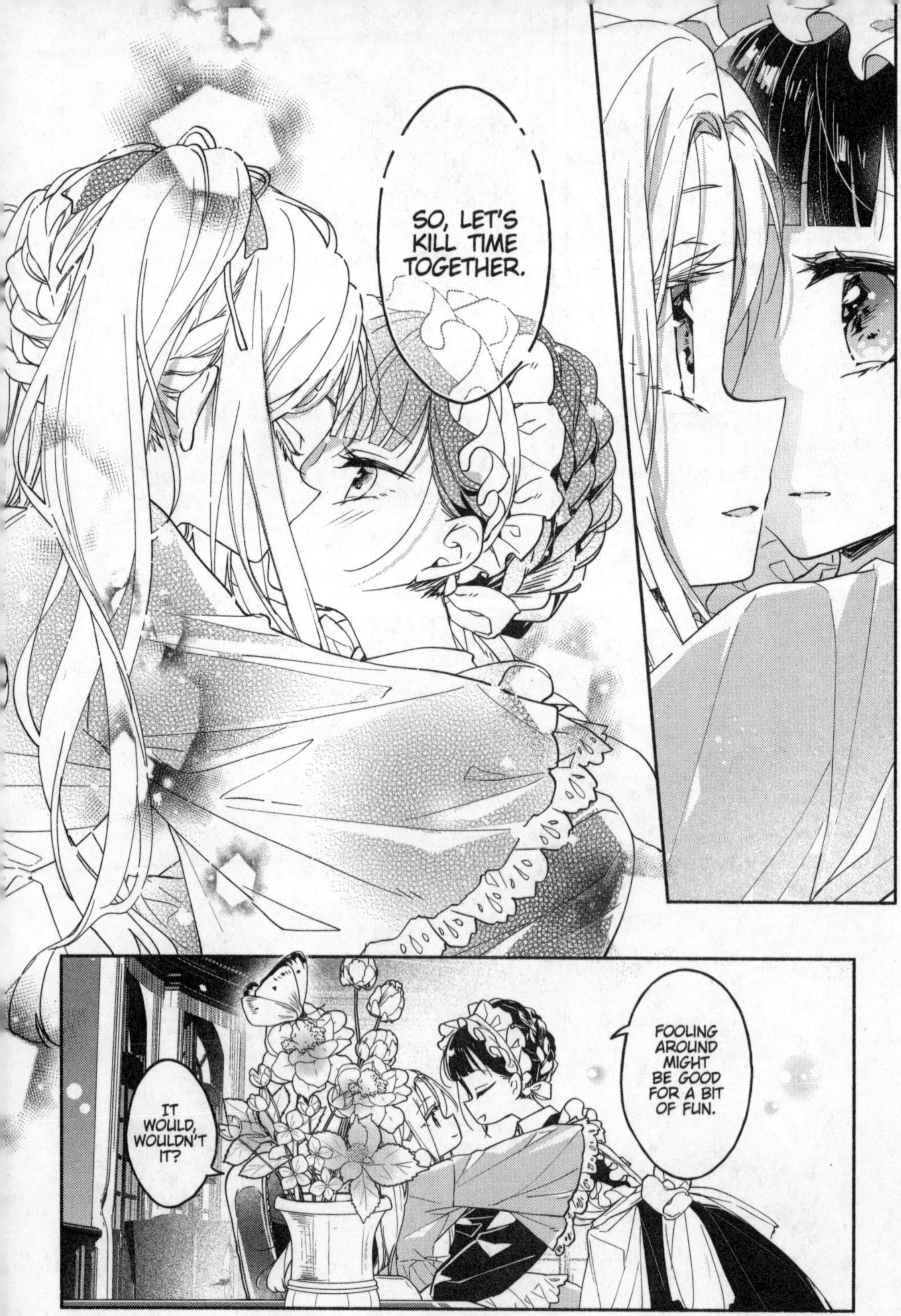
SO, LET'S KILL TIME TOGETHER.
FOOLING AROUND MIGHT BE GOOD FOR A BIT OF FUN.
IT WOULD, WOULDN'T IT?

END

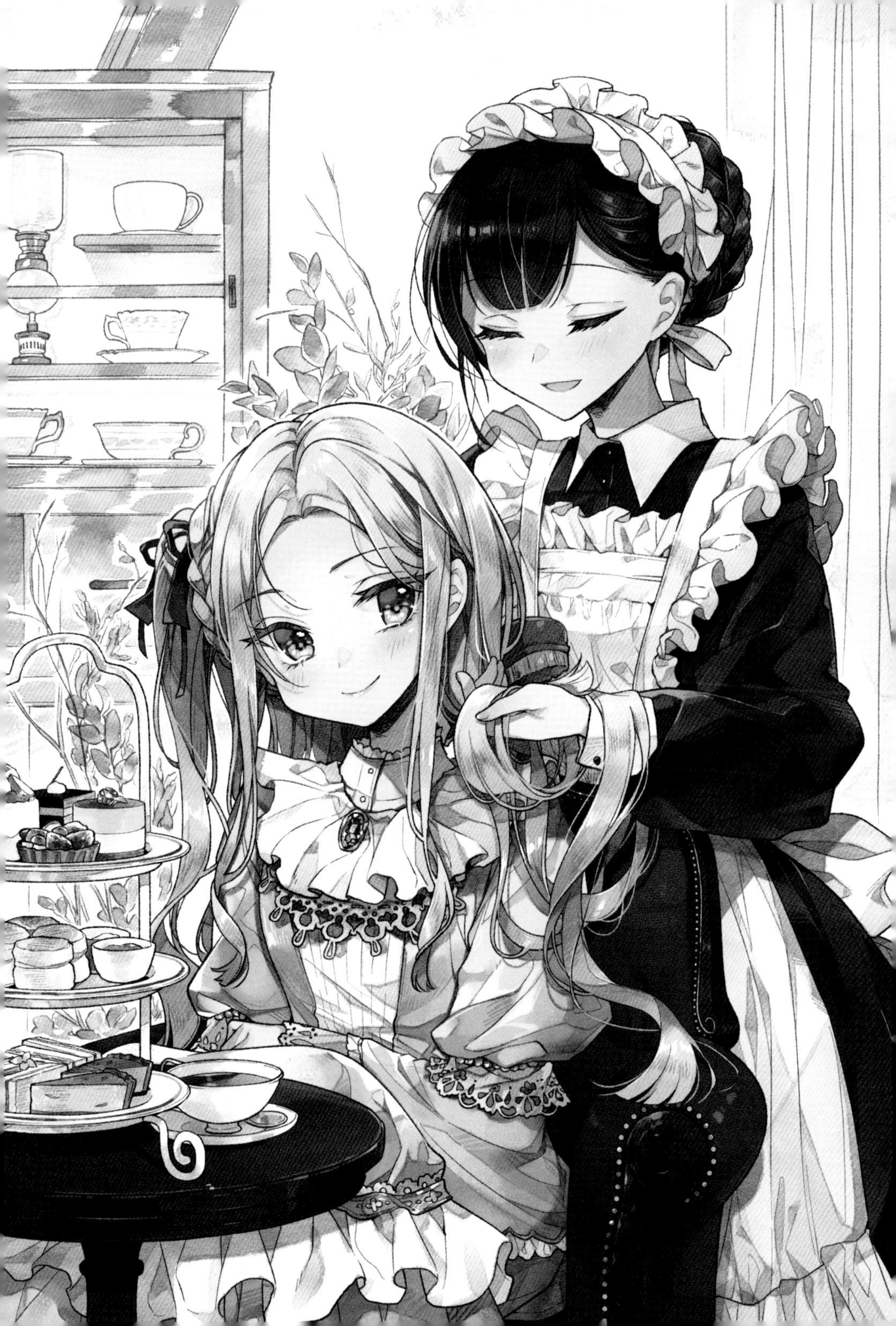

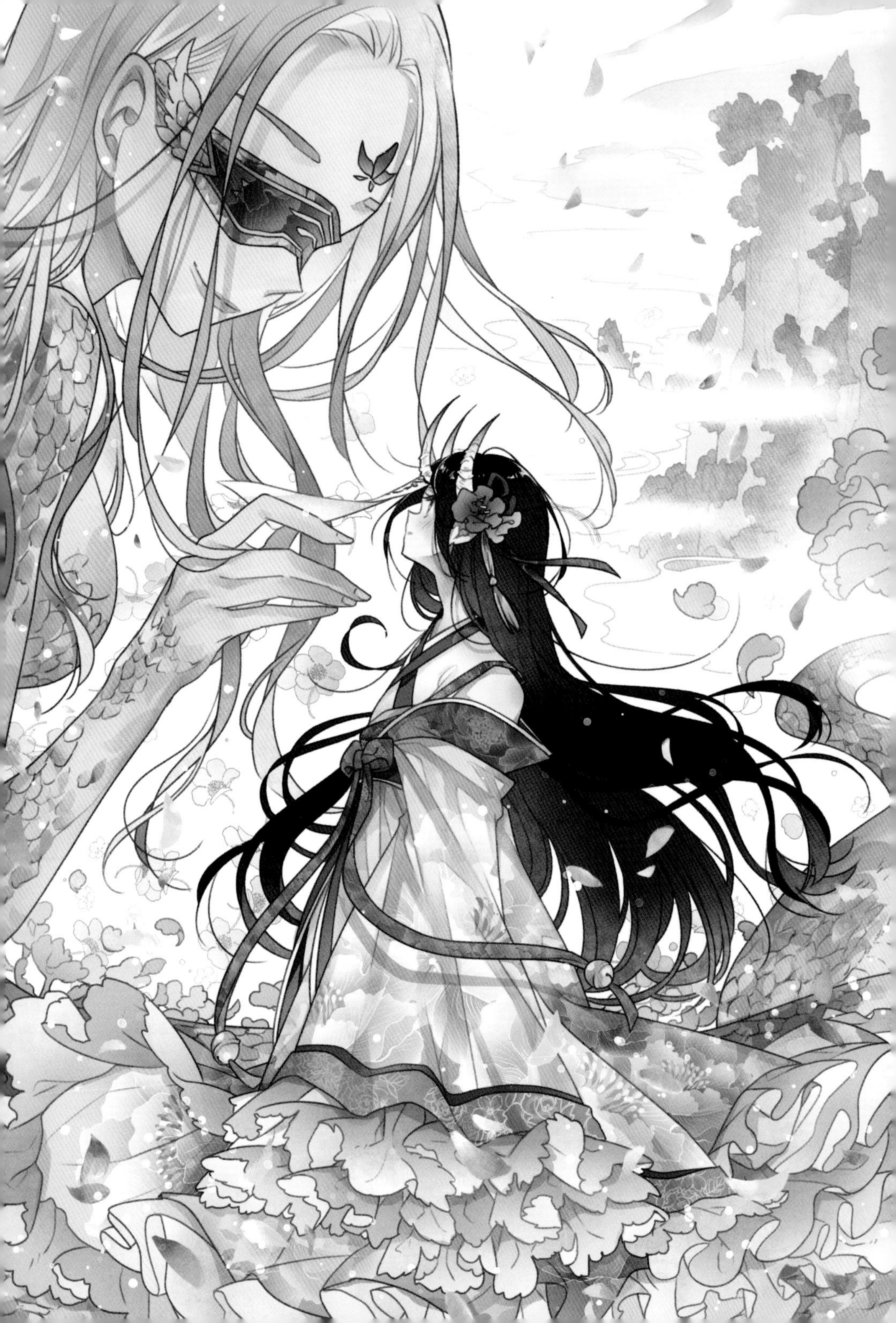

The Ogre and the Mountain God

Cats and Sugar Bowls

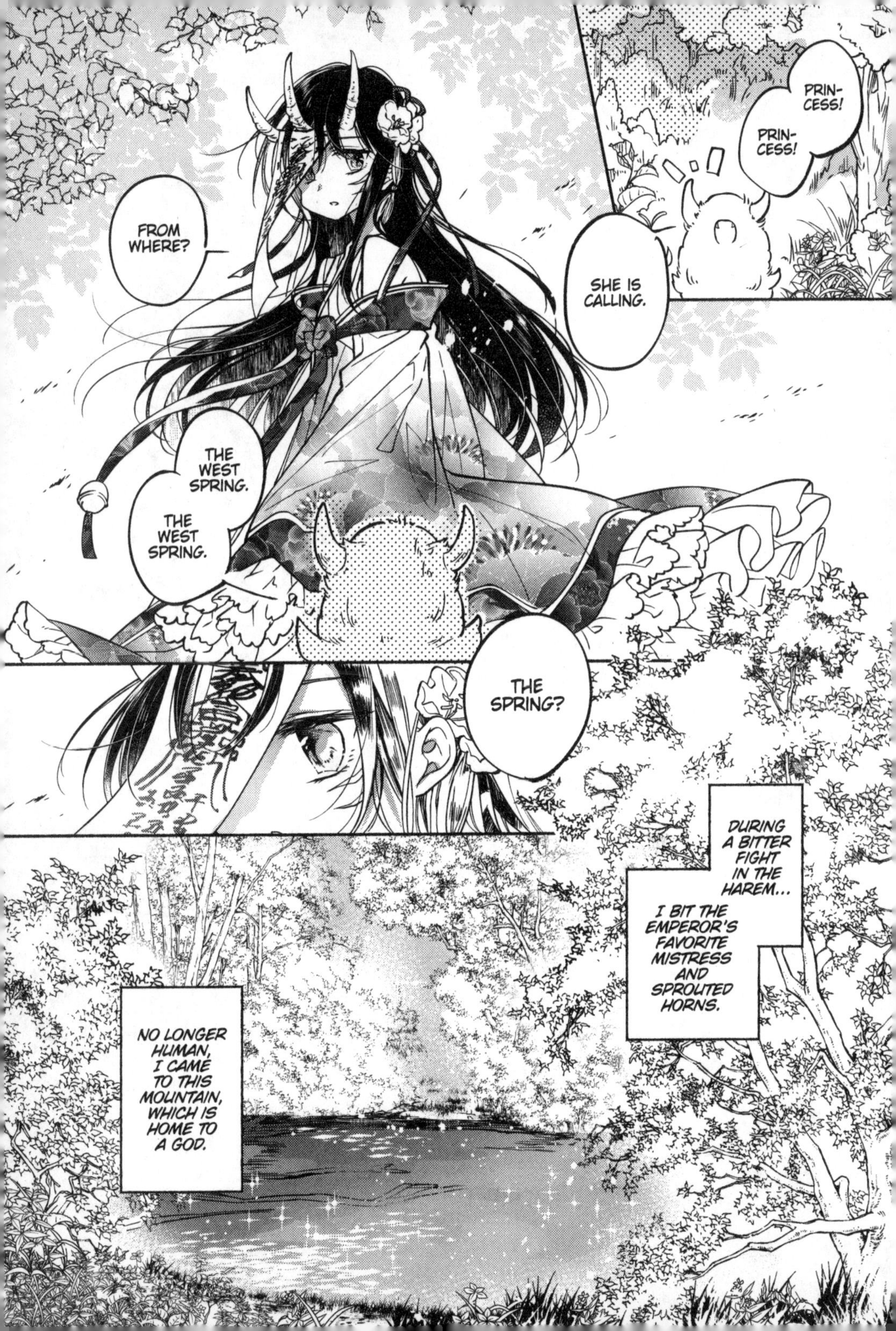
PRIN-CESS!
PRIN-CESS!
SHE IS CALLING.
FROM WHERE?
THE WEST SPRING.
THE WEST SPRING.
THE SPRING?
DURING A BITTER FIGHT IN THE HAREM...
I BIT THE EMPEROR'S FAVORITE MISTRESS AND SPROUTED HORNS.
NO LONGER HUMAN, I CAME TO THIS MOUNTAIN, WHICH IS HOME TO A GOD.

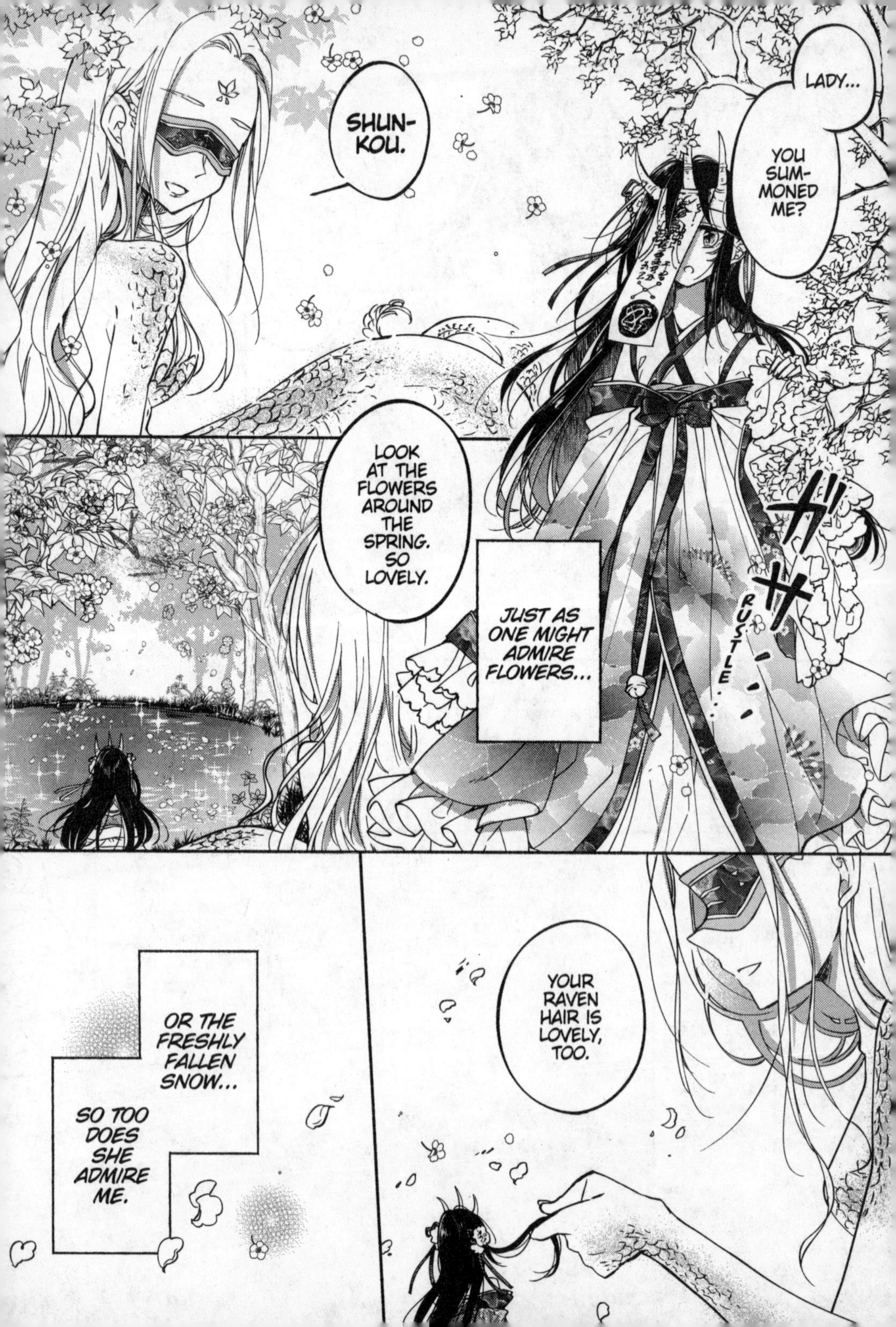
LADY...
YOU SUMMONED ME?
SHUN-KOU.
ザザ
RUSTLE...
LOOK AT THE FLOWERS AROUND THE SPRING. SO LOVELY.
JUST AS ONE MIGHT ADMIRE FLOWERS...
YOUR RAVEN HAIR IS LOVELY, TOO.
OR THE FRESHLY FALLEN SNOW...
SO TOO DOES SHE ADMIRE ME.

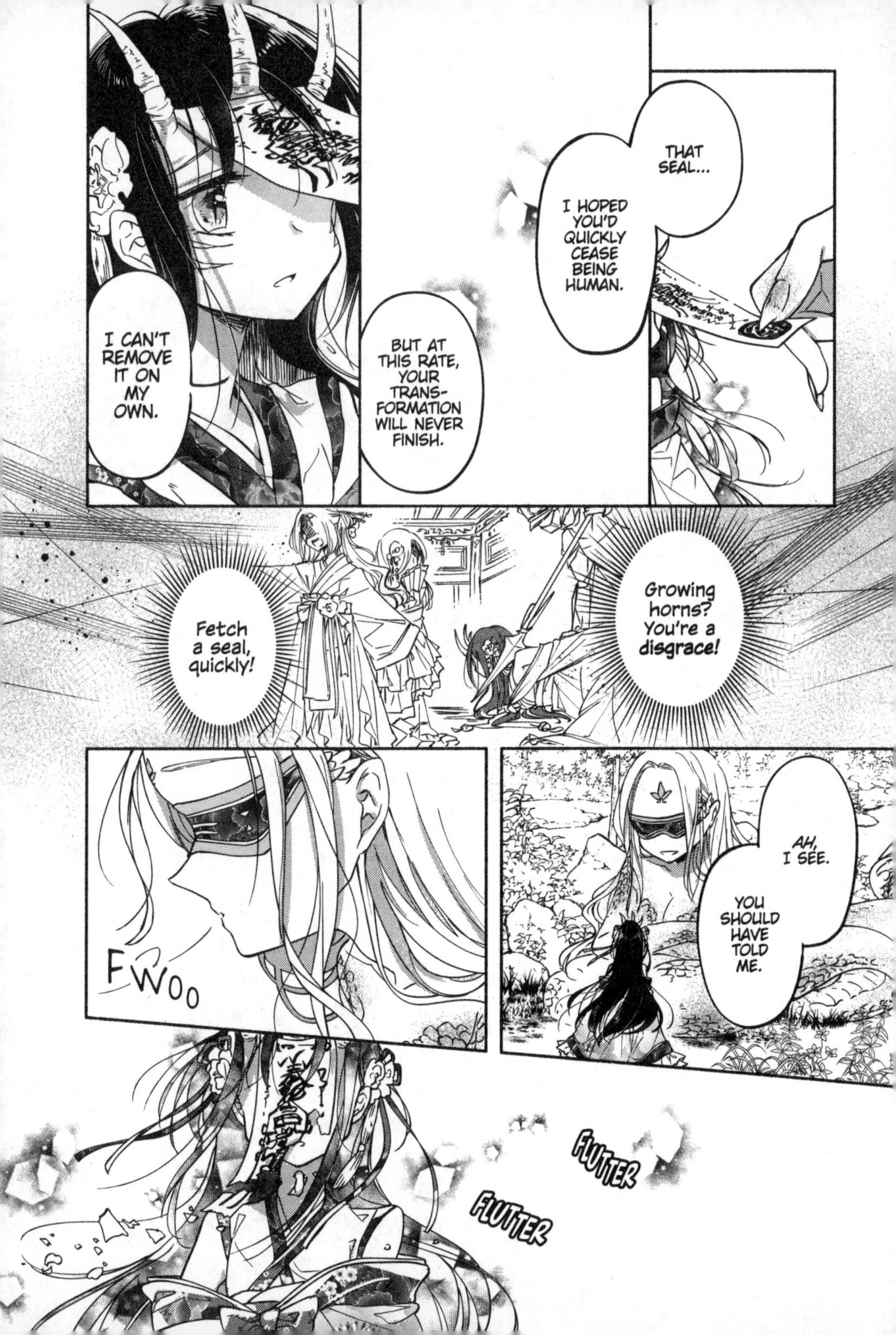
THAT SEAL...
I HOPED YOU'D QUICKLY CEASE BEING HUMAN.
BUT AT THIS RATE, YOUR TRANS-FORMATION WILL NEVER FINISH.
I CAN'T REMOVE IT ON MY OWN.
Growing horns? You're a **disgrace!**
Fetch a seal, quickly!
AH, I SEE.
YOU SHOULD HAVE TOLD ME.
FWOO
FLUTTER
FLUTTER

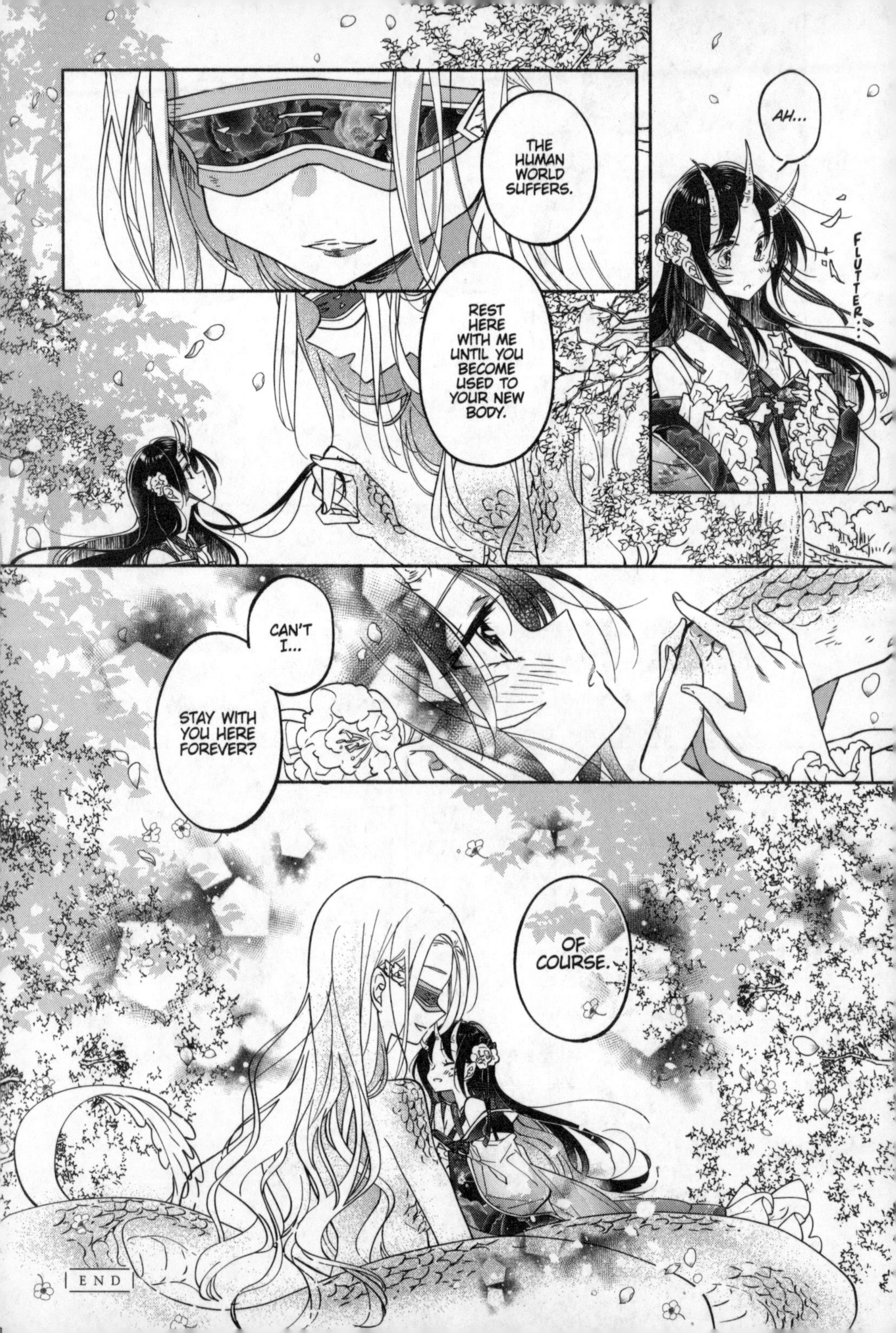
AH...
FLUTTER...
THE HUMAN WORLD SUFFERS.
REST HERE WITH ME UNTIL YOU BECOME USED TO YOUR NEW BODY.
CAN'T I...
STAY WITH YOU HERE FOREVER?
OF COURSE.
END

Cats *and* Sugar Bowls

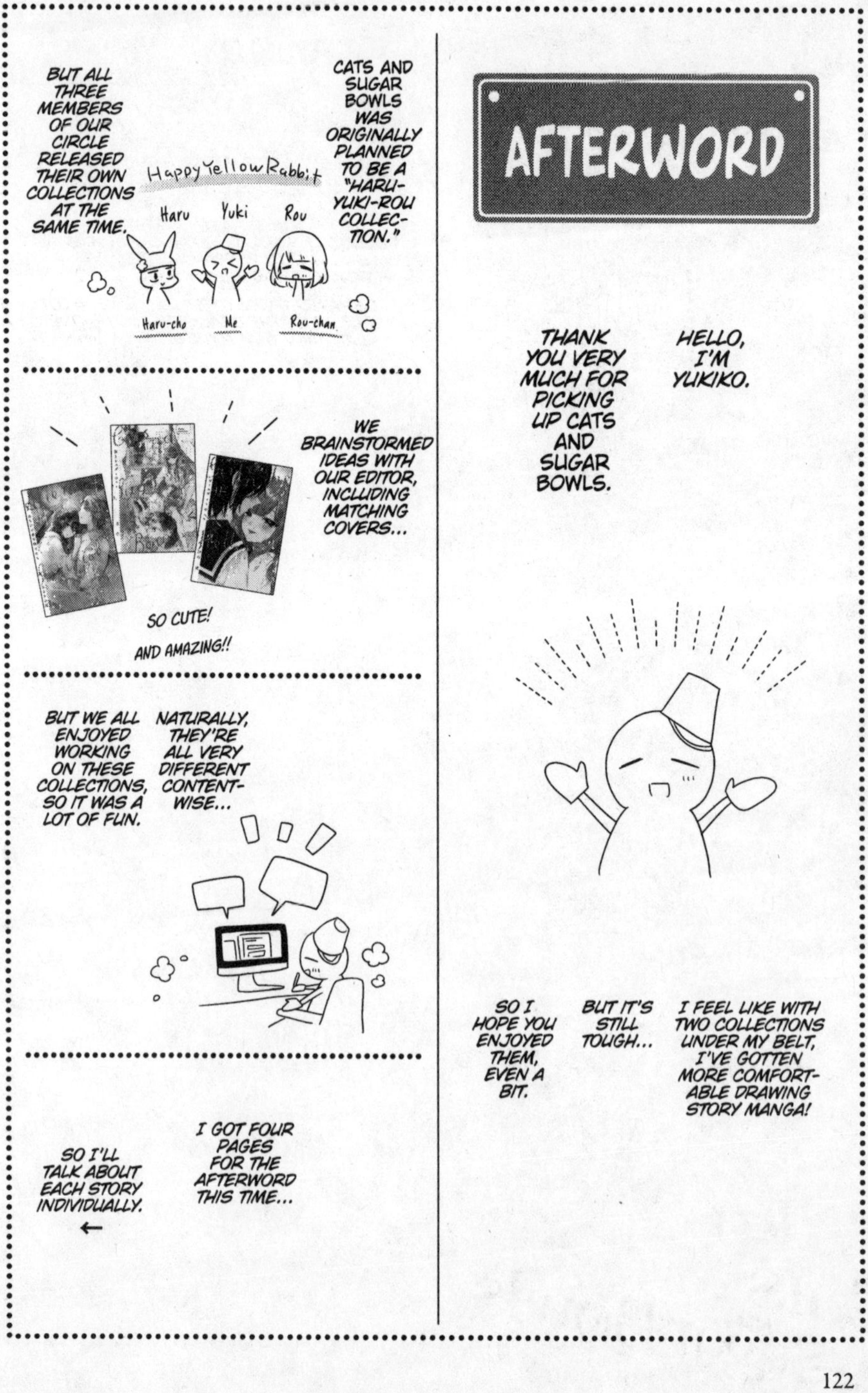
AFTERWORD
HELLO, I'M YUKIKO.
THANK YOU VERY MUCH FOR PICKING UP CATS AND SUGAR BOWLS.
I FEEL LIKE WITH TWO COLLECTIONS UNDER MY BELT, I'VE GOTTEN MORE COMFORTABLE DRAWING STORY MANGA!
BUT IT'S STILL TOUGH...
SO I HOPE YOU ENJOYED THEM, EVEN A BIT.
CATS AND SUGAR BOWLS WAS ORIGINALLY PLANNED TO BE A "HARU-YUKI-ROU COLLECTION."
BUT ALL THREE MEMBERS OF OUR CIRCLE RELEASED THEIR OWN COLLECTIONS AT THE SAME TIME.
HappyYellowRabbit
Haru
Yuki
Rou
Haru-cho
Me
Rou-chan
WE BRAINSTORMED IDEAS WITH OUR EDITOR, INCLUDING MATCHING COVERS...
SO CUTE!
AND AMAZING!!
NATURALLY, THEY'RE ALL VERY DIFFERENT CONTENT-WISE...
BUT WE ALL ENJOYED WORKING ON THESE COLLECTIONS, SO IT WAS A LOT OF FUN.
I GOT FOUR PAGES FOR THE AFTERWORD THIS TIME...
SO I'LL TALK ABOUT EACH STORY INDIVIDUALLY.
←

"CAT" TRILOGY

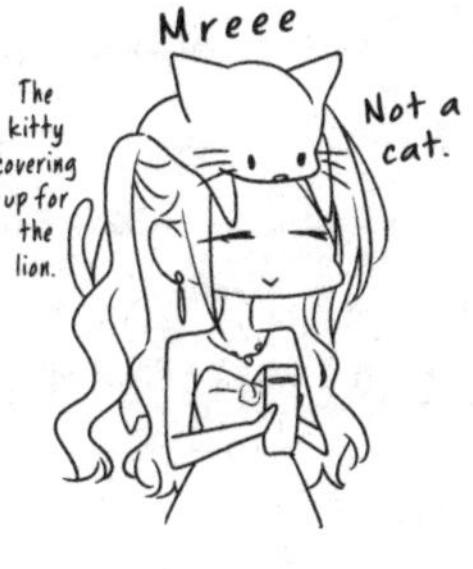
Mreee
The kitty covering up for the lion.
Not a cat.

THIS WAS A SET OF THREE STORIES I DREW FOR UNEMPLOYED YURI ANTHOLOGY AT THE "ADULT YURI ONLY" EVENT.

A CUTE GIRL TALKING TRASH IS A FETISH, SO I HAD HER TALK A LOT! MY REPERTOIRE WAS SMALL, SO I HAD TO RESEARCH TYPES OF TRASH TALK. (IT WAS PRETTY POINTLESS!)

WHEN I SHARED THESE STORIES ONLINE, A LOT OF PEOPLE SAID, "THE CRACKED SMARTPHONE WAS GREAT!" AND THAT MADE ME HAPPY.

UNBREAKABLE SUGAR BOWL

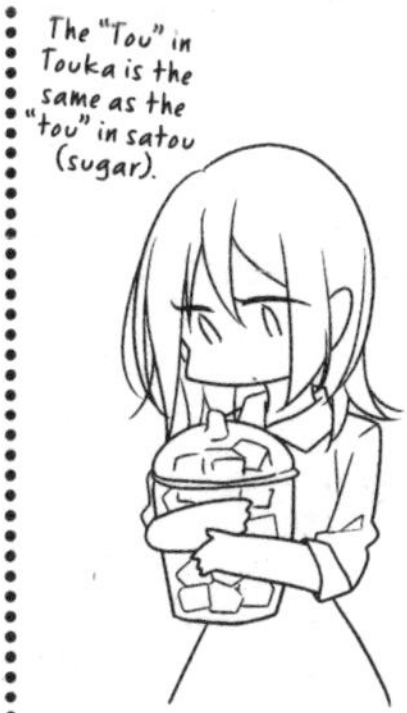
The "Tou" in Touka is the same as the "tou" in satou (sugar).

THIS ONE WAS DRAWN JUST FOR THIS VOLUME.

I HAD ONLY DRAWN SIXTEEN-PAGE SHORT STORIES BEFORE, SO I WORRIED ABOUT ITS LENGTH AND THE CONTENT.

ONCE I GET INTERESTED IN A THEME, I'LL DRAW IT OVER AND OVER AGAIN UNTIL I'M TIRED OF IT, SO I STILL WANT TO DRAW SOMETHING WITH S&M ELEMENTS.

THIS WAS THE FIRST TIME I DREW WORKING ADULTS ACTUALLY IN AN OFFICE SETTING.

SILKY

THIS PLOT FORCED ITSELF INTO MY HEAD ON THE BULLET TRAIN RIDE BACK FROM AN AUTOGRAPH EVENT FOR MY SERIALIZED MANGA.

I WAS BRAINSTORMING WHILE HALF-ASLEEP AND THIS IS WHAT CAME TO ME.

ONCE AGAIN, I FORGOT TO NAME THE PROTAGONIST.

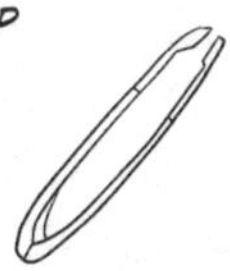

MY CHILDHOOD FRIEND

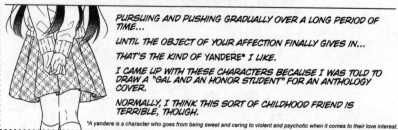

PURSUING AND PUSHING GRADUALLY OVER A LONG PERIOD OF TIME...

UNTIL THE OBJECT OF YOUR AFFECTION FINALLY GIVES IN...

THAT'S THE KIND OF YANDERE* I LIKE.

I CAME UP WITH THESE CHARACTERS BECAUSE I WAS TOLD TO DRAW A "GAL AND AN HONOR STUDENT" FOR AN ANTHOLOGY COVER.

NORMALLY, I THINK THIS SORT OF CHILDHOOD FRIEND IS TERRIBLE, THOUGH.

*A yandere is a character who goes from being sweet and caring to violent and psychotic when it comes to their love interest.

ONE AM AT THE LAUNDROMAT

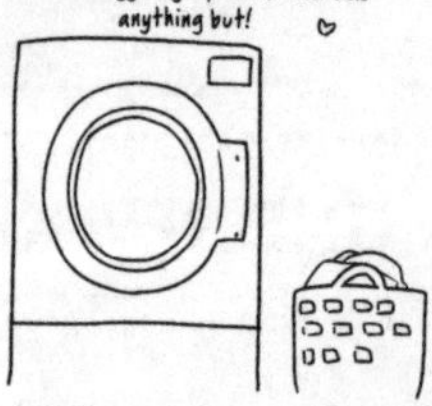

I SELDOM DRAW UNREMARKABLE FACES, BUT I WAS ABLE TO DO IT HERE.

I DEFINITELY LIKE LAUNDROMATS. THEY'RE SO NICE.

AND ONCE AGAIN, I DIDN'T NAME THE PROTAGONISTS.

Another entry for a "Working Adult Yuri Anthology" (Syrup Vol. 1) that was anything but! ♡

KILLING TIME OF THE BUTTERFLY

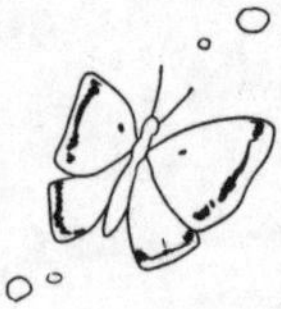

THESE WERE CHARACTERS I CAME UP WITH FOR A COVER ILLUSTRATION. THEY BECAME ONE OF THIS VOLUME'S COLORED PAGES.

I LOVE DRAWING FRILLS MORE THAN I LOVE TO EAT, SO I WAS SUPER HAPPY I GOT TO DRAW FRILLS ON A MAID OUTFIT.

THIS WAS FOR A "MASTER-AND-SERVANT" THEMED YURI ANTHOLOGY, BUT I HAVE A THING FOR BRAZEN SERVANTS, SO SHE WASN'T VERY SERVANT-LIKE IN THE END.

THE OGRE AND THE MOUNTAIN GOD

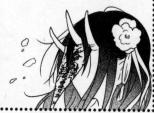

THE THEME WAS "NON-HUMAN X NON-HUMAN YURI."

I LIKE OGRES AND GODS AND OTHER MYSTERIOUS NON-HUMAN BEINGS...

SO I REALLY WANT TO DRAW THEM PROPERLY SOMEDAY.

THIS BOOK INCLUDES A COLOR ILLUSTRATION FOR THIS STORY, SO PLEASE TAKE A GOOD LOOK.

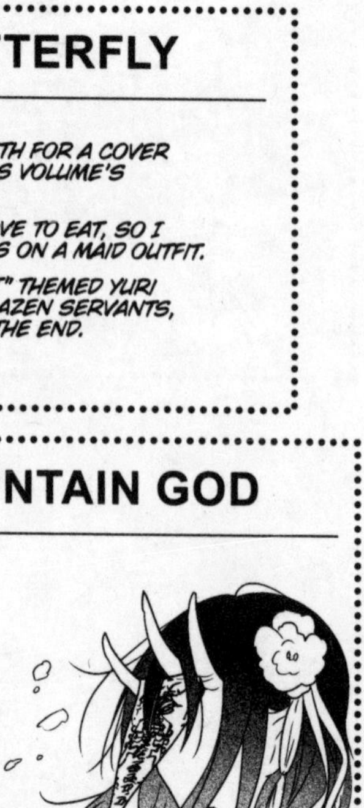

LATELY...

IT'S BEEN GETTING COLDER, SO I'VE BEEN HAVING HOTPOT EVERY NIGHT.

SOY MILK HOTPOT WITH NAPA CABBAGE, PORK, AND MUSHROOMS IS **REALLY** GOOD.

IT'S EVEN BETTER WITH A LOT OF EXTRA INGREDIENTS, LIKE PEA SPROUTS AND MIZUNA (A TYPE OF LEAFY GREEN).

I OFTEN WORK WHILE WATCHING HORROR MOVIES.

I LOVE HORROR, BUT I HAVE A HARD TIME WITH IT.

I WANT TO LOOK AWAY FROM SCARY SCENES AND FOCUS ON MY WORK.

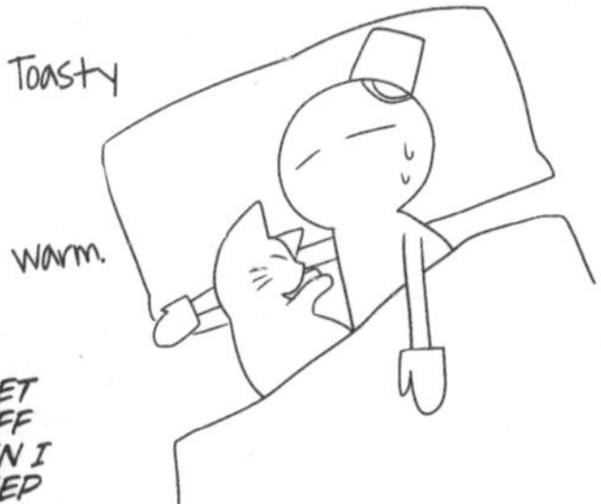
Toasty
warm.

I GET STIFF WHEN I SLEEP WITH MY CAT, BUT I LOVE IT.

WHEN I'M COMING UP WITH IDEAS FOR SHORT WORKS...

I THINK ABOUT WHAT MY READERS, WITH THEIR VARIOUS PROCLIVITIES, MIGHT WANT...

BUT THEN I REASSURE MYSELF THAT IT SHOULD BE OKAY AND DRAW WHAT I WANT.

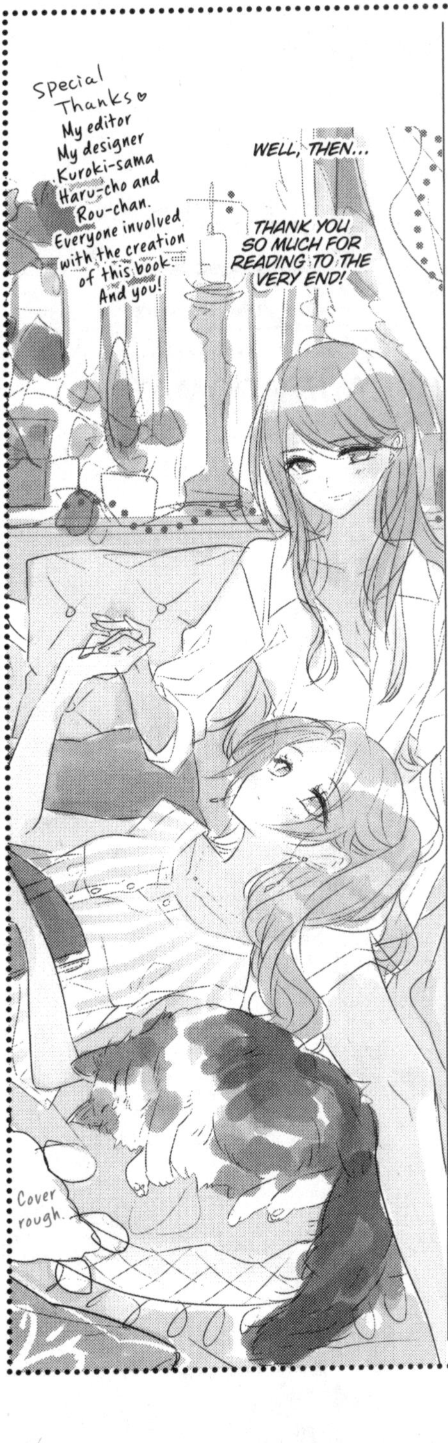
WELL, THEN...
THANK YOU SO MUCH FOR READING TO THE VERY END!
Special Thanks♡
My editor
My designer
Kuroki-sama
Haru-cho and
Rou-chan.
Everyone involved
with the creation
of this book
And you!
Cover rough.

Cats and Sugar Bowls

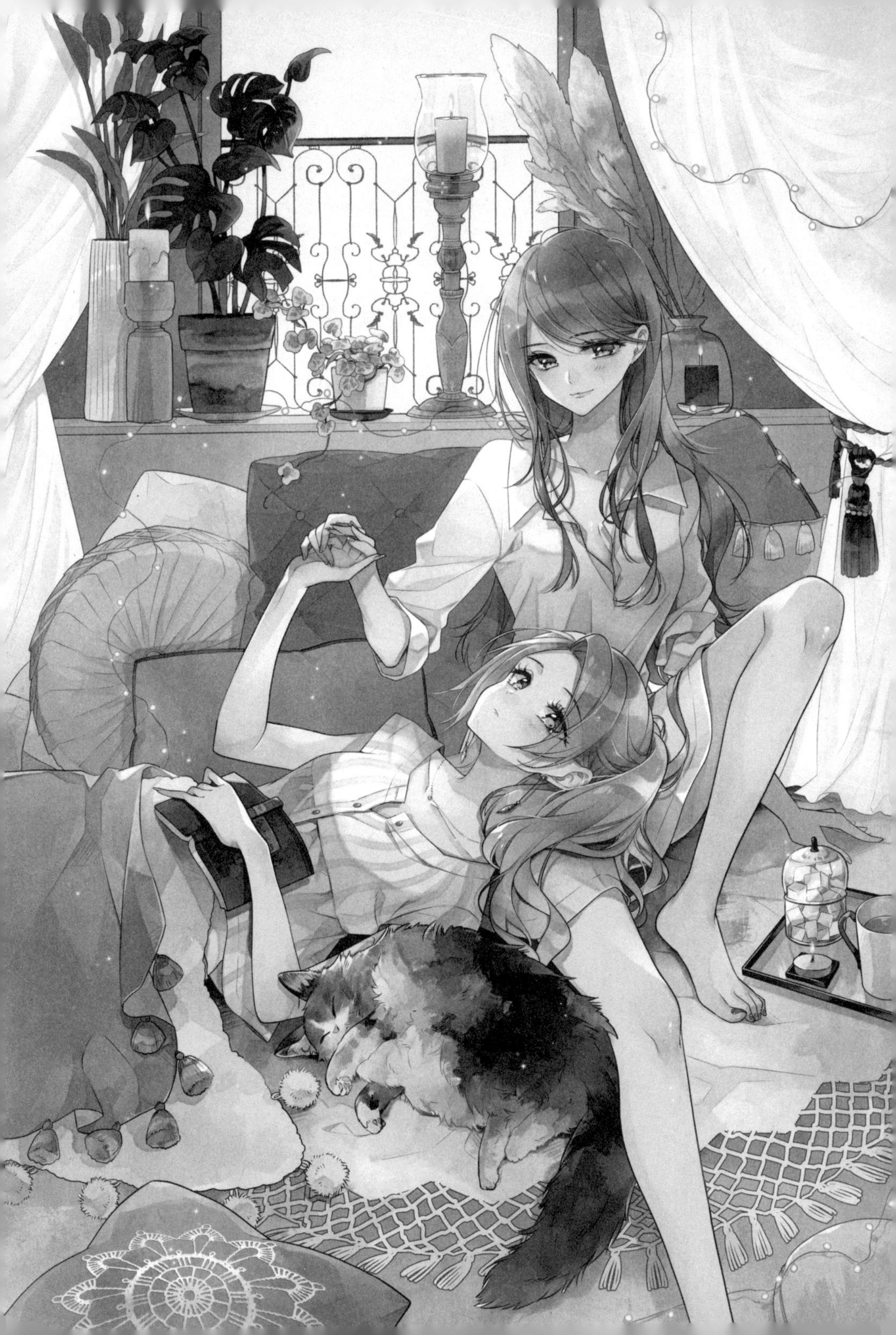

Cats and Sugar Bowls

SEVEN SEAS ENTERTAINMENT PRESENTS

Cats and Sugar Bowls

story and art by **YUKIKO**

TRANSLATION
Amber Tamosaitis

ADAPTATION
Asha Bardon

LETTERING
James Dashiell

COVER DESIGN
H. Qi

PROOFREADER
Alyssa Honsowetz

SENIOR EDITOR
Shanti Whitesides

PRODUCTION DESIGNER
Christina McKenzie

PRODUCTION MANAGER
Lissa Pattillo

PREPRESS TECHNICIAN
Jules Valera

PRINT MANAGER
Rhiannon Rasmussen-Silverstein

EDITOR-IN-CHIEF
Julie Davis

ASSOCIATE PUBLISHER
Adam Arnold

PUBLISHER
Jason DeAngelis

Seven Seas press and purchase enquiries can be sent to Marketing Manager Lianne Sentar at press@gomanga.com. Information regarding the distribution and purchase of digital editions is available from Digital Manager CK Russell at digital@gomanga.com.

ISBN: 978-1-68579-322-7
Printed in Canada
First Printing: September 2022
10 9 8 7 6 5 4 3 2 1

READING DIRECTIONS

This book reads from *right to left*, Japanese style. If this is your first time reading manga, you start reading from the top right panel on each page and take it from there. If you get lost, just follow the numbered diagram here. It may seem backwards at first, but you'll get the hang of it! Have fun!!

1
2
3
4
5
6
7
8
9

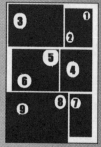

Follow us online: www.SevenSeasEntertainment.com